Dialogue in Places of Learning

Showing how youth from one of the poorest and most violent neighbourhoods in Cape Town, South Africa, learn differently in three educational contexts—in classrooms, in a community hip hop crew, on a youth radio show—this book illuminates how South African schools, like schools elsewhere, subtly reproduce inequalities by sorting students into social hierarchies linked to assessments of their use of language. Highlighting the voices and perspectives of young South Africans, this case study of youth in the Global South explores how language is linked to cultural mixing which occurred during colonialism and slavery and continues through patterns of global mobility. *Dialogue in Places of Learning: Youth Amplified in South Africa* demonstrates how language and learning are bound to space and place.

Adam Cooper is a research specialist at the Human Sciences Research Council in Cape Town, South Africa, a research associate in the Department of Education Policy Studies at Stellenbosch University, South Africa and a fellow of the Centre for Commonwealth Education, University of Cambridge.

Routledge Research in International and Comparative Education

This is a series that offers a global platform to engage scholars in continuous academic debate on key challenges and the latest thinking on issues in the fast-growing field of International and Comparative Education.

For a full list of titles in this series, please visit www.routledge.com

15 **Education and the State**
   International perspectives on a changing relationship
   Edited by Carla Aubry, Michael Geiss, Veronika Magyar-Haas and Jürgen Oelkers

16 **Conflict, Reconciliation and Peace Education**
   Moving Burundi Toward a Sustainable Future
   William M. Timpson, Elavie Ndura and Apollinaire Bangayimbaga

17 **Citizenship Education and Migrant Youth in China**
   Pathways to the Urban Underclass
   Miao Li

18 **International Service Learning**
   Engaging Host Communities
   Edited by Marianne A. Larsen

19 **Educational Borrowing in China**
   Looking West or Looking East?
   Charlene Tan

20 **Nationalism and History Education**
   Curricula and Textbooks in the United States and France
   Rachel D. Hutchins

21 **Global Literacy in Local Learning Contexts**
   Connecting Home and School
   Mary Faith Mount-Cors

22 **Dialogue in Places of Learning**
   Youth Amplified in South Africa
   Adam Cooper

Dialogue in Places of Learning

Youth Amplified in South Africa

Adam Cooper

NEW YORK AND LONDON

First published 2017
by Routledge
711 Third Avenue, New York, NY 10017

and by Routledge
2 Park Square, Milton Park, Abingdon, Oxon, OX14 4RN

First issued in paperback 2018

Routledge is an imprint of the Taylor & Francis Group, an informa business

© 2017 Taylor & Francis

The right of Adam Cooper to be identified as author of this work has been asserted by him in accordance with sections 77 and 78 of the Copyright, Designs and Patents Act 1988.

All rights reserved. No part of this book may be reprinted or reproduced or utilised in any form or by any electronic, mechanical, or other means, now known or hereafter invented, including photocopying and recording, or in any information storage or retrieval system, without permission in writing from the publishers.

Trademark notice: Product or corporate names may be trademarks or registered trademarks, and are used only for identification and explanation without intent to infringe.

Library of Congress Cataloguing-in-Publication Data
Names: Cooper, Adam, 1980- author.
Title: Dialogue in places of learning : youth amplified in South Africa / by Adam Cooper.
Description: New York : Routledge, 2016. | Series: Routledge research in international and comparative education ; no. 22 | Includes bibliographical references.
Identifiers: LCCN 2016008656 | ISBN 9781138194632
Subjects: LCSH: Urban poor—Education—South Africa—Cape Town. | Education—South Africa—Cape Town.
Classification: LCC LC5138.2.S6 C66 2016 | DDC 370.9173/20968—dc23
LC record available at http://lccn.loc.gov/2016008656

ISBN 13: 978-1-138-60021-8 (pbk)
ISBN 13: 978-1-138-19463-2 (hbk)

Typeset in Sabon
by Apex CoVantage, LLC

For my parents, Brenda and David, my sister Sara and my Lebogang

Contents

Figures and Tables — ix
Foreword: Becoming-With-Others by Michelle Fine — xi
Acknowledgements — xvii
Preface — xix

1 Opening Places — 1
2 Language, Race and Space in Cape Town — 21
3 Learning, Language and Dialogue — 34
4 Learning Places — 44
5 Dialogue and Learning at Rosemary Gardens High School — 59
6 Dialogue and Learning Amongst the Doodvenootskap — 83
7 Learning at Youth Amplified Radio Show — 102
8 The Centrality of Language in Places of Learning — 126
9 A New Educational Matrix — 139

Appendix A — 153
Appendix B — 157
Index — 161

Figures and Tables

Figures

1.1	South African income categories by race	3
2.1	Most spoken languages in each province	23
2.2	Growth of Cape Town's population by race	26
2.3	Cape Town residential areas by race	28
4.1	Premature departure from school by age and neighbourhood type in Cape Town	47
A1	Teesakkie se moses	153

Tables

1.1	Rosemary Gardens: Population and household size	10
1.2	Key results for 2011 Census Suburb Rosemary Gardens	10
2.1	South African languages spoken, 2011	22
2.2	Languages spoken in Rosemary Gardens	23
2.3	Languages spoken in Cape Town, 2011	23

Foreword: Becoming-With-Others

The self is made at the point of encounter with an Other. There is no self that is limited to itself. The Other is our origin by definition. What makes us human is our capacity to share our condition—including our wounds and injuries—with others. Anticipatory politics—as opposed to retrospective politics—is about reaching out to others. It is never about self-enclosure. The best of black radical thought has been about how we make sure that in the work of repair, certain compensations do not become pathological phenomena. It has been about nurturing the capacity to resume a human life in the aftermath of irreparable loss. Invoking Frantz Fanon, Steve Biko and countless others will come to nothing if this ethics of becoming-with-others is not the cornerstone of the new cycle of struggles.

Achille Mbembe, "On the State of South African Political Life," September 19, 2015

Dialogue in Places of Learning: Youth Amplified in South Africa is a literary experiment that both chronicles and provokes dialogues 'between'. A multi-sited ethnography authored by Adam Cooper, the text journeys from Rosemary Gardens High School to the Doodvenootskap hip hop crew to Youth Amplified, the youth-led radio show. The chapters gracefully move between colonial history, educational segmentation and intimate conversations among Adam Cooper and the youth, opening spaces of ease and (dis)ease. In skilful provocation, the conversations are pollenated by hauntings of colonialism and apartheid. To understand fully the precarious mo(u)rning after of multiracial democracy, Cooper says, "It would be impossible to consider Rosemary Gardens without first analyzing colonialism, apartheid, the policies and practices" of those times. The volume is an invitation, as Achille Mbembe suggests, to remake self and Other, to engage the "ethics of becoming-with-others" as we "nurture the capacity to resume a human life in the aftermath of irreparable loss". The book reveals much about healing, critical analysis, dialogic learning, and open wounds—between youth, between students and educators, and between these gifted young people and those of us who read the text.

The volume opens with a 'cast of characters', glides through social theory and history, is seasoned with youth poetry in what might be considered a 'mashed genre'. A critical post-colonial tour of tragedy then and now, punctuated with a careful ethnographic peering into three vibrant and contested spaces of educational praxis, and stitched together as a beautiful self-reflective text authored by a white man, caring educator, citizen of the globe and of Cape Town, narrating with generous reflection as whiteness and colouredness shift in treacherous racial waters of change and sedimentation.

With no romance, but exquisite respect for the words, passions and linguistic turns of these young people, Cooper accompanies them across place. He catalogues how history saturates their present, and he chronicles their dreams for tomorrow. Rosemary Gardens has 400 students in grade 7 and 60 in grade 12, even though the quality of the school pleasantly surprises the author. And so he begins a search: "I needed to understand why so many young people stopped attending this school". A linguistic excavation through, across and within places, he documents how the great-grandchildren of apartheid and democracy carry, and resist, (post)colonial contestations in school, in music and on the radio.

Cooper is a gifted ethnographer, an educator and researcher who cares for and enacts a debt to these young students who were good enough to let him hang out, sit with, write 'between'. Through a precise analysis of official and informal language, proper grammar expected in school and the lived discourses of youth media, Cooper reveals the historic, multi-generational scars of oppression, the sustained bruises of stratification and the lively, resisting creativity and imagination percolating despite/because of/in the shadow of/at the critical core of the South African life for coloured youth. As a reader I could hear how sensitively these youth analyse the cumulative effects of segregated schooling and sustained linguistic hierarchies. Students discuss what they call "schools from different races"—as though schools have races, which apparently they do in South Africa as in the United States. And they comment on white South Africans' linguistic surveillance as they "try to catch you out man . . . How good is your Afrikaans?" And surveillance doesn't just come from the outside, but penetrates within groups. We eavesdrop painfully on the policing within when Themba explains to his peers, "I think Greg has spend too much at that school that forced him to lose his colouredness." We hear echoes of colonial distinctions, internalised racism and fine wisdoms marinating at the radical margins.

Mbembe's opening quote, like Cooper's manuscript, invites us to consider a social ontology of becoming-with, a generous gesture in a nation where the white minority has viciously extracted and maintained money, soul, land, language and dignity from blacks and coloureds. I write from a nation where a small, white 1% has stolen/accumulated wealth, land and opportunity in the United States and globally, although critical theorist Jodi Melamed asks us to attend to the twists introduced in the United States by a performance of multicultural neoliberalism that deploys *diversity* as a fig leaf over the gross accumulation of wealth at the top. At this moment in time, how to *become-*, and *unbecome-with*, is a question for those of us in the Global North and South with uneven biographies of dispossession and privilege, as we walk in the world in very different hues.

Cooper, and now I, write to bear witness and gesture toward wit(h)ness, but I am never sure if these nods (for me at least) are anything more than softer shades of whiteness. And yet engage at the hyphen, we must.

I spent three weeks in South Africa during the summer of 2015, at a conference on Narrative and Memory at the University of Witwatersrand where most of the participants were brilliant young 'born free' generation black South African critical scholars. Twenty years after the fall of Apartheid, class and race still streak across the national consciousness, piercing the local poetry, penetrating social analysis and marking bodies, safety and fear with distinct material circumstances. Early in 2015, students at the University of Cape Town felled the statue of Rhodes, and then successfully resisted a rising of tuition fees. Gathered in solidarity with faculty and community activists, students demanded decolonizing the curriculum, integrating the faculty and transforming university culture to be racially inclusive. South Africa is a nation that knows how to struggle—against apartheid and HIV, against a Gini coefficient that rivals the inequality of the United States, against the ghostly colonial presence that lingers on university grounds.

In Johannesburg, my son and I visited Constitution Hall and the remarkable art collection of (in)justice in the foyer. One cannot help but be captivated by the bold and courageous, beautiful and complex wooden doors that open the space where democracy and justice beckon, doors carved in the 11 official languages of South Africa, cataloguing the human rights inscribed in the Constitution. In a quiet discussion with a justice, I asked, "What happened to education in this so-called bloodless revolution?" I was told, "We have not done enough; the commitments on the doors reflect our hope, but not yet our reality". Hope is a radical act, and so is humility.

This summer I witnessed white progressive South Africans step back, as if to try to resolve that which can't be resolved, as if to create reparative space for violence enacted and power denied and histories too big to redress, to honour the work of the next generation of scholars writing on narrative and memory, crafting poetry on the "tomorrow that never arrived". In a similar act of humility and gesture toward reparation, in this text Cooper opens the stage and steps aside. He does not erase himself or history, but as the book opens we meet the leading actors.

How does a white South African write with and beside coloured youth for largely white audiences occupied by fantasies of Africa then and now? Cooper invites readers into the pulsing belly of youth, race, education, hip hop, colonial language and creative aesthetic possibilities. He gently accompanies readers who may live in South Africa or other reaches of the British empire including the United States, into an intimate analysis of the infra-politics of youths' discursive worlds. And in those words we hear echoes of past, betrayals and disappointments of the present and yet a register of critical hope, linguistic playfulness and discursive mobility. Hip hop offers the "language of ideological combat", joining young people in South Africa with Palestinians, youth in South Central LA, New York City, Berlin and in Ferguson, Missouri. Just as language travels over continents, it mutates over history. Today we learn that among these young people, the language of 'race' signals not only skin colour but playfully marks sharp humour, attitude, 'cool', fashion and style. Because Cooper navigated across educational spaces, we hear how young people read the world in dialogue and in transition; critical consciousness—voiced in music and in the radio show—helps young people make sense of the sustained logics of oppression. The book closes, as it opens, with Mo referencing the film, *The Matrix*: "It's like Morpheus . . . if you can see through the system you can beat the system".

One more notable gift from this writer: Cooper asks us to listen to these discourses in the transition. Young people stitching a narrative across time as their bodies and futures ride the waves of post-apartheid neoliberal inequalities. His analysis sits firmly grounded in the soil of South Africa, blanketed in critical youth studies drawn from London and the United States, and yet he seeks to forge a field of critical youth studies rooted in the Global South. A subtle critique of the Northern-ist bias of critical youth studies, a refusal to essentialise but insistence on placing these stories in South Africa, *Youth Amplified* forges a path for critical youth studies situated and embodied in the racialised political economy, history, culture and subaltern spaces of the Global South. Theorizing from the voices of young people who live in communities where 9% of residents aged 20 and older have completed Grade 12 (or above), where only 58% of the labour force aged 15 to 64 is employed, sandwiched 'between' the multicultural economic 'top' and monoracial 'bottom,' these young people are bold and compelling in their discursive flexibility, creativity, critique and desires.

I am a white woman closer to the 'top' in the Global North, active in antiracist struggles and yet still privileged in all the ways you imagine, drafting a foreword, borrowing the analysis of a black South African–based Cameroonian, to comment on a powerful text written by a white South African educator working with youth considered 'coloured' analyzing voice, discourse, education and the fully fraught and never quite *post*colonial moment showered in the affects, structures, judgments and stratifications of the colonial yesterday. Proud and despairing about a revolution come and gone, furious at those who got a piece of the once only-white pie and then shut the doors on more generous and inclusive designs for justice, we write 'between'; we become-with; we can never fully unbecome but must refuse to erase the past or foreclose the future.

In borrowing and lending words and analytics in the messy and always fraught contact zone of critical scholarship, I/we reproduce white supremacist logics even as I try to resist them. I/we try to speak to each other across history, oceans, dialects and dangerous power lines without reifying the white stamp of legitimacy/legibility, and yet I fear there is no exit to the cul de sac of racialised violence in the academy or on the streets, even as we attempt to carve new circuits of solidarity.

As I write another black child was killed by police; another white police officer was acquitted; Black Lives Matter can be heard across the United States and our schools have been declared more segregated than in 1968. There are more African American men in prison than were enslaved in 1850.

I look forward to an ethnography, not yet a text, written by coloured youths of South Africa about white adults in the North. A full reversal of the gaze, this volume would chronicle the grotesque global biography of inhumanity and racialised violence and might even facilitate becoming-with-Others in the shadow of irreparable loss. Until then, thank you Adam.

Michelle Fine, Distinguished Professor of Critical Psychology,
Urban Education and American Studies,
The Graduate Center of the City University of New York

References

Mbembe, Achille. *On the state of South African political life*. 19 September 2015. Downloaded from http://africasacountry.com/2015/09/achille-mbembe-on-the-state-of-south-african-politics/.

Melamed, Jodi. 2011. *Represent and destroy*. Minnesota: University of Minnesota Press.

Acknowledgements

I would like to thank the Harry Crossley Foundation, the Oppenheimer Memorial Trust, the Commonwealth Scholarship Commission and Stellenbosch University for funding me during my PhD and the National Research Foundation of South Africa and Oppenheimer Memorial Trust for supporting my post-doctoral work. In Cambridge, Jo Dillabough gave me time, sustenance and guidance for which I am grateful. During my post-doc Michelle Fine showed me what it means to combine research and praxis and how scholars can be human beings too. The CUNY Graduate Center in New York was a wonderful space in which to write this book.

A big thank you goes to Azeem Badroodien, my PhD supervisor, as well as Aslam Fataar and all of their students in Education Policy Studies at Stellenbosch University who made such a lively, insightful and committed set of companions on this journey. The Vanderbilt University crew: Ben, Krista, Bernadette, Annie, Joanna, Holly and Maury helped with invaluable fieldwork and shared ideas generously, both of which contributed to this book.

I would like to thank my mom, who is now writing about pissflowers, pissfeathers and snarks, positioned within what she calls the 'lunatic fringe'. She never takes the road more travelled or less travelled, but takes her own road. My dad continues with his wonderful mixture of scepticism and eternal hope. He has always tried to open up places where dialogue might flourish and where people might work together (even though they rarely chose to do so), which are the topics of this book. My sister Sara is a constant source of support in my life. My partner Lebogang, who I met during this journey, makes my world look more and more different, as it becomes more familiar. I love you Lebz.

The educators at the school that I have called Rosemary Gardens High welcomed me into their school and homes and showed me unlimited kindness, in much the same way as they showed their learners every day. I cannot express how much I admired the patience, perseverance, humour and love that they showed the people around them.

This book is dedicated to all of the young people of Rosemary Gardens, 'wie het vir my gehulp om my Afrikaans te verbeter' (who helped me to improve my Afrikaans). Even though they said, "Please sir, please don't speak Afrikaans", when I ignored this advice they willingly taught me and never judged. And we learnt from each other. These young people never failed to dream. It is in that spirit that I have tried to write the pages that follow and from which I think the global and South African education machines could learn a great deal.

Preface

Mrs Chantal Peters

> *Our school is in the centre of the gangs. We lost a learner in 2002 one day after school. He was watching TV. He was in grade 1. He was sitting, um, at home, uh, the gangs were arguing outside, and one drew a gun and shot, and the bullet went through the door, and struck him, and he passed on. The gangs took ownership of Rosemary Gardens. We decided . . . we had to do something. . . . And, um, the only thing that we could think of was to start, or Mr Roberts could think of was to start a, um, a soccer team. And slowly, very slowly we became the soccer school. And, Mr Roberts would then arrange with other schools outside of the area, and those schools wouldn't come into Rosemary Gardens, because of this violence. I went to the gangsters' homes too. I went to them and I spoke to them, because I became angry now. It's not, uh, only about the child that was killed, but it involved us too.*

Chantal Peters is a tough, stoical woman. She is also kind. I remember one occasion when I was joking with her in her office and I heard faint giggles coming from behind a cupboard, only to realise that a misbehaving child had been stashed away behind the office furniture, serving his or her sentence while sharing the joke. Mrs Peters was the principal of Mountainside Primary School for over 30 years and her health deteriorated over that time; she has suffered from inactive tuberculosis throughout all of the years that I have known her. Like myself, Mrs Peters is a passionate Liverpool Football Club supporter.

Meeting Mrs Peters was one of a number of chance encounters that shaped my research in Rosemary Gardens between 2008 and 2012. I met Mrs Peters in 2008 at a workshop for teachers involved in the Cape Town–based Extra-Mural Education Project (EMEP), an NGO programme that developed after-school activities as a vehicle to enhance relationships between schools and their communities, as well as to provide young people with a more 'holistic' schooling experience. I worked for EMEP as a researcher from 2008 until 2012. At the workshop, Mrs Peters said that

Mountainside had suffered from 22 acts of vandalism in one school term in 2006. I decided to spend as much time as possible at Mountainside Primary, thinking that if I could comprehend a school like Mountainside, one with many social problems, I would be able to understand any under-resourced school in Cape Town. I've since realised that this logic was very naive: the 40 schools with which EMEP partnered were all vastly different institutions, located in different contexts, with different rhythms, ebbs and flows. Schools are also the products of different mixtures of people. I became very fond of the staff at Mountainside, and my EMEP colleagues often teased me that Mountainside was my favourite school, that I had a 'crush' on Mountainside.

One EMEP colleague who observed my interest in Mountainside asked if I would like to further my involvement in Rosemary Gardens by joining him on Saturday mornings at Rosemary Gardens High School, where he facilitated youth leadership sessions. Raymond had grown up in this neighbourhood and felt a personal connection to the school. I agreed to accompany him for the leadership workshops. During these sessions I often tried to converse with the young people in Afrikaans. The students thought that my Afrikaans sounded extremely comical. I have since been told that my Afrikaans has improved. I have also been schooled in Rosemary Gardens. Learners at Rosemary Gardens High School often asked me what country I am from. The only white people that these students encountered were Americans and Europeans who were completing internships at the school.

Mr Abdullah Williams

Through my involvement in this leadership programme I met a number of the Rosemary Gardens educators, as well as the principal, Mr Abdullah Williams. When he was anxious or thinking deeply, Mr Williams' eyebrows melted into a unitary entity, huddled together in solidarity. This often happened when I was trying to convince him of the value of another complicated idea, which I believed would benefit his school, an institution that was always already overflowing with people, projects and interventions attempting to 'save' the children of Rosemary Gardens.

During the anti-apartheid struggle Mr Williams was a devout African National Congress (ANC) cadre. He endured a spell in Victor Verster Prison as a result of his political activism. His MA thesis was an action-research project entitled, *Towards participatory teaching and learning processes in the English language classroom*, which he completed at the University of the Western Cape. Mr Williams explained the reasons for his interest in participatory teaching and learning in the following manner:

> At an early age I was an activist. My mother's cousin was on Robben Island for 15 years, for sabotage. We struggled economically. We weren't poor like as in Rosemary Gardens, but my mother was a single mother with six children in the 60s. These experiences hardened me,

but they made me empathise with the downtrodden, with the wretched of the earth kind of thing . . . As a 13 year old already you thought of boycotting white cricket, white sport. It's quite advanced by our standards or the standards of today. You know, 13 year olds are on mxit (a social networking forum), they're not political animals. I became a teacher because of our mentor Mr Checkly. When we didn't want him to teach we'd ask him "Mr Checkly, did you hear there was an increase in the price of bread" and then he'd go on for two periods trying to educate us politically and otherwise. I never wanted to become a teacher to talk about the demonstrative adjective, that is, the personal pronoun in its subjective case. I never wanted to talk about that. Even when I chose a poem or short story, I would introduce it in a way to make it politically relevant. Or to make them aware of the issues of life, whatever they may be. To look at things a bit deeper, beyond the superficial. As a teacher I wanted young people to be analytical, to think for themselves.

Mrs May Hughes

Through my EMEP work and by spending time at Rosemary Gardens High I also met May Hughes. May was a white, middle-class woman in her seventies. She was desperate to make a contribution to social development and transformation in Cape Town, something which she believed was possible through ensuring that more young people attended Rosemary Gardens High School for longer periods of time. She lived in a nearby gated community. May was highly efficient and determined, one of those people who will persist relentlessly until she attains the outcomes that she plans to achieve. May raised large amounts of money for the Rosemary Gardens Development Trust, an institution that aimed to support school projects through the provision of financial support. In 2005 May established the School Is Power project (SIP), with the intention of decreasing the number of youth in Rosemary Gardens who discontinue their schooling. As a means of illustrating the extent of school discontinuation amongst adolescents at Rosemary Gardens High, in 2012 there were over 400 grade 9s and only 60 grade 12s.

Through a contact I had made when I was employed at the Human Sciences Research Council, I facilitated a partnership between SIP and Vanderbilt University in the United States. In July of 2012, six doctoral students from Vanderbilt University travelled to Cape Town to help conduct a study for the SIP project. During this time a number of dialogues were held with community stakeholders. One such group that participated in the research was the provincial Department of Cultural Affairs and Sports coaching assistants (DCAS). DCAS had implemented a programme whereby young people from local communities were paid a stipend and in return they coached and facilitated a range of sporting and cultural activities after school, once the learners were dismissed from their academic classes. More than 10 such coaches were stationed at RGHS on weekday afternoons. The group was led by a smart, friendly and energetic young man called Clause. Clause was born in Rosemary Gardens and knew the community intimately. Clause brought a number of outspoken young people to a series of stakeholder dialogues that were conducted with the Vanderbilt students.

Fabio Julies

During one such afternoon session Fabio Julies, a young man of 17, reflected on his decision to stop attending school:

> When I'm at home I felt more stuff than I did at school because at school all I would do was read and write and not listen. I got bored after a while for me. Then after a while I just started writing poetry and that kind of stuff, and writing lyrics. When I'm at home I write better. When I'm at school I can't write because there's no activity or place for me to do that kind of stuff. So that was one of the, I can't say one of the main reasons, but yeah. I think I was the problem there, my mindset, where I was thinking.

Fabio is a member of the Doodvenootskap (meaning 'funeral service' or 'death partnership' literally, but a 'noot' is also the Afrikaans word for a musical note), a group of young hip hop artists, musicians and activists who aimed to bring about social change in Rosemary Gardens. Three members of the Doodvenootskap group were also employed by an NGO called Children's Rights and Anti-Abuse Group, or CRAAG, an organization that worked with victims of abuse, tried to improve gender relations in the neighbourhood and initiated community development projects. At times conflict existed between CRAAG and the Doodvenootskap, as CRAAG did not want Doodvenootskap members to rap about violence in a manner that the NGO felt was inappropriate. Dylan Aprils, who came from Rosemary Gardens himself, led the CRAAG team at the Rosemary Gardens Community site, which was situated in the Global Hope Foundation building, approximately 1 kilometer from Rosemary Gardens High. Dylan was a fiery, articulate man who was approximately 30 years old. He was very critical of outsiders who enter Rosemary Gardens without contributing to the community's development. Dylan was also a positive mentor for the Doodvenootskap.

Mr Adrian Louw

Adrian Louw is a big man. He is also well decorated: his tattoos took me by surprise one evening when he opened his front door without wearing a shirt. Adrian lives next door to me at number 69 Mountain Road. I live at number 71. He smokes Rothmans reds cigarettes outside on his front porch in the evenings and I often chat to him in passing. My cat Bella defecates in his rosemary bush, which looks very healthy, probably in some small part due to the expensive 'science diet' I feed Bella. Adrian is the station manager at a Cape Town community radio station. One evening he complained that the station could not secure a facilitator for the Children's Radio Education Workshop and that the Saturday morning slot was thus left open. Having worked for four years conducting similar projects through the Extra-Mural Education Project, I believed that I could start a programme with youth during this time slot and use activity-based research in order to stimulate dialogue between young people from different backgrounds. I invited Mr Williams to select five Rosemary Gardens High School students to participate in the programme. I also approached staff at three other schools, and asked them if they would like for their students to be involved in the youth radio show. A few months later the young people agreed on the name 'Youth Amplified' for the show.

1 Opening Places

> *A perspective on place enables us to consider how a particular locale—a classroom, community, town, after school club, or website—is not an isolated container, but positioned in a nexus of relations to other such locales . . . as classrooms or other sites of learning are seen less as parking lots and more as intersections, then the particular mobilities of people moving through them become a key issue for evidence and equity.*
>
> Leander, Phillips & Taylor, 2010: 336

> *Just as our skin provides us with a means to negotiate our interactions with the world—both in how we perceive our surroundings and in how those around us perceive us—our language plays an equally pivotal role in determining who we are:* **it is The Skin That We Speak** *(original emphasis).*
>
> Delpit, 2002: xvii

A Study of Youth in Contemporary South Africa

This book explores how young people from one Cape Town neighbourhood, an area that was constructed during apartheid, learnt differently in classrooms, by comparison with when they were participating in other educational places. For three years I followed students into the local high school and interacted with a hip hop crew that wrote lyrics and performed in the same community. I also facilitated a radio show where youth from this area shared their thoughts and ideas live on air, in conversation with peers from other schools. I have used these three educational sites to create a journey that moves across the lives of young people from this neighbourhood, illuminating the progress made in post-apartheid South Africa by highlighting some of the opportunities available to its young citizens. The different sites are held together by the fact that young people from Rosemary Gardens[1] engaged with a range of ideas and people and expressed their own views, through language, in each of the three places.

These three interlinked sites shed light on how youth in troubled, unequal societies, like South Africa, learn in different educational places. Since the beginning of the South African democracy, the world has watched this new country unfold, amazed at the largely bloodless negotiated settlement, but wondering whether the racial reconciliation is genuine and if sustainable economic redress is possible for one of the world's most unequal societies. South Africa represents a testing ground or case study for racial and economic justice everywhere. I did the research for this book believing that there is no better way to observe developments in this multiracial social experiment than to interact with the generation who are growing up in it, listening to their dreams and frustrations and assessing what their futures may hold.

Young people born in the post-apartheid era, such as those who feature in this study, long for an improved quality of life and the chance to become upwardly mobile, valued members of their society. These are opportunities that many South Africans assumed would accompany democracy. Yet change has been slow. Some changes have taken place. Old draconian laws that separated and oppressed people labeled by the apartheid government as 'black', 'Indian' and 'coloured' have now been replaced by some of the most progressive legislation in the world. For example, the new Child Justice Act (2008) is underpinned by a restorative justice framework that does not advocate for retribution for child offenders. Instead the act stipulates that perpetrators and victims of crime should be reconciled. The South African Schools Act (1996) ensures that local communities, in the form of parents, constitute a majority on School Governing Bodies.

Besides developing new legislation, there have been other achievements. The new government, led by the ruling African National Congress, has delivered services to large numbers of the population. Some 85% of households now use electricity for lighting, compared to 58% in 1996. In 2011, 77% of the population lived in formal dwellings, with the government building 2.6 million houses between 1994 and 2009 (Statistics South Africa, 2011).

The government's social assistance programme consists of a number of non-contributory social grants, including pensions for the elderly, disability for those who cannot work and a child grant for parents. Some 16.1 million people now receive social grants, which make up the main source of income for 22% of households (Republic of South Africa, 2013).

Despite these admirable legislative and service delivery developments, material transformation has been frustratingly slow. The average annual household income for black South Africans is R60,600 (approximately USD $4,500),[2] whereas it is R365,000 (approximately USD $24,000) for white South Africans (Statistics South Africa, 2011). Sixty percent of South African children grow up in households with a monthly income of less than R575 (approximately US$40) per person per month, with 67% of black children growing up in households that live below the poverty line compared to just 2% of white children (Hall & Chennells, 2011). Income inequality is also increasing rapidly within race groups. Significant numbers of black South Africans have joined the upper classes, yet inequality and the number of

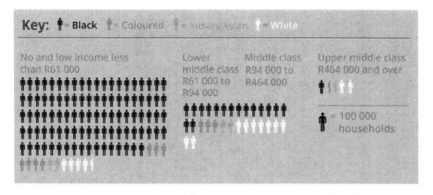

Figure 1.1 South African income categories by race
Source: *Mail & Guardian*, 26 September 2014

poor and unemployed people have grown exponentially (Seekings & Nattrass, 2005).

These class- and race-based divisions are rife in Cape Town, the city that forms the focus of this book. Cape Town is essentially two cities: a wealthy one that lures foreign capital and tourists, and one characterized by urban ghettos of underdevelopment. Mcdonald (2008) says that Cape Town may in fact be *the* most unequal city in the world. The very high rates of violent crime are indicative of these unresolved class- and race-based inequalities.

For the young, urban poor these outcomes are infuriating. They do not dream about owning a two-bedroom government-built brick house and having access to electricity and a social grant. These young people want challenging and exciting jobs. They want to own houses in nice neighbourhoods. The lifestyles and commodities they observe in the media and which adorn middle- and upper-class youth remain largely unattainable for most of the urban poor. Neither are these young people fooled by glib terms that the new state creates, concepts like the 'rainbow nation'. There is a general air of disappointment, of great expectations and small gains that have been acquired very slowly.

Three Interconnected Learning Places

The media, government and large sections of the general public perceive education to be vital to remedying these setbacks and accelerating transformation. Many of the 'born free' generation, as the group born post 1994 is sometimes called, buy into this belief that schooling is the best way to escape poverty and realise their aspirations. It is certainly true that the qualifications that schools confer remain essential in the global era, as it is very difficult to obtain a good job without completing high school. However, it is also true that schools, like most social institutions, reproduce power relations such that poor children go to poor schools and get badly paid jobs. It was important for me to investigate how school may create and/or limit opportunities for youth in Rosemary Gardens, meaning that this institution was an important research site. I tried to capture this group's experiences of 'the school' by spending time in classrooms, listening to their interactions with educators.

School is not the only place that stirs hope in young people. Youth often experiment with who they are and who they would like to become in informal educational places. These sites allow them to explore their passions through activities like music, dance and grappling with new ideas. In informal educational sites youth engage with products from global and local popular culture and are often able to learn on their own terms. Hip hop rap songs are one example of how youth mix, play with and reinvent language in many parts of the world (Alim, 2009). Hip hop is now the world's most popular subculture, with young men and women using this genre to experiment with forms of language and identity in diverse settings like Palestine, Senegal and Brazil. Hip hop is especially appealing to poor black youth, who use this cultural form to occupy public space through their words, graphic art and breakdancing. I stumbled upon the Doodvenootskap hip hop crew through spending time in Rosemary Gardens. It was obvious to me that the young men involved in this group carried a great sense of purpose in the work that they performed and that they perceived enormous potential in participating in this forum, making it an important research site.

The third and final place that features on this journey is a youth radio show that was broadcast live and made use of interactive social networking tools. Youth Amplified had an accompanying Facebook page and participants interacted with the public through text messages and telephone calls. Informal learning places, like this radio show, in conjunction with new technologies such as the Internet, cellular telephones and social networking sites, provide young people with opportunities to express themselves through using language to reclaim public places. The three sites therefore formed a unique expedition across the lives of young people from one Cape Town neighbourhood.

I have used these formal and informal educational contexts to illuminate the lives of youth from Rosemary Gardens, providing glimpses into how they learnt in and between sites, as they assessed and optimised the potential that these places held. The three places were selected through an unfolding, organic process. Or, perhaps I should say that this is one interpretation of the research 'plan'. Interesting sites emerged as I was introduced to new people, as I traced and followed social connections and networks across different locations. On the other hand, the research that makes up this book could be understood as a project that I pre-designed, arranging interactions with people and making 'customised' contexts, such as the radio show. It would also be true to say that part of the story I tell in this book emerged in retrospect, as I pieced together different people, activities and histories, creating a coherent narrative. Each of these three interpretations of the research process that makes up this book is partially true. Research is a messy business, particularly in low-income South African neighbourhoods where 'quiet' is a scarce commodity and convenient places for conducting interview conversations tend to be elusive. What I can say, with confidence, is that I spent a great deal of time in one poor neighbourhood that I will call Rosemary Gardens, 'following' a range of people, primarily youth, in an effort to tell a larger story. This larger story is about how young South Africans learnt in different places as they participated in dialogues with other people, in the hope of one day realising their aspirations. Let me give a little bit more detail about the three places.

Site 1: Rosemary Gardens High School

At the time I started this study I was employed by a Cape Town–based NGO called the Extra-Mural Education Project (EMEP), an organisation that worked at a local primary school in Rosemary Gardens. EMEP facilitated extra-murals at more than 40 schools in the Western Cape province, using these activities to promote schools as hubs of their communities. I developed a special relationship with a number of the staff at a school in Rosemary Gardens, a school I will call Mountainview Primary. This led to my facilitating leadership sessions at the high school in the area, in collaboration with a colleague who had grown up in Rosemary Gardens. Together we tried to create an orientation programme for students entering the high school from Mountainview Primary.

The Rosemary Gardens High School that I became familiar with was very different from the caricatured South African township school that exists in the media. In the media and in the imaginations of many who make up the South African middle- and upper-classes, schools in neighbourhoods that were formerly reserved for 'black' and working-class 'coloured'[3] children are generally thought to be dysfunctional places. These schools are associated with textbooks that do not arrive until late in the academic year, if at all, as demonstrated by the widely publicised 'Limpopo textbook crisis' (Veriava, 2013). It is assumed that large numbers of teachers at such schools are regularly absent and that they rarely spend time teaching in the classroom. Students are believed to learn very little at township schools and it is thought that they instead dedicate most of their time either to criminal and/or gang-affiliated activities, being pregnant or abusing various substances.

There is indeed some truth to these perceptions, but this picture is only one view of township schools. The whole truth is far more complex. Rosemary Gardens High School (RGHS) had access to textbooks, as well as to sports fields and coaches. At the school there were two computer laboratories, a library and a gymnasium. On most days, one or two of the 38 educators may well have been absent, but the vast majority arrived at school and spent a great deal of time in classrooms, delivering the school curriculum. The school offered a large number of activities and resources to its students. A free meal was available to all students who wanted to eat at school and many chose to receive food through this programme known as the 'feeding scheme'. The school offered a range of afternoon activities, as well as access to resources like books and computers. A number of entrepreneurial projects took place on the school grounds. Ben 10, an NGO that refurbished, rented out and sold bicycles, operated from a prefabricated structure at the front of the premises, and the school farmed lavender, a plant that was used to produce cosmetics and beauty products.

Despite offering this array of activities and services, the school suffered from very high rates of discontinuation. There were over 400 grade 7s and only 60 grade 12s in 2012, a consistent trend in recent years. This confused me. How could a school that offered dance, music, sports, extra lessons in the afternoons, as well as computer laboratories, a Virgin Active gym and a free meal, be so unappealing to young people who had access to few opportunities and resources?

The school appeared to have the benefit of good leadership, moreover, which increased my bewilderment as to why so many youth did not want to spend time at school. The principal, with whom I became close, was a man I greatly admired. He was a political activist during the apartheid era and held a MA degree which focused on participatory teaching and learning at RGHS. RGHS has also had stability in its leadership, another factor that experts pinpoint as important for school effectiveness. The school was erected in 1978 and has only ever had two school principals during its existence.

I needed to understand why so many young people stopped attending this high school and so I spent as much time as possible in classrooms and at school-related activities. I interviewed 15 teachers one-on-one and conducted focus groups with half of the grade 12 learners. Thirty students participated in the focus groups: one of the two matriculating classes was chosen at random and then divided into groups of four or five. I asked the students questions regarding what they enjoyed and did not enjoy about school and encouraged them to describe life in their classrooms and neighbourhood. I also probed what learning meant to them.

I was often invited to functions at the school, including the prize-giving, as well as other events that involved dignitaries from the Western Cape Education Department and speeches by the patron of the School Improvement Programme (SIP), who is a prominent academic. In these meetings I met a number of local education department officials and later interviewed some of them, probing their personal perceptions of the school and the learners. I served as a co-opted trustee on the Rosemary Gardens Development Trust, which was created to help raise money to develop the school's infrastructure. My involvement at the school, with educators and students, therefore extended beyond my role as researcher as I tried to piece together how students learnt at school and how this institution fitted into their worldviews and aspirations.

Site 2: The Doodvenootskap

My participation at RGHS led to my path crossing with the activities of the local hip hop group called the Doodvenootskap (DVS). My first extensive interaction with the crew occurred when May Hughes, the founder of the SIP programme, invited a group of different people to attend a teatime discussion on 'school dropout', or 'school discontinuation', as I prefer to call it. The discussion took place at May's home in a nearby middle-class, previously whites-only neighbourhood. What captivated me about the Doodvenootskap members was their level of self-confidence and the intelligence and clarity of many of their contributions to the discussion. I was further struck by how comfortable the DVS members appeared to be in themselves, their confidence to speak and contribute to the conversation, and their readiness to disagree if that was required. Their sense of entitlement to speak in this white woman's home struck me as being exceptional.

I decided to engage the DVS members in conversations and follow them as they worked, in different contexts, over the following months. The crew granted me permission to observe them in their various activities and to conduct interviews with each of them on a one-to-one basis. In the months that followed we built up a healthy relationship. I was invited to attend events that they held in Rosemary Gardens; for example, the group hosted a 'coffee bar' discussion on the topic of 'identity' with youth from the area. DVS was involved in a number of different activities that included public performances of their music and, for some members of the group, employed work for a local NGO called Children's Rights and Anti-Abuse Group (CRAAG). Their partnership with CRAAG allowed the crew to work with Rosemary Gardens residents on a number of projects, helping to improve the status and rights of children and youth in the area. CRAAG provided DVS with a small office in the local community centre. Use of this office exposed the group to the range of people, such as local government officials and other NGO staff, who moved through this place.

I was drawn to the Doodvenootskap because of their sense of pride and confidence to speak in public forums, which struck me as very different from the way that students behaved at Rosemary Gardens High School. There seemed to be a sense of purpose to the work that DVS conducted, an unspoken belief that these activities were meaningful and that involvement in this informal structure would lead to future opportunities.

Site 3: Youth Amplified

I wondered whether the students who attended Rosemary Gardens High School might become more animated and learn better if they were exposed to an 'alternative curriculum' that spoke directly to the hardships that they experienced in their lives. They were certainly aware that society operates in ways that are oppressive to groups such as themselves, but they were not given a place in which to speak about or interrogate social inequalities.

The serendipitous opportunity to facilitate the youth radio show allowed me to experiment with an alternative curriculum, in an informal educational place, using a form of critical pedagogy. Critical pedagogy is an approach to teaching and learning that calls for oppressed peoples to reflect on the conditions of their oppression, a process which may lead to social change. This approach shares similarities with Gloria Ladson-Billings' (1995) theory of a culturally relevant pedagogy, one that connects with the cultural resources of poor students and stimulates their sociopolitical consciousness. The way that I conceptualised the radio show was therefore shaped by my interest in engaging marginalised young people in the realm of ideas, in a way that stimulated their interests and addressed some of their concerns.

On a practical level, I first became involved in starting up the radio show after a conversation with my next-door neighbour, who could not find a facilitator for a children's educational slot at the radio station that he managed. The original idea was that I would help develop a format for the programme, which would focus on participants engaging with a variety of materials, such as documentary films, newspaper articles, musical inserts, and contributions from guests. These activities would then form the basis for critical discussions. Given my background of working for an educational NGO, I suggested we work with materials that mostly explored themes of 'education in South Africa', but that we would also choose themes selected by the participants in the programme.

In the 18 months that followed I worked alongside the young people on the programme, as we watched documentaries, read newspaper articles and academic texts and interviewed guests live on air. Some of these guests included members of the Doodvenootskap, as well as the junior mayor of Cape Town. I interviewed each of the participants one-on-one, asking them questions about what they enjoyed and did not enjoy about the programme and what they learnt at the show. The participants offered opinions on students from the other schools in these interviews. My involvement and research on the radio programme provided interesting insights into how students from quite different Cape Town schools and residential areas engaged with one another, in relation to an alternative curriculum which attempted to stimulate sociopolitical consciousness.

Students from four schools participated in the programme. These schools included Rosemary Gardens High School; a former 'black', English medium but isiXhosa-dominated school that I call Lukhanyo High; and the Cape Institute of Education, a focus school recently established by the Western

Cape Education Department to enhance the academic development of gifted learners reared in the townships. In 2012 a fourth school was invited into the emerging space, as the radio station did not want the show to become stigmatised as solely consisting of 'marginalised youth'.

A former model C school[4] that I call Barry Hertzog High School (BHHS) was decided upon. The students auditioned for the role of host/hostess and the show was broadcast live on Saturday mornings in 2012.

The programme led to conflict and cooperation, much laughing and some crying, as well as an unusual opportunity for young people from radically different backgrounds to engage in dialogues across the lines of race, class, gender and residential location. What was most useful to me about the radio show was that it provided opportunities to observe youth from Rosemary Gardens in an informal educational setting as they interacted with a diverse range of peers and engaged with issues related to social justice.

Cut and Paste: Placing the Three Sites Side by Side

The three places described in this book were very different from one another. My challenge lay in comparing and integrating them into a connected journey that moved across the lives of youth from one neighbourhood, illuminating their aspirations and educational experiences. This meant developing a set of concepts that could connect the different sites, enabling me to tell a bigger story about their lives and learning endeavours.

The three sites are connected by the fact that Rosemary Gardens youth participated in all of them, using language and engaging in dialogues. Rosemary Gardens was built for people classified as 'coloured' in the 1970s, a time when people were taken from their homes and dumped in hastily erected areas with low-cost housing or no accommodation at all. This neighbourhood is located approximately 20 km from Cape Town's city centre and was constructed between 1972 and 1974, more than 20 years after Group Areas Act (1950) legislation separated 'white', 'black', 'coloured' and 'Indian' people residentially. Apartheid legislation meant that people who owned land in areas deemed by the state to be legally reserved for race groups other than the landowner, were forced to sell their property, usually for an amount far less than it was worth, and to relocate to other, often inadequate housing, in areas like Rosemary Gardens (Adhikari, 2006).

In Cape Town, thousands of people were forcibly removed from areas like the cosmopolitan District Six in the inner city and from places in the suburbs. These areas were conveniently located in close proximity to transport networks and employment nodes and became exclusively reserved for 'white' people. Many people were forced to begin new lives on the Cape Flats, the barren, sandy, windswept area in Cape Town that was designated to be inhabited by 'black', 'Indian' and 'coloured' people.

This history has resulted in contemporary social problems that impacted on Rosemary Gardens High School and other places that youth in this study frequented. Apartheid-era legislation catalysed dislocation and created ruptures in the social fabric of families and communities, fissures which are still apparent in the second decade of the 21st century. Today, Rosemary Gardens suffers from poverty and community violence, gangsterism and drug abuse, overcrowded conditions, lack of access to social services, high levels of unemployment and low incomes for those who are able to find employment (Statistics South Africa, 2011). Demographically, Rosemary Gardens has not changed significantly in the democratic period. According to the 2011 census this neighbourhood is still inhabited by a vast majority (95%) of people who classify themselves as coloured in census data and less than 1% white people. Thirty-five percent of adults have only primary schooling and less than a quarter of a percentile of residents have attended tertiary education institutions. Some 59% of the households in this neighbourhood live on a total of less than R3,200 (approximately $200) income per month.

These statistics do not represent the whole or only picture of this neighbourhood, as many positive social interactions take place and people find innovative, creative and unique ways to live their daily lives. My description of RGHS, for example, shows a different kind of place that exists in the neighbourhood of Rosemary Gardens. However, this information is important when trying to understand some of the historical forces that have shaped the lives of people from Rosemary Gardens.

Table 1.1 Rosemary Gardens: Population and household size

Population	32,598
Households	6,504
Average Household Size	5.01

Source: Statistics South Africa, Census, 2011

Table 1.2 Key results for 2011 Census Suburb Rosemary Gardens

The population is predominantly coloured (95%).
9% of those aged 20 years and older have completed Grade 12 or higher.
58% of the labour force (aged 15 to 64) is employed.
59% of households have a monthly income of R3,200 or less.
82% of households live in formal dwellings.
91% of households have access to piped water in their dwelling or inside their yard.
83% of households have access to a flush toilet connected to the public sewer system.
94% of households have their refuse removed at least once a week.
99% of households use electricity for lighting in their dwelling.

Source: Statistics South Africa Census, 2011

Place Matters

Places, like Rosemary Gardens, are produced by history. Places do not only consist of the bricks and mortar that make up the rooms of a house, or the grass that forms a sports field. They are not empty containers waiting to be filled by objects and people. History shapes places through the politics, policies and social relationships that operate in and beyond the borders of specific sites. Places are therefore 'social' in the sense that they consist of the relationships and histories that lead to their becoming 'a place'. Henri Lefebvre (1991) explored, in great detail, the idea that space can be thought of as a social phenomenon and not only as a physical, geographical area. Lefebvre (1991) introduced and described three forms of space, which he believed could be used together to understand how social space functions in its totality.

I will call the three concepts of Lefebvre's (1991) spatial triad, which I use to understand the three places in this book, 'material', 'imagined' and 'lived' space.[5] Material space . . . "is the space of social practice"; it is the way that physical space is organised under the dominant economic and political systems. In the global era this usually refers to the spatial forms and patterns that emerge in capitalist social democracies. Examples of material space that are related to learning include school transport routes, everyday teaching and learning routines, employment relations that determine which schools students attend and the erection of particular kinds of neighbourhoods and their associated schools.

'Imagined' space is the ways that space is conceived in the mind of scientists, architects and planners, "a certain type of artist with a scientific bent" (Lefebvre, 1991: 38). It is how space is *imagined* in the minds of human beings. Imagined space is the dominant spatial form in any society, manifesting in the languages, signs and symbols that operate in schools, other informal learning places and society more broadly.

Lived space is forged through the interactions between material and imagined space, as people find 'ways of being', which they create through navigating these other spatial forms. For example, students endure school routines, and try to use and understand the languages of the school, as they find ways to 'live' school partly on their own terms, on a daily basis. Lived space may also manifest through social resistance, independent from these other kinds of space (Lefebvre, 1991). Lived space is directly experienced, can be observed in art and other nonverbal forms and is often linked to the clandestine or underground aspects of life that the imagination depicts and transforms.

Graffiti at Rosemary Gardens High School is a good example of lived space. Graffiti existed all over the school, on the walls, school uniforms and desks. Students therefore accepted material spatial routines, such as wearing uniforms and sitting in rows in their desks. They listened to the teachers deliver the curriculum, using the specialised languages that make the classroom a particular kind of imagined space. However, they left their mark, evidence of their lived experiences, on these material and imagined forms of space by writing their own words wherever possible, in the form of graffiti.

Specific combinations of material, imagined and lived social relations intersected to produce RGHS, the Doodvenootskap and Youth Amplified. Unpacking the ways in which these places functioned as educational settings involved analysing how material, imagined and lived space affected each of these places. A focus on 'place' allows the classroom to be seen as one educational context amongst the range of learning places that exist within local neighbourhoods. The classroom is not an isolated site where the education department conducts specialised pedagogical work. Learning places are constructed historically and are shaped by relationships that exist inside and beyond their borders. I return to this idea in Chapter Four, naming the key material, imagined and lived relations that combined to form RGHS, the Doodvenootskap and Youth Amplified. Material, imagined and lived space help us understand how young people learn in context-specific ways and how they make sense of the opportunities that may be extracted from different sites.

Language Varieties and Kaapse Afrikaans

The other main commonality between these different learning places was that youth used language somewhat differently depending on the place. The use of language was intimately connected to learning in these sites, as well as to the value youth placed on these settings. In other words, young people spoke in different ways and with different regularity at RGHS, amongst the Doodvenootskap and at Youth Amplified, and other people evaluated and made sense of their words. The use and assessment of forms of language therefore shaped learning everywhere.

The specific variety of Afrikaans that youth from Rosemary Gardens spoke held particular significance for their learning endeavours. Young people from Rosemary Gardens mainly spoke an informal variety of Afrikaans that I will call 'Kaapse' (Cape) Afrikaans. Kaapse Afrikaans emerged through the mixture of indigenous Khoi and San languages, British and Dutch colonial settlers and slaves from East Africa and Asia, a history I explore in more detail in the next chapter. Kaapse Afrikaans is a good example of how language use, and communication in general, is increasingly becoming understood as 'translingual practice' or 'translanguaging' (Canagarajah, 2013; García & Wei, 2013). Translingual practice implies that communication transcends individual languages. People do not use *a* language, neither do they simply code-switch between a number of distinct languages. Communication consists of the ways that people use a range of signs and symbols from different places, signs and symbols which are differentially empowered (Blommaert, 2010; Canagarajah, 2013; Martin-Jones,

Blackledge & Creese, 2012). The frequent contact between groups of people and their languages, under globalization, precipitated the idea of translanguaging. However, examples like Kaapse Afrikaans demonstrate that these processes of linguistic mixing have occurred for centuries, especially in colonial contexts. Kaapse Afrikaans is not generally understood to comprise *a language*, but is instead a mixture of words from different sources that are used in context dependent ways.

The language, signs and symbols used by young people in Rosemary Gardens are associated with working-class coloured people in Cape Town, generating negative stereotypes of its users being uneducated and uncouth. Their language carried a low status, linked to its origins in interactions between slaves at the Cape and the ways that its speakers were given the status of second-class citizens during colonialism and under apartheid. Language is the most important mobile resource which young people use to learn in the various settings of their lives (Blommaert, 2010). However, languages are inscribed with social significance and not equally valued, with implications for learning in different sites. The languages that youth like those in Rosemary Gardens use are bound up in the places where they grow up, as well as the histories and social hierarchies of these places. While young people are experts at creatively using a wide range of words from different sources to assert their identities and ideas, their words carry the scars of past injustices and are often interpreted as evidence of inferiority. The ways in which young people from Rosemary Gardens used language was assessed differently in the three places.

Dialogic Learning

The three places all contained and shaped linguistic interactions between people, exchanges that were fundamental to how young people learnt in these sites. A range of interacting perspectives may be called a 'dialogue'. Dialogues that did or did not occur in each place were most important for how young people from Rosemary Gardens learnt in interactions with educators, peers and others. Dialogic learning occurs when conversations consist of a range of different, unsynthesised perspectives existing side by side. These different opinions or views encourage people to compare and assess a variety of viewpoints and to develop their own opinions (Wegerif, 2008, 2011). Put another way, dialogic learning promotes the examination of different, unintegrated answers, unlike other learning exercises in which a single, final solution is desirable, such as with mathematical problems.

A range of perspectives, in dialogue, may lead to forms of knowledge being co-produced by people, as they work side by side (Alexander, 2008). Dialogic learning is therefore not, primarily, an individual process, as it involves all of the participants learning from one another, co-constructing knowledge and engaging in dialogues communally. Dialogic learning differs from cognitivist learning theories that focus on thought processes as they occur *within* individuals. These theories are sometimes called 'jug and mug', 'banking' or 'transmission' approaches to learning, implying that knowledge is able, metaphorically, to be poured into, or deposited/banked, within the heads of passive learners (Freire, 1970).

Dialogic learning theories also differ from sociocultural approaches to learning that focus on interactions between people and learning environments. Sociocultural learning theories, such as the work of Lev Vygotsky, analyse how person-environment interactions lead to pathways of development for individual people, producing concept development, improved language use and higher mental functions (Vygotsky, 1978, 1986; Wegerif, 2011). Vygotsky's focus was primarily on individual person outcomes and how these may be improved through, for example, the 'zone of proximal development'. The zone of proximal development represents the difference between what an individual person may achieve on their own, in comparison to their development when aided by relevant others, such as teachers.

From a dialogical perspective, teachers and students are both teacher-students (Freire, 1970). Dialogic learning happens when people learn from each other as they share different perspectives, adjust their own views and create a joint product, in the form of a dialogue. Dialogues occurred in a variety of forms at RGHS, Youth Amplified and amongst the Doodvenootskap, offering youth from Rosemary Gardens different kinds of learning experiences.

I unpack dialogic learning in more detail in Chapter Three, looking at language ideologies and speech genres, exploring how these and other ideas applied to RGHS, the Doodvenootskap and Youth Amplified. The concepts of lived space and language— understood as a resource for dialogic learning and not as something which poor youth of colour lack or are deficient in— are crucial tools for conducting an insightful study of young people's lived educational experiences in different places in contemporary South Africa.

A Study of Youth in the Global South

While this book follows in a tradition of Youth Studies research that has been pioneered and dominated by scholars in the Global North, it demonstrates profound differences between conditions of youth in the Global North and South. I have prioritised young people's agency in relation to the social, political and historical contexts in which they live, an approach to Youth Studies that began with the Birmingham School, as it was known, in the 1970s. Prior to the Birmingham School, the study of youth was almost always framed by the idea that 'youth are a problem', with young men typically depicted as 'gangsters', 'delinquents' and 'criminals' and young women cast as 'sexual deviants'. The Birmingham School broke with earlier work that represented youth as a threat to the modern nation-state, interpreting young people's actions as intentional responses to their socio-historical milieu. These scholars showed how working-class British youth tried to find solutions to material inequalities through youth cultures or 'subcultures' (Clarke et al., 1976; Dillabough & Kennelly, 2010). In the United States, a series of critical ethnographers followed the spirit of the Birmingham school, not 'othering' or pathologising groups of youth, combining deep descriptive accounts of young people with sharp political and ideological critiques (Dimitriadis, 2009; Fine, 1991; MacLeod, 1995; Weis, 1990).

Important African studies of youth have followed the Birmingham School approach, highlighting how colonialism, post-colonial state failure and a troubled relationship with material modernity produce the tumultuous conditions in which African youth grow up (Abbink, 2005; de Boeck, 2005). A good recent example of this approach, in the African context, is Honwana (2012), who uses the concept of 'waithood' to describe the liminal state, the involuntary delay in reaching adulthood that most African youth experience due to the lack of skills, resources and opportunities that would ensure independence. She argues that youth in the Global South experience this condition most emphatically because of neoliberal structural adjustment policies that have plagued their countries. Waithood extends to civic participation, family life and learning opportunities. It involves creativity and agency, as youth hustle to survive.

It would be impossible meaningfully to understand the lives of Rosemary Gardens youth without first analysing colonialism, apartheid and the policies and practices that accompanied those periods. The neighbourhood of Rosemary Gardens was formed after apartheid legislation ensured that people were forcibly removed from central Cape Town and dumped elsewhere. The languages that these young people speak are products of interactions between indigenous peoples, slaves and colonizers. The way that I have conceptualised 'space' and 'language' is an attempt to demonstrate how these structural forces are part of the everyday contexts that frame, limit and enable young people's praxis. Their forms of lived space and use of language are woven through their material and imagined conditions.

Despite, or in addition to sharing a heritage with Youth Studies from the Global North, I believe that a study of youth in the Global South is compelled more aggressively to seek solutions to social problems like unemployment, educational attainment and inequality. A conservative World Bank figure estimates that South Africa suffers from 54% youth (15–24-year-olds) unemployment, compared to the United States with 16%, Britain 20%, China 10%, Chile 16%, Brazil 14% and Russia 15%. For the period 2011–2015, only Spain had a higher youth unemployment rate (http://data.worldbank.org/indicator/SL.UEM.1524.ZS). South African youth, like other Southern youth, do not receive the levels of state support and social security from which young people in more developed contexts benefit. If youth in developing countries do find work, they are more likely than their Northern counterparts to find casual, irregular employment and they are less likely to try to find work through official channels. Erratic opportunities to obtain work and leaving education earlier than Northern youth are two of the most important employment related differences between youth in the Global North and South (International Labour Organisation, 2013).

Frustrations that result from these insecurities and a lack of attractive opportunities are beginning to show. In 2015 student protests raged across South African campuses. In contexts that suffer from urgent challenges we have a responsibility to look for solutions. We cannot only analyse historical contexts. However, I am not advocating a 'back to basics' educational approach. Reading, writing and arithmetic are essential but insufficient to address the challenges of youth in contexts like South Africa. Instead, I am proposing that partial solutions might lie in exploring the ways that history, politics and economics become relevant to and emerge out of young people's praxis. One form that this takes is their words, their forms of language, their most intimate and potentially powerful form of cultural capital. We need to listen, carefully, to what young people themselves say about the challenges they face and the resources that they have at their disposal. The title of this book refers to the name of the radio show, but it is also being used as a metaphor, implying that the volume of young people's words needs to be increased in each of these educational sites and that adults should listen to what youth have to say. Listening to young people illuminates how their lives consist of much more than a series of deficits, like a lack of education, unhealthy bodies, unproductive activities and damaging relationships.

Young people's words and actions should be interpreted in relation to the multiple contexts they inhabit, the lived spaces that form the meaningful parts of their lives. This strategy makes it possible to mobilise a range of interconnected resources and people. Many valuable educational sites exist in poor communities. These places are produced by social relationships and historical forces that operate both inside and beyond their borders. Instead of approaching educational solutions like trying to heal a malignant body part, I am proposing that we listen to, work with and attempt to nourish the entire body. Transformation is possible, but only if we look at education in radically new ways and only if we listen, carefully, to the people who have most to gain and lose in the future of our society.

****

This sets the scene that is continued in the following chapters. Chapter Two is a historical account of language, race and space in Cape Town, showing how the words that Rosemary Gardens youth have inherited are entangled with social interactions that occurred between colonisers, indigenous peoples and imported slaves. Their words carry low social status, due to their position in this history, which impacts on how they engage in dialogues and learn in different settings. How young people learn through dialogue, in educational places, is the topic Chapter Three. Language ideologies, ideas about the value of various languages, play a substantial part in this process. I explore the impact of macro linguistic ideologies and more immediate factors that shape dialogic learning. Chapter Four explores the concept of 'place' as it relates to learning. The three learning places are unpacked in terms of the key sets of material, imagined and lived social relations that created and reproduced these sites.

While Chapters Two, Three and Four are theoretical chapters in which the conceptual tools are sharpened against the backdrop of the three places, Chapter Five is the first in-depth portrayal of a key place, one in which the young people's words come alive. This chapter launches us into classrooms at Rosemary Gardens High School. In Chapter Six I analyse the words and actions of the Doodvenootskap (DVS), the hip hop crew that used terms that they were exposed to in interactions with local NGOs and concepts that they accessed from global and local hip hop culture. Chapter Seven moves out of the Rosemary Gardens community to the Youth Amplified radio show. I describe the Rosemary Gardens learners involved in Youth Amplified and unpack themes and conflicts that emerged in this place. I compare 'learning' in each of the three places in Chapter Eight, concentrating on the role of language. In the final chapter I reinsert issues that were raised in the different sites of the study into current, global debates on education and language.

Notes

1 All of the names of people, places and organisations in this book are pseudonyms.
2 Exchange rate used is R1= USD 15 as at December 2015.
3 In this book I try to avoid using racial categories wherever possible. When I refer to suburbs or schools that were formerly reserved for particular groups as designated by the apartheid state, I place the racial category in inverted commas, for example: "areas reserved for 'coloured' people during apartheid". When referring to census data it should be noted that these statistics are based on the ways that people classify themselves in census surveys, based on the options from which they are forced to choose.

Many of the references to race in this book were made by the young participants in the study. Racial categories continue to have relevance in contemporary South Africa because forms of subtle and blatant racism continue to exist. Race is still intimately related to social class and residential neighbourhoods. Neighbourhoods that were reserved for people classified as 'black' or 'coloured' under apartheid continue to be inhabited by people who classify themselves as members of these groups in census data. Most 'white' people continue to be relatively rich and live in well-resourced areas, and most people (or their families) who are poor, were classified as 'coloured' or 'black' under apartheid.

When I use the term 'coloured' I am not referring to an essentialised racial category, but rather as, following Erasmus (2001: 21): "cultural identities comprising detailed bodies of knowledge, specific cultural practices, memories, rituals and modes of being... formed in the colonial encounter between colonists (Dutch and British), slaves from East and South India and from East Africa and conquered indigenous peoples, the Khoi and the San. The result has been a highly specific and recognisable cultural formation—not just a 'mixture' but a very particular mixture comprising elements of Dutch, British, Malaysian, Khoi and other forms of African culture appropriated, translated and articulated in complex and subtle ways. These elements acquire their specific cultural meaning only once fused and translated".

4 In the final years of the apartheid era, parents at 'white' public schools were given the option to convert their governance structure to a semi-private form called Model C, and many of these schools changed their admissions policies to accept children of other races. These schools could also establish school fee policies (Sayed, 1999). Following the transition to democracy, the legal form of 'Model C' was abolished, however, the term continues to be used in public discourse to describe government schools formerly reserved for 'white' children.

5 Lefebvre (1991) called the three forms of space in his triad 'spatial practices', 'representations of space' and 'representational spaces' (Lefebvre, 1991: 33). At other times, he referred to these three forms of space as 'perceived', 'conceived' and 'lived' space. My renaming Lefebvre's (1991) three moments of social space as 'material', 'imagined' and 'lived' space is an attempt to make my research project clear and understandable, but also to remain faithful to Lefebvre's original scholarship. I believe that I have retained scholarly faithfulness because Lefebvre (1991) thought that the labels used to refer to forms of space were less important than capturing the way that space operates in its totality. Lefebvre (1991) believed that this could be achieved through describing the process through which space is produced, which is the title of his major work. In *The production of space* Lefebvre outlined his spatial trialectic or the three forms of space in an extremely abstract, fleeting and non-linear way, because he believed that space operates in this kind of fragmented, changing fashion. My descriptions of the interaction between 'material', 'imagined' and 'lived' space attempt to convey this process as it relates to learning in particular places.

I have used three terms, like Lefebvre, remaining true to his broader scholastic project, which extended beyond theories of space. Lefebvre's spatial trialectic—the three forms of space—was used to militate against binary thinking that he believed plagued theories of space and the social sciences more generally. Lefebvre tried to move social scientific thinking beyond **either** a material, empirical, measuring exercise **or** a meaning-making, representational, hermeneutic approach, to something more fluid and complex. His spatial trialectic attempts to convey such an approach. Soja (1996: 9) reports that in personal contact with Lefebvre he described his work as a 'heuristic approximation'. He was using this typology to illustrate an alternative way of thinking, rather than to map or describe empirical phenomena. The actual terms used were less important than providing a glimpse into his alternative vision. I believe that the terms 'material', 'imagined' and 'lived' space, as they are used in this book, remain true to that vision. As Lefebvre's most distinguished scholar, Edward Soja (1996: 2) says (Soja used the terms 'Firstspace, Secondspace and Thirdspace'): "Thirdspace is a purposefully tentative and flexible term that attempts to capture what is a constantly shifting and changing milieu of ideas, events, appearances, meanings. If you would like to invent a different term to capture what I am trying to convey, go ahead and do so".

References

Abbink, J. 2005. Being young in Africa: the politics of despair and renewal. In J. Abbink & I. Van Kessel (Eds.), *Vanguard or vandals: youth, politics and conflict in Africa (pp. 1–36)*. Leiden: Brill.

Adhikari, M. 2006. Hope, fear, shame, frustration: continuity and change in the expression of coloured identity in white supremacist South Africa, 1910-1994. *Journal of Southern African Studies, 32*(3), 467–487.

Alexander, R. 2008. *Towards dialogic teaching: rethinking classroom talk (4th ed.)*. York: Dialogos.
Alim, H. 2009. Creating 'an empire within an empire': critical hip hop, language pedagogies and the role of sociolinguistics. In S. Alim, A. Ibrahim & A. Pennycook (Eds.), *Global linguistic flows: hip hop cultures, youth identities, and the politics of language (pp. 213–230)*. London: Routledge.
Blommaert, J. 2010. *The sociolinguistics of globalization*. Cambridge: Cambridge University Press.
Canagarajah, A. 2013. *Literacy as translingual practice: between communities and classrooms*. London: Routledge.
Clarke, J., Hall, S., Jefferson, T. & Roberts, B. 1976. Subcultures, cultures & class. In S. Hall & T. Jefferson (Eds.), *Resistance through rituals (pp. 9–75)*. London: Hutchinson & Co.
de Boeck, F. 2005. Introduction: children and youth in Africa. In A. Honwana & F. de Boeck (Eds.), *Makers and breakers: children and youth in postcolonial Africa (pp. 1–18)*. London: James Currey.
Delpit, L. 2002. No kinda sense. In L. Delpit & J. K. Dowdy (Eds.), *The skin that we speak: thoughts on language and culture in the classroom (pp. 31–48)*. New York: New Press.
Dillabough, J. & Kennelly, J. 2010. *Lost youth in the global city: class, culture and the urban imaginary*. New York: Routledge.
Dimitriadis, G. 2009. *Performing identity/performing culture: hip hop as text, pedagogy and lived practice*. New York: Peter Lang.
Erasmus, Z. 2001. Introduction: re-imagining coloured identities in post-apartheid South Africa. In Z. Erasmus (Ed.), *Coloured by history, shaped by place: new perspectives on coloured identities in Cape Town (pp. 13–28)*. Cape Town: Kwela Books & South African History Online.
Fine, M. 1991. *Framing dropouts: notes on the politics of an urban public high school*. Albany: SUNY Press.
Freire, P. 1970. *Pedagogy of the oppressed*. New York: Continuum International Publishing.
García, O. & Wei, L. 2013. *Translanguaging: language, bilingualism and education*. New York: Palgrave Macmillan.
Hall, K. & Chennells, M. 2011. *Children and income poverty: a brief update. Children count brief*. Cape Town: Children's Institute, University of Cape Town.
Honwana, A. 2012. *The time of youth: work, social change, and politics in Africa*. West Hartford: Kumarian Press Pub.
International Labour Office (ILO). 2013. *Global employment trends for youth*. Geneva: International Labour Organisation.
Ladson-Billings, G. 1995. Toward a theory of culturally relevant pedagogy. *American Educational Research Journal, 32*, 465–491.
Leander, K., Phillips, N. & Taylor, K. 2010. The changing social spaces of learning: mapping new mobilities. *Review of Research in Education, 34*, 329–394.
Lefebvre, H. 1991. *The production of space*. Oxford: Blackwell.
MacLeod, J. 1995. *Ain't no makin' it: levelled aspirations in a low-income neighbourhood*. Boulder, CO: Westview Press.
Martin-Jones, M., Blackledge, A. & Creese, A. 2012. Introduction: a sociolinguistics of multilingualism for our times. In M. Martin-Jones, A. Blackledge & A. Creese (Eds.), *The Routledge handbook of multilingualism (pp. 1–26)*. London: Routledge.
McDonald, A. 2008. *World city syndrome: neoliberalism and inequality in Cape Town*. New York: Routledge.
Republic of South Africa. 1996. The South African Schools Act No. 84, 1996. Government Gazette, 15 November 1996. No. 17579.
Republic of South Africa. 2008. Child Justice Act (Act No. 75 of 2008). Pretoria: Government Printer.

Republic of South Africa. 2013. *Budget review, national treasury.* Downloaded on 25 February 2015 from: http://www.treasury.gov.za/documents/national%20 budget/2013/review.

Sayed, Y. 1999. Discourses of the policy of educational decentralisation in South Africa since 1994: an examination of the South African Schools Act. *Compare: A Journal of Comparative and International Education,* 29(2), 141–152.

Seekings, J. & Natrass, N. 2005. *Class, race and inequality in South Africa.* New Haven: Yale University Press.

Soja, E. W. 1996. *Thirdspace: journeys to Los Angeles and other real-and-imagined places.* Oxford: Blackwell.

Statistics South Africa. 2011. Downloaded on 12 July 2013 from: www.statssa.gov.za/Census2011.

Veriava, F. 2013. *The 2012 Limpopo textbook crisis: a study in rights-based advocacy, the raising of rights consciousness and governance.* Downloaded on 6 June 2014 from: http://www.section27.org.za/wp-content/uploads/2013/10/The-2012-Limpopo-Textbook-Crisis1.pdf.

Vygotsky, L. 1978. *Mind in Society: the development of higher psychological processes.* Cambridge, MA: Harvard University Press.

Vygotsky, L. 1986. *Thought and language.* Cambridge, MA: MIT Press.

Wegerif, R. 2008. Reason and dialogue in education. In B. van Oers, E. Elbers, W. Wardekker & R. van der Veer (Eds.), *The transformation of learning (pp. 273–288).* Cambridge: Cambridge University Press.

Wegerif, R. 2011. From dialectic to dialogic. In T. Koschmann (Ed.), *Theories of learning and studies of instructional practice (pp. 201–221).* New York: Springer.

Weis, L. 1990. *Working class without work: high school students in a de-industrializing economy.* New York: Routledge.

The World Bank. Downloaded on 20 November 2015 from: http://data.worldbank.org/indicator/SL.UEM.1524.ZS.

2 Language, Race and Space in Cape Town

Being so-called 'coloured' is the most confusing and mind-boggling thing there is.

Emile Jansen, member of the Black Noise hip hop crew, quoted in Battersby, 2003: 123

If Afrikaans is to be re-constructed into a symbol of non-racialism, the belief that propriety, authority and legitimacy is somehow (exclusively) related to proficiency in standard Afrikaans can obviously not be sustained, and a 'new' ideology about Afrikaans needs to be formulated and propagated, conveying the understanding that speakers of other varieties of Afrikaans (generally black, coloured or Indian/Asian speakers) are not backward, inferior or less intelligent.

Webb, 2010: 115

Where we come from Afrikaans is the language of the working class, the language of poor people and the language of the downtrodden. It is the language of the marginalised. Yet, one cannot work in Afrikaans Studies without living ironically. The novelist Jan Rabie said, "Afrikaans is South Africa's most non-racial achievement," but we also know that it bears the imprint of power and the abuse of state power.

Willemse, 2013: 126

South African Languages

The fact that young people from Rosemary Gardens spoke Kaapse Afrikaans had a profound impact on their learning endeavours in the three places. Kaapse Afrikaans is inscribed with social significance that is entangled with the history of Cape Town. Some background information on languages at the Cape is necessary to understand how Rosemary Gardens youth used their language to participate and learn, through dialogue, and how other people evaluated their words and ideas. This chapter focuses on the language used by the group studied in this book, while Chapter Three looks at a general theory of dialogic learning and the role that language plays in that process.

The genesis and evolution of Kaapse Afrikaans can be traced back into the bowels of Cape Town. It is linked to the city's most notorious periods and practices. At the same time this language has been produced by interactions between diverse groups of people, forming a spicy blend of expressive, emotive and malleable words. The term 'Kaaps' ('Kaapse' is an adjective, 'Kaaps' is the noun) was coined by the playwright Adam Small, but is not widely used. It has been used more frequently since the performance of a recent dramatic production at the Baxter Theatre and a documentary, both called *Afrikaaps*. I call this language variety 'Kaapse Afrikaans' because other names for it, like Kombuistaal (kitchen language) and Gam (derived from 'ham'; 'Gamtaal' means lower-class language) have derogatory connotations, unless used by the speakers themselves.

Kaapse Afrikaans is a close, but often embarrassing relative for white Afrikaners, quite different from the version of Afrikaans that has been standardised and is protected by the South African constitution. Standard Afrikaans evolved from Dutch and is one of the 11 official South African languages. The other 10 languages include English and nine indigenous African languages. According to the 2011 national census, isiZulu is the most widely spoken language (22.7%) in the country, followed by isiXhosa (16%), Afrikaans (13.5%) and English (9.6%).

As the name Kaapse (Cape) Afrikaans suggests, there are distinct regional differences to the languages spoken in South Africa. IsiZulu is mainly

Table 2.1 South African languages spoken, 2011

Language	% of total population
Afrikaans	13.5%
English	9.6%
isiNdebele	2.1%
isiXhosa	16%
isiZulu	22.7%
Sepedi	9.1%
Sesotho	7.6%
Setswana	8%
Sign language	0.5%
SiSwati	2.5%
Tshivenda	2.4%
Xitsonga	4.5%
Other	1.6%
TOTAL	100%

Source: Statistics South Africa, Census (2011)

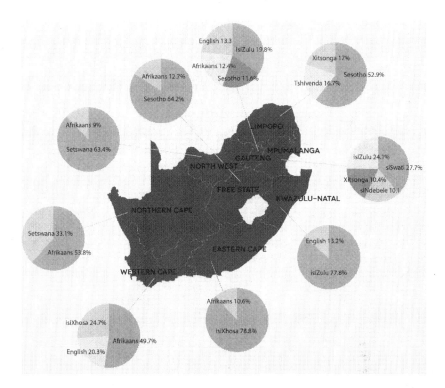

Figure 2.1 Most spoken languages in each province
Graphic: Meghan Judge

Table 2.2 Languages spoken in Rosemary Gardens

Language	People	% of Total Population
Afrikaans	23,041	81.33%
English	5215	18.41%
isiXhosa	40	0.14%
Other African	33	0.12%

Source: Statistics South Africa Census (2011)

Table 2.3 Languages spoken in Cape Town, 2011

Language	% of Total Population
Afrikaans	35.7%
English	28.4%
isiXhosa	29.8%
Other	6.1%
TOTAL	100%

Source: Census (2011)

spoken in KwaZulu Natal and in Gauteng. In the Western Cape province, where the current study takes place, Afrikaans is by far the most widely spoken language (49.7%), with isiXhosa (24.7%) and English (20.3%) less spoken (Statistics South Africa, 2011). This statistic includes all versions of Afrikaans, as census data does not differentiate.

These regional differences in language use reflect ethnic differences in the diverse South African population. The predominance of isiXhosa in the Eastern Cape, isiZulu in KwaZulu Natal, Setswana in the Northwest province and Sesotho in the Free State, indicate where the majority of Xhosa, Zulu, Tswana and Sotho people live, respectively. Despite these differences, much linguistic fluidity takes place, as contact between groups has occurred for centuries; and in contemporary South Africa people regularly speak multiple languages, mixing and matching as the context dictates (Mesthrie, 2002). This is particularly the case in urban contexts, where much language contact occurs.

A History of Language at the Cape: The Early Colonial Period

Afrikaans is the most widely spoken language in the Western Cape due to the social history of this region. Cape Town's population, and the languages it speaks, is markedly different from the inhabitants of other South African cities. It is impossible to understand the significance of the language used by young people in Rosemary Gardens and the other components of this book without unpacking how this language is related to race and space in the city. Kaapse Afrikaans emerged through interactions between groups of people at the Cape Colony; its development is bound up in specific spaces of contact and policies of segregation that occurred in the city during the colonial and apartheid periods.

The Dutch East India Company (DEIC) arrived at the Cape in 1652, with the intention to establish a refreshment station between Europe and the East Indies. The voyage from Europe to the East took approximately six months, meaning that many sailors perished due to the lack of fresh food and water. When they arrived, the Dutch encountered two distinct groups, the pastoralist, livestock-owning Khoi and the hunter-gathering San (McCormick, 2002). Under colonialism there were almost no Bantu-speaking peoples, like the Xhosa or Zulu, in the Western Cape.

The Dutch initially had no intention of settling at the Cape, but when bartering with the Khoi proved to be unreliable, a number of farms were established. Slaves were imported from Angola and Dahomey (present-day Benin) to work on the farms, with the first group of slaves arriving in 1658 (Western, 1981). Later, slaves were brought from other parts of Africa, including Zanzibar, Madagascar and Mozambique and from South India, Ceylon and the Indonesian Archipelago in Asia (McCormick, 2002). The slave population of the Cape Colony was one of the most diverse in the world in terms of origins, culture, religion and language. The existence of a diverse group of slaves meant that a great deal of contact occurred between languages at the DEIC slave lodge, at DEIC employees' homes and on farms. It was common for up to five languages to be spoken in an 18th-century Cape household (McCormick, 2002).

Between 1652 and 1795, which began the period of British colonial rule (a transition period lasted until 1815), the Dutch language dominated the new settlement, although Khoi was regularly heard in the city. By the end of the 1700s it was unusual to hear Khoi in Cape Town, as smallpox and colonial rule had destroyed most of its speakers (McCormick, 2002). Portuguese creole was particularly common during the 18th century amongst Malay slaves and those from the Indian and East African coasts.

The settlement at the Cape was still relatively small by the time the British assumed control, consisting of approximately 1,200 houses. Although English became the language of government, finance and commerce with the commencement of British colonial rule, attempts to Anglicise the society were mainly aimed at the middle and upper classes. Despite English speakers assuming political and economic supremacy and the number of immigrants from the Netherlands decreasing, Cape Dutch continued to grow and comprised the home language for most of the slave descendants (McCormick, 2002). British rule coincided with freedom of religion and the increased influence of Islam in the city. By the beginning of 1800, one fifth of Cape Town was Muslim, with Cape Dutch or Afrikaans becoming the dominant language for interactions between Muslim people in the early 1800s. Cape Dutch was even used as a medium of instruction in many madrasahs, and the first substantial pieces of written Afrikaans were completed by Muslim slaves in the Arabic script (McCormick, 2002; Mesthrie, 2002).

Cape Town After the Emancipation of Slaves

Contemporary Kaapse Afrikaans is almost exclusively spoken by coloured people, a collective identity that emerged in the aftermath of emancipation, in the context of fierce working-class competition for employment after the inland mineral discoveries. Cape Town's population is different from other South African cities: while coloured people make up 8.9% of the national population, 49% of people in the Western Cape described themselves as coloured in the 2011 census and 42% of Cape Town is made up of this group. Forty percent of the South African coloured population lives in Cape Town, including 95% of the population of Rosemary Gardens (Western, 1981). Kaapse Afrikaans and coloured identities are therefore intimately related to the Cape and its history.

The term 'coloured' was first used in the second half of the 19th century and initially referred to freed slaves (Western, 1981). Slavery was abolished in 1834, with 5,607 slaves or 29% of the city's population being freed. Most of those manumitted spoke Cape Dutch as their home language.

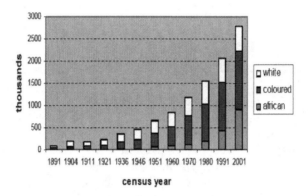

Figure 2.2 Growth of Cape Town's population by race
Source: Seekings (2007)

Emancipation was shortly followed by the discovery of precious minerals. Diamonds were first found in Kimberly in 1867, and gold was initially struck on the Witwatersrand in 1886. The Cape was transformed by the precious mineral mining industry and the resultant burgeoning industrialization as a new wave of immigrants arrived in the region. The population of Cape Town expanded almost six-fold from 33,239 in 1875 to 168,257 in 1911. The discovery of gold and diamonds led to South Africa's equivalent of the Industrial Revolution and with it a radical transformation of the social and economic structures at the Cape.

The discovery of minerals and industrialisation led to intense competition for labour. The black working classes of the Cape colony began to forge a shared identity based on a common socio-economic status and a cultural heritage that had emerged during the colonial period, including a shared language. Many in this group claimed to have a familiarity with and espousal of Western cultural forms and stated that they were, at least partly, the descendants of colonists from Europe (Adhikari, 2005). Some of the black people who had lived through the colonial period at the Cape therefore asserted a separate identity as coloured people, claiming relative privileges ahead of black people from other parts of the country. The history of coloured people at the Cape is therefore immersed in the ways in which whites have conquered, divided, ruled and exploited other groups. Under these circumstances, oppressed people have not been passive in their oppression, using different strategies in attempts to alleviate some of their harsh life circumstances. Some of these strategies included attempts to gain higher status and more resources than others perceived as lower in the colonial and apartheid hierarchies.

Coloured people should not be seen as 'mixed-race': the stereotype of coloured as based on hybridity and miscegenation implies that there are such things as 'pure races', which is clearly not true. Instead, leading scholars argue that coloured identities are creole identities forged in the colonial encounter—not just any mixture, but a particular mixture that occurred through contact between the Khoi and San, Dutch and British colonial settlers and slaves from East and North Africa and Asia. It is only in the particular mixture and the ways that it is fused and translated that coloured identities can be meaningfully understood as "detailed bodies of knowledge, specific cultural practices, memories, rituals and modes of being" (Erasmus, 2001: 21).

Although distinct coloured identities emerged in the mid-19th century, many people have rejected being classified or classifying themselves in this way, especially during the era in which Black Consciousness united different groups which were not classified as white, forging a common front to fight apartheid. However, many coloured people have also aspired to distance themselves from the black majority, assimilate with whiteness and leverage the relative privileges that were granted by a succession of white supremacist governments (Adhikari, 2005).

These divisions continue to have relevance in contemporary South Africa and in Rosemary Gardens. Many coloured Capetonians feel that they exist in a very precarious position, often claiming to be *Not white enough, not black enough*, the title of Mohamed Adhikari's book on this subject. This has led to forms of deeply conservative politics, exemplified by the fact that the Western Cape is currently the only one of the nine provinces to be ruled by the national opposition party, the Democratic Alliance (DA). The DA was formed through a merger of the New National Party—the 'Old' National Party being the institution that invented apartheid and the Democratic Party, made up mainly of white liberals. The election of the DA in 2009 was facilitated by the coloured vote, as coloured people form a majority in the Western Cape. To simplify these developments, coloured voters in the Western Cape have been instrumental in electing a ruling party with strong links to the architects of apartheid.

Language and Space in Cape Town After the Discovery of Gold and Diamonds

I am interested in the history of social relations at the Cape because of the link it has to the status of Kaapse Afrikaans, the language spoken by young people in Rosemary Gardens. The status of this language had a profound impact on how these young people learnt through educational dialogues, a process which is described in detail in the next chapter. The status of Kaapse Afrikaans was forged through political, social and linguistic forces that played out in the late 19th and early 20th centuries. In the late 1800s a white-led movement campaigning for Afrikaans to be officially recognised culminated in this group's version of the language becoming a medium of instruction in schools from 1914 and, along with Dutch and English, an official national language in 1926 (McCormick, 2002).

Increased linguistic divergence between white and non-white Afrikaans speakers was enmeshed with political events and apartheid legislation. The civil rights that were bestowed on coloured people in the mid-19th century began to be eroded at the beginning of the 20th century and were more aggressively taken away during apartheid. The British colonial authorities had not perceived the relatively small coloured population at the Cape as posing a threat and even felt a sense of "bounded liberality" to the non-whites who lived in the city (Western, 1981: 33). This resulted in equality before the law at the Cape and no legal restrictions in terms of where people were allowed to live. However, in 1887 new legislation declared a restricted franchise, segregated education systems were created, and coloured people were denied permission to be elected to parliament (Adhikari, 2005). Later, the Population Registration Act classified 'coloured' people as second-class citizens; the Group Areas Act (1950) led to the removal of people from areas like District Six, and in 1951 'coloured' voters were struck off the common voters roll.

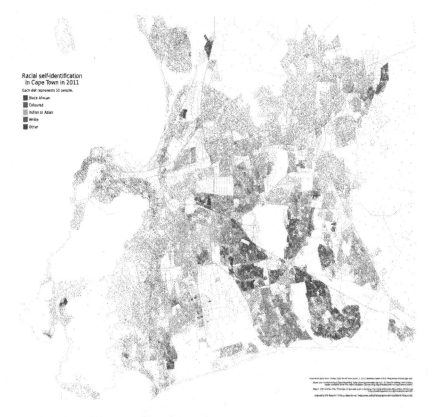

Figure 2.3 Cape Town residential areas by race
Graphic: Adrian Frith

The erosion of civil rights and the construction of laws that further entrenched an emphatically racist regime paved the way for the spatial geography of Cape Town to be radically transformed and for the construction of neighbourhoods like Rosemary Gardens. Prior to 1948, Cape Town was the most racially integrated city in Southern and possibly Sub-Saharan Africa, with one third of the city's population living in mixed neighbourhoods (Western, 1981). The Group Areas Act changed all that. Between 1966 and 1980, 60,000 people were removed from District Six, with almost all of the houses and shops bulldozed to the ground. In all, 150,000 people were forced to relocate from the city centre and southern suburbs, places like Mowbray, Claremont, Rondebosch and Harfield Village (www.capetown.at/heritage/city/district%206.htm). Apartheid Cape Town was designed such that the white population would be 'protected' by the mountain, the sea and the railway line, with further buffering provided by 'tracts' of coloured areas that formed a barrier between whites and the black African population.

As the map above illustrates, the demographic make-up of contemporary Cape Town neighbourhoods has not changed much in the post-apartheid era.

Second-Class Citizens, Second-Class Language

The lowly status of Kaapse Afrikaans is linked to its speakers' slave heritage and the fact that this group was cast as second-class citizens through draconian legislation that was implemented in the late nineteenth and mid-twentieth centuries. This language has connotations of its speakers being lower class, having dubious moral tendencies, and it is generally not perceived as an erudite language used by people who are 'well educated'.

The standardisation of Afrikaans by whites excluded the Afrikaans spoken by coloured and black speakers (Battersby, 2003). The standard Afrikaans that is used in school curricula is the culmination of the Afrikaner nationalist movement's attempts to entrench political and economic power. On the other hand, Kaapse Afrikaans is a creole language that is largely spoken by working-class Capetonians (Stone, 1991, 1995). This language formed as a result of the multiple cosmopolitan spaces in which slaves moved, the role of Islam at the Cape and the Cape's divided history of English and Dutch colonial rule. White Afrikaners resisted the mixing of English and Afrikaans, or for that matter standardised Afrikaans and any other language, due to their political project (McCormick, 2002). However, coloured people in Cape Town had a very different political, and hence linguistic agenda, contributing to their use of a different form of Afrikaans. Kaapse Afrikaans has never aspired to remain 'pure' (Dyers, 2008).

The difference between standard and Kaapse Afrikaans is only one example of how history and politics determine how specific varieties of a language become standardised over time, while other less esteemed versions of a language are given the status of 'pidgin', 'creole' and 'informal language' (Bourdieu, 1991; Mesthrie et al., 2009). In France, for example, the elite

Parisian version of French gained ascendency from other dialectics from the fourteenth century onwards. The language used in elite Parisian circles was elevated to the status of the official language and was widely used in written form, while other regional and rural dialects were classified as forms of *patois*, with relatively lower status (Bourdieu, 1991). In England, the variety of English spoken in the political and economic centre of London, as well the English used in the academic centres of Oxford and Cambridge, formed a prestigious geographical triangle in the East Midlands within which the basis for standardised, modern forms of English were agreed upon (Mesthrie et al., 2009). The relative statuses of different varieties of Afrikaans is but one example of this phenomenon.

The language spoken by young people from Rosemary Gardens was inherited from the linguistic legacy of the Cape Town underclasses. Rosemary Gardens was established through the removal of people classified as 'coloured' from areas like District Six and other parts of the Cape Town inner city and suburbs. Most of these people spoke, and their descendants continue to speak, Kaapse Afrikaans as their home language, mixed with and in addition to informal English. The vast majority of the students and all of the educators at RGHS would have been classified as 'coloured' during apartheid. Six of the teaching staff grew up in the area, but none continued to live in this neighbourhood. The variety of Afrikaans that these young people used impacted how others evaluated their language and ideas; it shaped whether these young people felt comfortable engaging in educational sites, and it influenced whether they perceived themselves as legitimate students. These perceptions varied across the three places.

Differences Between Standard Afrikaans and Kaapse Afrikaans

Speakers use Kaapse Afrikaans to play with, disrupt and assert a subordinate identity, maintaining social cohesion between people who use this language (Stone, 1995). This is different from white Afrikaners' relationship with standard Afrikaans, which represents a pertinent marker of one version of white South African identity, holding strong emotional attachment for its speakers. Coloured people generally view standard Afrikaans as a language of "arrogance and cruelty" (Webb, 2010: 112). The use of standard English or Afrikaans amongst people who predominantly speak 'Kaaps' is likely to be interpreted as the speaker attempting to distance him or herself in order to gain social ascendency. People who primarily speak Kaapse Afrikaans acknowledge that gaining upward mobility requires code-switching to middle-class English/Afrikaans in certain contexts.

The use of this language is heavily influenced by context. Rap artist Ready D says that writing a dictionary of what he calls 'gamtaal' would be impossible due to its changing nature and the fact that it is so malleable in different spaces, such as prisons, communities, schools and homes (quoted in

Marlin-Curiel, 2003: 71). Speaking Kaapse Afrikaans requires careful navigation and it is used very differently when speaking to, for example one's mother, versus speaking to a teenage peer. Middle-class people generally reject Kaapse Afrikaans as a language and discourage their children from speaking it. Rural coloured people perceive this language as a result of the moral degeneration that is linked to urban life and instead strive to maintain respectability and speak 'pure' or 'suiwer' Afrikaans. These negative appraisals of their language made it difficult for youth from Rosemary Gardens to speak in a way that felt natural to them and to be respected in educational sites.

Connecting the Cape Colony Case Study to Other Contexts

The Cape case study may seem like an extreme and unusual example of languages mixing and forming hierarchies between different versions as groups interact. However, Kaapse Afrikaans is in fact only one example of translingual practice: people use words from a range of sources as they come into contact with different groups of people. In the aftermath of slavery, colonialism and with recent high levels of migration, mixing languages appears to be a normal part of communication.

For example, 'Singlish', a mixture of Hokkien and English, is wildly popular amongst young people in Singapore and was used in hit television shows (Rubdy, 2005). The Singaporean government's *Speak English Well* campaign, attempted to suppress creative, hybrid language forms like 'Singlish'. Similarly, Indonesian nationalists have used the media and education to promote 'Indonesian', a specific, 'high' variety of Malay developed from linguistic planning conducted by scholars and administrators under Dutch colonial rule. Other varieties and creolised versions of Malay have been suppressed (Ewing, 2005).

Cameroon provides an excellent example of the multiplicity and mixed nature of languages that exist in post-colonial states, particularly in Africa. Today Cameroon has two official languages, English and French. In addition, 286 local languages are spoken amongst the population of approximately 20 million, as well as Pidgin English and a hybrid language *Camfranglais* (Nkwain, 2013). The term *Camfranglais* is made up of the French words Camerounais, Francais and Anglais, indicating that this language is a mixture of those three languages. Camerounais, a truly hybrid language, is a combination of Cameroonian Pidgin English and words from other local languages. This language is most popular amongst the youth in urban centres, spreading in the late 90s through its use by musicians.

In Morocco, a prominent philanthropist, Noureddine Ayouch, proposed several policy changes to the language of instruction in Moroccan public education (Schulthies, 2014). The proposed changes were related to debate on whether Modern Standard Arabic and Moroccan Arabic comprise different languages, or they should be understood as varieties on a linguistic continuum (Schulthies, 2014). In India, 'Hinglish', a mixture of Hindi and

English, is described in the edited collected *Chutnifying English*, a reference to linguistic hybridity coined by Salman Rushdie (Trivedi, 2011). In the foreword to that volume Hinglish is said to have existed since the British arrived in India, as languages mixed with the interactions of people. Hinglish is most commonly found in Mumbai, a city that was founded by the British.

Linguistic hybridity is not restricted to post-colonial contexts. The history of slavery in the United States created interesting language mixtures that have implications for classrooms in the 21st century. In the United States what has come to be known as the 'ebonics debate' has led to heated discussions after an Oakland court resolution recognised the legitimacy of 'ebonics' or African American Vernacular English (AAVE). The court ruled that some instruction should take place in AAVE, but that educators also need to facilitate the acquisition of standard English-language skills and learn aspects of AAVE themselves (Delpit, 1997).

In the contemporary United States people refer to the lived realities of 'Spanglish' (Morales, 2002), a hybrid of English and Spanish. The large numbers of Turks arriving in Germany since the 1960s has led to a linguistic mélange of the two languages. German parents have concerns that their children should not learn German that has been tainted by 'Turkish' (Horrocks & Kolinsky, 1996).

Many examples of languages mixing and forming hierarchies between different versions therefore exist, as people engage in forms of translingual practice. Kaapse Afrikaans is only one example of this phenomenon. As groups of people come into contact with one another, their languages cross-pollinate. The ways that languages change and are used in everyday life are bound up in the places where they interact. These different threads and snippets of language are not equally valued; they are inscribed with meaning and indicate the classed, raced and gendered identities of the speaker. Youth, such as those in this study, participate in educational settings primarily through contributing their words to the verbal discussions that occur in these places. Their words have different origins and statuses and are given different values based on ideologies pertaining to language. Young people on the margins of society usually have access to words that are not esteemed in the same ways as those of middle- and upper-class children. The evaluation of language use and by extension young people's learning endeavours are closely related to linguistic ideologies, a concept that is unpacked in detail in the next chapter.

References

Adhikari, M. 2005. *Not white enough, not black enough: racial identity in the South African 'Coloured' community*. Cape Town: Double Storey Books.

Battersby, J. 2003. 'Sometimes it feels like I'm not black enough': recast(e)ing coloured through South African hip hop as a postcolonial text. In S. Jacobs & H. Wasserman & S. Jacobs (Eds.), *Shifting selves: post-apartheid essays on mass media, culture and identity (pp. 109–129)*. Cape Town: Kwela Books.

Bourdieu, P. 1991. *Language and symbolic power*. Cambridge: Polity Press.

Delpit, L. 1997. Ebonics and culturally responsive instruction: what should teachers do? *Rethinking Schools Online, 12*(1). Downloaded from: http://www.rethinkingschools.org/archive/12_1/ebdelpit_shtml.

Dyers, C. 2008. Language shift or maintenance? Factors determining the use of Afrikaans among some township youth in South Africa. *Stellenbosch Papers in Linguistics, 38*, 49–72.

Erasmus, Z. 2001. Introduction: re-imagining coloured identities in post-apartheid South Africa. In Z. Erasmus (Ed.), *Coloured by history, shaped by place: new perspectives on coloured identities in Cape Town (pp. 13–28)*. Cape Town: Kwela Books & South African History Online.

Ewing, M. C. 2005. Colloquial Indonesian: the Austronesian languages of Asia and Madagascar. In K. Adelaar & N. Himmelmann (Eds.), *The Austronesian languages of Asia and Madagascar (pp. 227–258)*. East Sussex: Psychology Press.

Horrocks, D. & Kolinsky, E. 1996. *Turkish culture in German society today* (Vol. 1). New York: Berghahn Books.

Marlin-Curiel, S. 2003. Sampling the past: sound, language and identity in the new South Africa. In H. Wasserman & S. Jacobs (Eds.), *Shifting selves: post-apartheid essays on mass media, culture and identity (pp. 55–78)*. Cape Town: Kwela Books.

McCormick, K. 2002. *Language in Cape Town's district six*. Oxford: Oxford University Press.

Mesthrie, R. 2002. *Language in South Africa*. Cambridge: Cambridge University Press.

Mesthrie, R., Swann, J., Deumert, A. & Leap, W. 2009. *Introducing sociolinguistics*. Edinburgh: Edinburgh University Press.

Morales, E. 2002. *Living in Spanglish: the search for Latino identity in America*. New York: Macmillan.

Nkwain, J. 2013. Does language contact necessarily engender conflict? The case of Cameroonian Quadrilingualism. *Linguistik Online, 43*(3/10), 82.

Rubdy, R. 2005. Remaking Singapore for the new age: official ideology and the realities of practice in language-in-education. In A. Lin & P. Martin (Eds.), *Decolonisation, globalisation: language-in-education policy and practice (pp. 55–75)*. Clevedon: Multilingual Matters.

Schulties, B. 2014. *Reviving official language debates in Morocco*. Downloaded on 25 March from: www.anthropology-news.org/index.php/2014/03/13the-language-ofinstruction-or-the-instruction-of-language/.

Seekings, J. 2007. *Poverty and inequality after apartheid*. Working paper 200. Cape Town: Centre for Social Science Research, University of Cape Town.

Statistics South Africa. 2011. Downloaded on 12 July 2013 from: www.statssa.gov.za/Census2011.

Stone, G. 1991. *An ethnographic and socio-semantic analysis of lexis among working-class Afrikaans-speaking coloured adolescent and young adult males in the Cape Peninsula, 1963–1990*. Unpublished Masters Thesis. University of Cape Town, Cape Town.

Stone, G. 1995. The lexicon and socio-linguistic codes of the working-class Afrikaans-speaking Cape Peninsula coloured community. In R. Mesthrie (Ed.), *Language and social history: studies in South African sociolinguistics (pp. 277–290)*. Cape Town: David Phillip.

Trivedi, H. 2011. Foreword. In R. Kothari & R. Snell (Eds.), *Chutnefying English: the phenomenon of Hinglish*. India: Penguin Books.

Webb, V. 2010. Constructing an inclusive speech community from two mutually excluding ones: the third Afrikaans language movement. *Tydskrif vir letterkunde, 47*(1), 106–120.

Western, J. 1981. *Outcast Cape Town*. California: University of California Press.

Willemse, H. 2013. Jakes Gerwel (1946–2012). *Tydskrif vir letterkunde, 50*(1), 126–130. Downloaded on 10 December 2015 from: www.capetown.at/heritage/city/district%206.htm.

3 Learning, Language and Dialogue

> *It (dialogue) is the art of forming concepts through working out the common meaning. What characterizes a dialogue . . . is precisely this: that in dialogue spoken language—in the process of question and answer, giving and taking, talking at cross purposes and seeing each other's point—performs the communication of meaning.*
>
> Gadamer, 1975: 361

> *If it is in speaking their word that people, by naming the world, transform it, dialogue imposes itself as the way by which they achieve significance as human beings.*
>
> Freire, 1970: 88

Who Spoke Where

The first thing that I noticed at Youth Amplified was who spoke, how they spoke and what kind of reaction was elicited from peers. The young people arrived from scattered parts of the city and attended schools with contrasting histories. They sussed one another out, sometimes subtly, sometimes confrontationally, often suspiciously. The kids from ID Mkhize were quiet and shy. Of all the participants they were the least comfortable speaking in English. On a number of occasions Rosemary Gardens High School students became defensive when others spoke in ways that they experienced as intimidating.

At Rosemary Gardens High School I was struck by how infrequently students spoke in classrooms. Learners almost never asked questions. On the other hand, during the first full afternoon that I spent with the Doodvenootskap I was surprised by how forcefully these young people spoke, in the fairly lavish home of May Hughes, an older white woman. Members of the group were not afraid to speak openly in this setting. One or two of their inputs were even a bit rude. One member of the crew, Damian, tried to explain the value of peer education by saying that amongst his friends he speaks about "cars", but that in a discussion with May Hughes it would perhaps be more appropriate to talk about "cows". The group thought that this cheeky comment was hilarious. DVS members were not silenced in potentially intimidating places.

The ways that the young people were able to use language, in the three places, was intimately related to their learning endeavours. Language use illuminated worldviews, cultural backgrounds and social statuses. It elicited a range of emotions and insecurities, demonstrating power relations that transcended the specific sites. Young people from Rosemary Gardens have inherited the linguistic legacy that was described in the previous chapter, a history that is enmeshed with the ways that different groups of people have treated one another, as the city of Cape Town developed. This language shaped their contributions to dialogues in the three educational sites and the ways that others evaluated their words.

Language and Learning: Towards a Dialogical Theory

Language is important for learning because it is the basis for social interactions in educational sites. Together, different people's linguistic contributions coalesce to form dialogues. Dialogues crystalise through the interaction of different people's perspectives, contributions that exist in the form of language. Through exposure to new and different viewpoints, young people may reflect on their own positions, leading to forms of learning that are interactive. The utterance is the basic unit of dialogue, marking the contribution of a single speaker. Utterances exist in the form of language, which is bound up in ideologies that promote some ways of speaking as 'better' and more learned than others.

A language ideology is a belief system about what is appropriate and valuable regarding the use of language. These belief systems shape speakers' behaviour and understanding of 'appropriate' use of language. Language ideologies need to be seen in historical context (McGroarty, 2010). In the 19th century linguists were obsessed with the standardization and codification of languages. Linguists insisted that languages were bounded, unified entities that were best used with consistency and rigid grammar (Blommaert, 2010; Canagarajah, 2013; Martin-Jones, Blackledge & Creese, 2012). These ideologies of language were linked to the formation and aspirations of nations, states and empires. The development of nation-states was central to official versions of languages gaining power and status, varieties that have become institutionally supported and nationally/internationally recognised. The ways in which particular versions of French, English and Afrikaans became standardised were described in the previous chapter, linked to the political ambitions of specific groups of people. The standardisation of particular varieties of language leads to different versions becoming inscribed with varying statuses, a process which has relevance to dialogic learning in educational sites.

A substantial component of dialogic learning involves participants reflecting on the value of utterances. Language is a mobile resource that young people use to contribute opinions and learn in a range of sites. However, utterances hold different values, with words and phrases that form part of standardised dialects generally more empowered than other versions. People on the margins of society, like the young people in Rosemary Gardens, are unlikely to speak standardised versions of language. If youth and others perceive their language to hold little value, this diminishes the likelihood of their contributing utterances to dialogues, understanding their opinions in relation to those of others and co-constructing knowledge. To fully engage in dialogues youth need the confidence and opportunities to make utterances that militate against, or add to, the opinions of others, as they compare their views to different standpoints.

A useful set of concepts for analysing language ideologies and the value of forms of language is outlined by Bourdieu (1991). Bourdieu borrowed terms from the field of economics, such as linguistic 'capital' and linguistic 'products' with contingent 'value', which collectively form the linguistic 'market'. Linguistic capital is the value of the language-related resources that a person has at his/her disposal and which they use in educational sites, such as the three described in this book. Bourdieu (1991) showed how language is used to maintain power and status; the ways in which the upper classes speak and the words they use provide them with linguistic resources that enable social elevation.

The state generally supports these linguistic ideologies, endorsing standardised forms of language, validating particular linguistic conventions and enabling certain groups to acquire and accumulate linguistic capital. Governments regulate what is linguistically acceptable in formal educational settings through policies of mass schooling. Future citizens are taught to speak in specific ways and to value particular forms of language rather than others. Linguistic competence is linked to how powerful groups define what counts as excellent language usage (Bourdieu, 1991). Symbolic domination happens when groups of people begin to see their language as inherently less valuable.

Research has found that a different linguistic market exists in hip hop circles, a youth subculture which has, to some degree, interrogated and resisted the dominant linguistic market (Alim, 2009). Hip hop is the largest youth subculture globally and it fundamentally involves youth experimenting with, and asserting, new forms of language. Hip hop ciphers, the human circles in which lyrics are 'spat' and 'battles fought', have become cross-national places where linguistic identities and ideologies are produced and contested, where language is altered and recreated. The production of rap lyrics challenges hip hoppers to assess and confront linguistic ideologies. In each of the three places I carefully examined and compared the effects of the linguistic market and language ideologies on young people's participation in dialogues.

Speech Genres

The linguistic market and the value of different words fluctuates depending on the social context in which words are used. While certain kinds of linguistic capital hold value in the 'market' of, for example, gang or prison life, or in pubs in working-class neighbourhoods, particular forms of linguistic capital are most valued nationally, internationally and in powerful educational institutions.

Languages are therefore shaped by the environments in which they are used, both at a macro-societal level, but also in terms of more immediate, micro-social dynamics (Hornberger & Hult, 2008). It was unsurprising that language was used differently in classrooms at RGHS, amongst the Doodvenootskap and at Youth Amplified.

A useful concept for understanding the more localised aspects of dialogue is the notion of 'speech genres'. A speech genre is the way that language use in specific places, such as schools, leads to linguistic norms and patterns developing, observed in greetings, ways of addressing others, style of speech and word usage. Speech genres include particular content and styles of speech (Gardiner, 1992). The social position of speakers and the personal relationships that shape any given dialogue are fundamental to producing speech genres (Bakhtin, 1986).

An example of a classroom speech genre documented in international research on schooling, is known as 'Information, Response and Feedback' (IRF) (Flanders, 1970; Sinclair & Coulthard, 1975). In the form of IRF, an educator typically initiates social interactions in the classroom, the students then respond to what was initiated and the educator evaluates their responses, providing them with feedback. The educator controls this type of interaction, limiting spontaneous dialogue or learning exchanges that students may otherwise initiate. Research has shown that it is common for two thirds of all classroom talk to consist of IRF.

The IRF speech genre has emerged in relation to the role of the modern teacher, who delivers a standardised curriculum designed by an education department and who is expected to demonstrate that students have achieved predetermined learning outcomes. Some classroom-based interventions have tried to experiment with changing the predominance of IRF-type speech genres. Such programmes introduce and develop small groupwork strategies for students, as well as stipulating sets of 'ground rules': norms, values and practices that emerge or are instilled in a given place. Classroom ground rules encourage students to take turns speaking, listen to others, ask questions and give reasons for opinions (Dawes, Mercer & Wegerif, 2004; Mercer & Littleton, 2007).

Research on student groupwork has found that young people either position themselves in competition with one another, may simply agree with others, or their individual identities could be suspended in the interests of the best argument 'winning' (Mercer, 2005; Mercer & Littleton, 2007; Rojas-Drummond & Mercer, 2004; Wegerif & Mercer, 1997). This third scenario is called exploratory talk; it involves competition between ideas and not between people, with the best argument being a communal achievement that emerges through synergy between group members. Exploratory talk offers students opportunities to think collectively and find new ways of interpreting already existing knowledge (Barnes, 2008). It creates a safe space where participants may experiment with putting ideas into words, free from the threat of belittlement from others. Every participant is assumed to have the equal right to participate and to question claims that are made (Habermas, 1990; Wegerif, 2008).[1] Group decisions are based on rational agreement, as people debate which perspectives contain the most value. Researchers generally agree that exploratory talk is ideal for promoting classroom-based learning.

Hip hop and talk radio contain different speech genres that affect dialogue and learning. Hip hop ciphers are the circles in which rappers 'spit' their lyrics as they interact with one another by demonstrating their lyrical prowess. The fact that rappers position themselves within circular ciphas (sometimes spelled 'cypher' or 'cypha'), such that a hierarchy does not exist, and that they take turns speaking, hints at a speech genre that is democratic, encouraging dialogue. However, the 'battles' that are fought in these circles have a reputation for frequently containing personal insults and gratuitous 'dissing', which do not facilitate dialogic learning. Although DVS did not take part in battles and I did not observe them participating in ciphas, I looked for evidence of the kinds of speech genres that the group utilised in interactions with each other and with me. I also explored their written lyrics, hunting for clues about the kinds of dialogues the group valued and in which they engaged.

Talk radio encourages a speech genre that seeks out different opinions and attempts to stimulate debate. Youth Amplified was facilitated by the young people, another factor which potentially offered opportunities for a speech genre that was non-hierarchical and unintimidating for the participants. On the other hand, the show was broadcast across the entire city of Cape Town, which may have inhibited dialogue and led to a repressed speech genre. A range of patterns of utterances emerged in each of the places, speech genres that inhibited or enabled dialogic learning.

Authoritative and Internally Persuasive Discourses

Speech genres and opportunities to participate in dialogue are shaped by what Bakhtin (1981) called authoritative and internally persuasive discourses.[2] Authoritative discourses demand acknowledgement, may not be questioned or changed and can be thought of as the "word of the father" (Bakhtin, 1981: 342–346). This form of discourse insists on unconditional loyalty to its content and values; it is taboo to play with its content, as it must be completely accepted or rejected. In terms of its subject matter, authoritative discourse often consists of 'traditions', the 'official line' or in the acknowledged truths of, for example, religion or science. On the other hand, internally persuasive discourse is very important for dialogic learning, as it invites responses through catalysing people to respond with new words or ideas of their own. Internally persuasive discourse evokes the imagination and often involves forms of play.

At RGHS, Youth Amplified and amongst the Doodvenootskap, young people were exposed to forms of authoritative and internally persuasive discourse that affected how and whether they were drawn into dialogues. A crucial initial question that I asked in each of the three places was whether young people were actually provided with opportunities to speak, respond and engage in dialogues. Were they able to place their perspectives alongside those of others and participate in discussions? Were these youth able to make statements that went against the grain and challenged other perspectives? Sometimes young people need first to be exposed to new ideas in a structured manner through authoritative discourse before they are able to play with and amend these forms of knowledge. Used strategically and in combination, both authoritative and internally persuasive discourse may therefore stimulate thinking and learning (Matusov, 2007). However, places where authoritative discourses operate exclusively can silence young people and result in their feeling bored, inadequate and unable or unwilling to contribute to educational discussions.

Dialogic learning is substantially shaped by the language-related ideologies that exist in a society, as well as the more immediate ways that language is shaped by learning places, factors like speech genres and authoritative/internally persuasive discourse. These macro-ideological and more immediate influences shape whether young people are willing and able to make sense of the relationships between their own ideas and those of others. If these contextual factors enable opportunities for dialogic learning, young people may then attempt to insert themselves into dialogues and begin to understand other opinions, perspectives and ideas.

Building Bridges and 'Double-Voicedness': Learning Through Dialogue

The process through which educational dialogues lead to learning is illuminated by the concepts of *fusing horizons* and *double-voicedness*. Understanding in dialogue involves metaphorically laying down a bridge between different perspectives, fusing or connecting two separate 'horizons'. This 'bridge' helps to transcend the hiatus between what initially appears as two distinct 'horizons'. Other people's words, located across this metaphorical bridge, need to resonate with something 'close' to one's personal experiences or imagination. Different horizons therefore represent gaps in understanding between a person's own perspectives and the opinions of others. The fusion of horizons requires a form of linguistic mediation, a transfer of language and meaning from one horizon to the other, such that something common is expressed (Gadamer, 1975: 306). Knowledge is co-constructed by generating similarities between two separate but related concepts or viewpoints. The metaphor of a horizon demonstrates that this process involves points of view or 'lenses' that allow people to understand certain perspectives, ideas and concepts in relation to others. A person needs to be able to connect their experiences or words to a new perspective, in the process understanding similarities and differences. This does not mean that a generic, universal experience or concept is arrived at through this comparison, but rather that a person's previous understanding is refined.

For example, I might understand the word 'pretentious' to mean a person trying to impress others through driving a flashy car and wearing expensive clothes. Somebody else may use the term in a different context, applying it to intellectuals trying to be impressive through using obscure words. Dialogic learning involves using my understanding of 'pretentious' to observe something common to the different uses of this concept. I may realise that (possibly underserved) self-importance can be applied to intellectual and other social contexts. By using my understanding of the term I build a bridge and link it to another meaning, refining and expanding my original knowledge of the concept 'pretentious', through interactions with somebody else and their knowledge. In this way a joint product emerges through the dialogue.

'Building a bridge' and linking common understanding may lead to young people appropriating the words of others, incorporating them into their own repertoires through a process called 'double-voicedness' (Bakhtin, 1981). Double-voicedness refers to integrating the words of another into one's own linguistic resources. For example, a student may hear a word used by a teacher without understanding its meaning. The child could then ask a parent to explain the meaning of the word and s/he may provide them with a different explanation. Over time they attempt to amalgamate the perspectives or voices of teachers and parents into their own words, fusing these different horizons through the process of double-voicedness. The words that are appropriated are always partly theirs, partly somebody else's, partly the product of the historical context.

In the classroom, I examined how ideas and concepts were introduced and formed part of lessons, how students responded to teachers' utterances and whether they acquired new ideas and concepts through classroom discussions. At Youth Amplified, the materials the group engaged with, such as documentaries, written pieces and interviews, generated a range of perspectives that were used in discussions and which held potential for learning. Doodvenootskap members' interacted with nongovernmental organisations (NGOs) and global hip hop culture, providing insight into the ways in which these young people developed their own ideas, double-voicing these after discussions with others.

A substantial component of dialogic learning therefore consists of young people assessing different perspectives and explaining concepts or theories in 'their own words'. Doing so successfully demonstrates that the essence of the concept or theory has been understood, through using one's own language to describe the words of another. People demonstrate understanding by assimilating knowledge into personal conceptual frameworks and explaining terms in their own words, not simply reiterating the thinking of somebody else (Alexander, 2008; Nystrand, 1997). Through this process, subjective understandings are refined. However, it is also important that people listen to, and understand, what others say, as this provides them with different perspectives. Dialogic learning takes place when young people adapt the core meaning of other people's utterances to produce something new; double-voicedness is an integral part of this process.

Conclusion

Learning is a social process forged through interactions between people. Language is central to these interactions, allowing communication to flow, but, simultaneously, reinforcing societal power relations through linguistic ideologies. Speech genres, patterns of interactions between people demonstrate the norms and practices that become re-enacted in particular contexts, producing particular kinds of social interactions and learning experiences. Even individual learning processes, exemplified by the concepts of 'fusing horizons' and 'double voicedness', illustrate the fundamentally social nature of learning, involving multiple interacting horizons and the voices of different people. In a recent collection entitled *Contemporary theories of learning*, the editor Knud Illeris (2009) argues that learning involves the interaction of a person's internal processes with external, environmental factors. Illeris (2009) believes that a comprehensive theory of learning requires integrating these two very different sets of processes. This kind of approach to learning assumes that the individual and her environment are two separate variables to begin with. Through the concepts of language and place I have tried to show how people and contexts are always already part of and subsumed within each other. Places *are* the social relations that lead to their becoming thought of as 'this place' or 'that place' in the first place. Places are underpinned by sets of social relations that shape who learns, how they learn and why they learn. While this chapter has focussed on *dialogic learning*, the next will unpack the *places* in which it did or did not happen for youth from Rosemary Gardens.

Notes

1 Habermas calls this form of communication the 'ideal speech situation'. In the ideal speech situation, 'rational' debates are strived for, discussions are intended not to be hampered by individuals physically or emotionally coercing others in the group.
2 In this case discourse refers to the relationship between different utterances that together make up forms of communication. This meaning of the term differs from Foucauldian 'discourse', which is concerned with the relationship between power and knowledge.

References

Alexander, R. 2008. *Towards dialogic teaching: rethinking classroom talk (4th ed.)*. York: Dialogos.

Alim, H. 2009. Creating 'an empire within an empire': critical hip hop, language pedagogies and the role of sociolinguistics. In S. Alim, A. Ibrahim & A. Pennycook (Eds.), *Global linguistic flows: hip hop cultures, youth identities, and the politics of language (pp. 213–230)*. London: Routledge.

Bakhtin, M. 1981. *The dialogic imagination: four essays by M. M. Bakhtin*. Austin: University of Texas Press.

Bakhtin, M. 1986. *Speech genres and other late essays*. Austin: University of Texas Press.

Barnes, D. 2008. Exploratory talk for learning. In N. Mercer & S. Hodgkinson (Eds.), *Exploring talk in school (pp. 1–17)*. London: SAGE.

Blommaert, J. 2010. *The sociolinguistics of globalization*. Cambridge: Cambridge University Press.

Bourdieu, P. 1991. *Language and symbolic power*. Cambridge: Polity Press.

Canagarajah, A. S. 2013. *Literacy as translingual practice: between communities and classrooms*. London: Routledge.

Dawes, L., Mercer, N. & Wegerif, R. 2004. *Thinking together: a programme of activities for developing speaking, listening and thinking skills*. Birmingham: Imaginative Minds Ltd.

Flanders, N. 1970. *Analysing teacher behaviour*. Reading, MA: Addison-Wesley.

Freire, P. 1970. *Pedagogy of the oppressed*. New York: Continuum International Publishing.

Gadamer, H. 1975. *Truth and method*. London: Continuum.

Gardiner, M. 1992. *The dialogics of critique: M.M. Bakhtin and the theory of ideology*. London: Routledge.

Habermas, J. 1990. *Discourse ethics: notes on a program of philosophical justification, moral consciousness and communicative action*. Cambridge: MIT Press.

Hornberger, N. & Hult, F. 2008. Ecological language education policy. In B. Spolsky & F. Hult (Eds.), *The handbook of educational linguistics (pp. 280–296)*. United Kingdom: John Wiley & Sons.

Illeris, K. 2009. A comprehensive understanding of human learning. In K. Illeris (Ed.), *Contemporary theories of learning: learning theorists . . . in their own words (pp. 7–21)*. London: Routledge.

Martin-Jones, M., Blackledge, A. & Creese, A. 2012. Introduction: a sociolinguistics of multilingualism for our times. In M. Martin-Jones, A. Blackledge & A. Creese (Eds.), *The Routledge handbook of multilingualism (pp. 1–26)*. London: Routledge.

Matusov, E. 2007. Applying Bakhtin Scholarship on discourse in education: a critical review essay. *Educational Theory*, 57(2), 215–237.

McGroarty, M. 2010. Language and ideologies. In N. Hornberger (Ed.), *Sociolinguistics and language education (pp. 3–39)*. Bristol: Multilingual Matters.

Mercer, N. 2005. Sociocultural discourse analysis: analysing classroom talk as a social mode of thinking. *Journal of Applied Linguistics*, 1(2), 137–168.

Mercer, N. & Littleton, K. 2007. *Dialogue and the development of children's thinking*. London: Routledge.

Nystrand, M. 1997. *Opening dialogue: understanding the dynamics of language and learning in the English classroom*. New York: Teachers College Press.

Rojas-Drummond, S. & Mercer, N. 2004. Scaffolding the development of effective collaboration and learning. *International Journal of Educational Research*, 39, 99–111.

Sinclair, J. M. & Coulthard, R. M. 1975. *Toward an analysis of discourse.* New York: Oxford University Press.

Wegerif, R. 2008. Reason and dialogue in education. In B. van Oers, E. Elbers, W. Wardekker & R. van der Veer (Eds.), *The transformation of learning (pp. 273–288).* Cambridge: Cambridge University Press.

Wegerif, R. & Mercer, N. 1997. A dialogical framework for researching peer talk. In R. Wegerif & P. Scrimshaw (Eds.), *Computers and talk in the primary classroom (pp. 49–65).* Clevedon: Multilingual Matters.

4 Learning Places

> *Consider a house ... The house has ... an air of stability about it ... the epitome of immobility, with its concrete and its stark, cold and rigid outlines ... Now, a critical analysis would doubtless destroy the appearance of solidity ... stripping it, of its concrete slabs and its thin non-load-bearing walls, which are really glorified screens, and uncovering a very different picture. ... Our house would emerge as permeated from every direction by streams of energy which run in and out of it by every imaginable route: water, gas, electricity, telephone lines, radio and television signals. ... Its image of immobility would then be replaced by an image of a complex of mobilities, a nexus of in and out conduits.*
>
> Lefebvre, 1991: 92–93

'Places Without Borders'

Language ideologies and other context-specific processes related to language, like speech genres, shaped learning in the three places. However, these were not the only factors that influenced these educational sites. A thorough understanding of how dialogic learning operated at RGHS, Youth Amplified and amongst the Doodvenootskap, required unpacking what these places consisted of. As should now be obvious, I am not using place only to refer to a physical zone with a perimeter around it, or, like in Euclidean geometry, a location on a two-dimensional Cartesian plane. Places are actually produced through sets of social relations (Lefebvre, 1991). Relations between teachers and students partly produce classrooms: a room with only desks and a chalkboard and no people would not be a classroom in any meaningful way. It is helpful to think of places as junctions, points of intersection within networks of social relations. Many of the social relations associated with the place in question primarily occur outside of its geographical location. Places are historically located too; the moment when geographical locations become officially recognised as 'this' place or 'that' place they develop norms, values and associated power relations. Place is therefore inseparable from time, as places do not pre-exist social relations. Assuming that places are ready-made physical settings within which learning happens excludes analyses of how and why these sites 'got there' in the first place (Sheehy & Leander, 2004).

RGHS, the Doodvenootskap and Youth Amplified can therefore be thought of as porous, evolving constellations of social relations that met at a specific moment and evolved over time. For example, the school was not an enclosed container, separated from the surrounding neighbourhood and students' home environments. Young people arrived at school from homes that contained caregivers, siblings and particular economic circumstances. They travelled to school through neighbourhoods with specific social problems and resources. The school was connected to an education department that devised curricula and prescribed the behaviour of school personnel; it was a component of a nation that shaped educational policy documents and, in the process, envisioned its ideal citizenry. Learning places are therefore connected to and produced by a range of social relations that operate at different levels. Analysing how learning did or did not happen in these places required an understanding of the key sets of social relations at work in each place. One way of systematically exploring the three learning places is to unpack how material, imagined and lived space contributed to producing these sites and shaped their potential for dialogic learning.

'Place, Rosemary & Time': Material Space, Learning and Rosemary Gardens High School

The ways in which residential areas were divided and rearranged in Cape Town led to the construction and evolution of Rosemary Gardens High School as a learning place. Apartheid legislation enabled the forced removal of people from certain areas and their relocation to more remote, less well-resourced, newly constructed neighbourhoods. This had a profound impact on where Capetonians lived, found employment and attended schools in the second half of the 20th century. These laws shaped spatial routes, routines and forms of mobility in the city, with ramifications for schooling in the past and present. A map of where people of different race groups lived in 2011 closely resembles apartheid era divisions (see map page 43).

While schools everywhere generally reproduce inequalities, apartheid spatial segregation produced extreme forms of class- and race-based inequalities that were and continue to be significantly spatialised. Some youth who live in areas previously reserved for 'black' and 'coloured' children do attend schools elsewhere, but school fees, transportation costs and fears of public humiliation, due to not being able to afford, for example, school outings, prevent many young people from attending schools in middle-class suburbs (Bray et al., 2010).

These divisions and inequalities are perpetuated in post-apartheid Cape Town. The city is divided into a global cosmopolitan coastal paradise where shopping malls and other services support work and leisure for a global elite, separate from the slums or townships that exist on the outskirts of the city. The townships supply cheap labour for the wealthy sectors of Cape Town. These divisions have been exacerbated by the creation of City Improvement Districts (CIDs), demarcated zones in which taxpayers contribute additional funds in order to gain access to higher-quality services, including security. Material spatial divisions that began under apartheid and continue in the post-apartheid city impact heavily on schools in neighbourhoods previously reserved for people classified as 'black', 'Indian' and 'coloured'.

'Imagine All the Rosemary Gardens People': Imagined Space and Learning at RGHS

Material and imagined space constantly intersect. One example of this is the ways that physical places or neighbourhoods, and by extension schools, that were constructed for 'coloured' people under the Group Areas Act (1950) are associated with a wide range of racialised stereotypes and prejudices. Stereotypes related to schools and youth in these areas include a lack of learning at school, as well as widespread immorality, criminality, drug use, school dropout and illicit sexual activity amongst youth in these neighbourhoods. Depictions of 'colouredness' have been tainted by the rise of gangs or 'brotherhoods' after forced removals (Pinnock, 1984; Scharf, 1986). Through these brotherhoods some young coloured men found ways of recreating social cohesion following the state's rupturing of communities like District Six. However, coloured youth involved in organised armed violence remain a small minority of the total population.

Social problems, like young men involved in organised armed violence, are a direct result of oppressive policies and inequalities in both the past and present. Yet these social challenges are not generally perceived as a consequence of disparities: they are instead understood as a direct threat to the credibility and allure of the 'global city'. This results in youth of colour being constructed as a problem that needs to be solved, part of, for example, a 'war that needs to be waged on crime' (Samara, 2011). Regular depictions, in the media and the general social imaginary of working-class coloured youth as gangsters may have a damaging effect on young people at schools like RGHS (Samara, 2011). These portrayals are likely to affect young people's self-perceptions, as well as what they believe is possible for people like themselves. Material spatial divisions created by apartheid legislation and subsequent processes that perpetuate inequality have therefore led to places like Rosemary Gardens becoming imagined as filled with criminality and danger. Township schools that these youth attend, like RGHS, are conceived as dysfunctional, criminalised spaces associated with 'blackness' and 'colouredness' in the media and in the imaginations of the middle and upper classes of Cape Town (Fataar, 2007). These perceptions have an effect on teachers' and students' attitudes, contributing to the kinds of learning places that township schools become.

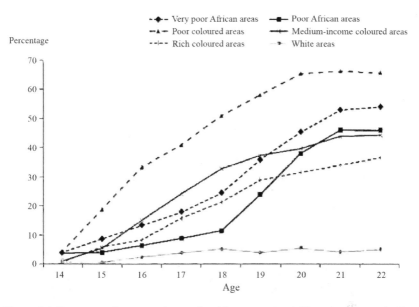

Figure 4.1 Premature departure from school by age and neighbourhood type in Cape Town

Source: Bray et al. (2010)

The ways that people in neighbourhoods like Rosemary Gardens imagine their place in democratic South Africa impacts on their perceptions of schools. Bray et al. (2010) found that coloured youth were far more likely to discontinue their schooling than black youth (Bray et al., 2010). Using data from the representative Cape Area Panel Study, they show that approximately 10% of learners at schools in poor, formerly 'black' areas had left school by age 17, yet in excess of 40% of learners of the same age in formerly 'coloured' areas no longer attended school.

High rates of coloured youth discontinuing their schooling implies that this group does not believe that genuine opportunities exist for them in post-apartheid South Africa and that they feel alienated in the new democratic dispensation. On the other hand, many black youth continue to believe that education offers opportunities for improved social and economic status and therefore persevere with their schooling. Black Capetonian youth invest in the widely accepted ideological position that if you go to school and work hard, you will be rewarded with upward social mobility, whereas, in general, coloured youth are not convinced by this rhetoric. All of the educators and almost all of the students at RGHS would have been classified as 'coloured' during apartheid. RGHS as a place of learning cannot be understood in isolation from the material spatial practices that have divided people in the greater Cape Town area and the effects this segregation has had on the perceptions of different groups.

'Learning to Live': Schooling and Lived Space

Students are not passive in relation to oppressive forms of material and imagined space. International research shows many examples of how marginalised youth create lived space through forms of resistance to schooling. In his classic study *Learning to Labour: why working class kids get working class jobs*, Paul Willis (1977) showed how working-class British men exert some agency through constructing oppositional school identities or cultures. Willis' 'lads' resisted the authority of their teachers, making fun of middle-class men and their 'book-learning' and rejecting educational achievement ideology. This was observed in, for example, their refusal to be quiet in class or read books, practices they associated with 'soft', middle-class men.

This study did not use a spatial analysis but, in the terms that I am using, the 'lads' instead created lived space through favouring places like the shop floor and the pub, reproducing 'authentic' class and gender-specific practices and identities in these sites. Their oppositional identities and rejection of formal education ultimately resulted in their perpetuating the class-based structure of their society, as these 'working-class kids got working-class jobs', the subtitle of Willis' book. Identities that exhibit elements of lived space, forged in opposition to mainstream culture, may eventually be self-defeating. At the same time, the school's inability to engage with marginalised young people's class-culture backgrounds suppresses dialogue and learning, reproducing societal inequalities. A form of lived space for working-class youth, in relation to RGHS, may therefore consist of rejecting the school and its ideologies, as was suggested by the high rates of coloured youth who stop attending school. The consequences of this course of action may ultimately be self-defeating.

Evidence exists that school discontinuation is not an empowering process for poor urban youth. Fine (1991) found that young black students in inner-city New York stopped coming to school as a consequence of the numerous ways that school practices, policies and ideologies function to push young people out of school and effectively silence them. Silencing occurred through classroom-based practices of quelling dissenting opinions, rewarding conformity, repressing certain forms of participation and the teacher ultimately providing the 'correct' answer that students needed to remember and then recite when they were evaluated (Fine, 1991). Silencing "signifies a terror of words, a fear of talk" (Fine, 1991: 32). This description does not invoke an empowering image of lived space, created through oppositional identities and rejecting the school. Young people's decisions and practices, such as discontinuing their schooling, therefore need to be carefully analysed to assess whether these actions constitute empowering forms of lived space. Although oppositional identities and forms of resistance may initially appear to comprise forms of agency, they may ultimately function to perpetuate inequalities.

A more empowering form of school opposition is youth who maintain high educational aspirations and persist with schooling, but, simultaneously, resist education in its institutionalised form. Mac an Ghaill (1988) describes the 'black sisters', a group of Asian and Afro-Caribbean girls in the United Kingdom who displayed a pro-education but anti-school stance: they saw the value of education in terms of the potential it held for their advancement in society, but rejected education in its institutionalised form due to their experiences of racist schools (Mac an Ghaill, 1988). These young women created lived space, resisting their school through being late for classes, poor attendance, not completing their homework and by speaking in their mother-tongue language while at school. Concurrently, the 'black sisters' strived to achieve at school in order to subvert racist societal stereotypes of black girls being associated with intellectual inferiority. These youth displayed high educational aspirations, but disengaged from the school, in so doing utilising lived space to resist the school's institutional culture. Finding empowering forms of lived space for poor urban youth of colour often means resisting powerful forces that result in an alienating school experience, but simultaneously being able to endure the school system and extract the codes and qualifications it offers.

Conceptualising Rosemary Gardens High School as a place made up of sets of intersecting material, imagined and lived socio-spatial relations that coalesce in a particular moment, helped to understand how the school inhibited or enhanced learning. Material, historical forces, such as forced removals, have violently subjugated groups of people who live in Rosemary Gardens. The school was also shaped by imagined forces that constructed RGHS as a particular kind of place associated with coloured youth, ideologies that generally evoked stereotypical connotations of criminality, substance abuse, teenage pregnancy and a lack of learning. Research has shown that lived space crystalises in schools like RGHS through young people's oppositional identities and resistance to schooling. Resistance is not the only form of lived space, as youth may produce lived space by, for example, using combinations of real and imagined space. Succeeding against the odds, in educational contexts, may also be a form of lived space. However, research has shown how marginalised young people are often attracted to forms of resistance in order to express themselves, demonstrating their disdain for alienating educational institutions. These practices may ultimately be self-defeating in terms of youth not acquiring powerful forms of knowledge and failing to obtain formal education qualifications that may be used for upward social mobility.

'Two Weddings and a Funeral Service': The Doodvenootskap as a Site of Learning

The subtitle of this section is a play on the title of the popular movie *Four Weddings and a Funeral*. In this context it refers to the committed relationships the Doodvenootskap had with the NGO called the Children's Rights and Anti-Abuse Group (CRAAG) and with hip hop culture, as well as the literal translation of the Afrikaans term Doodvenootskap, which means 'funeral service'. To further explain the Doodvenootskap's relationship with CRAAG, three members of the crew were employed by this organisation. As CRAAG employees they helped conduct research with young people in Rosemary Gardens and advocated for the nonviolent treatment of children from this neighbourhood. They facilitated youth participation in decision-making forums at school and in the community. The Doodvenootskap's relationships with CRAAG and hip hop culture shaped the kind of learning that occurred amongst the group, as did the way the crew imagined itself to be a funeral service, cleaning up the 'mess' made by gang affiliation.

Doodvenootskap Learning Practices Enabled by Material Office Space

DVS was not a 'place' in the same ways that Youth Amplified and RGHS were places. Youth Amplified and RGHS had definite physical locations in which most of the learning-related activities occurred, namely the building on Spindal Road, Rosemary Gardens (RGHS) and the radio station on Main Road, Salt River (Youth Amplified). The Doodvenootskap did not have a similar central meeting point; it is better thought of as a metaphorical 'place'. However, DVS did conduct a substantial proportion of its work at the community centre in Rosemary Gardens, where CRAAG provided them with an office, Internet access and a telephone line. This was the place where I usually interacted with the group. This community centre was known as the *Global Hope Foundation* building. Global Hope Foundation (GHF) is an international NGO that operates in Rosemary Gardens; its premises were built in 1982 through a partnership between the United Reformed Church from Germany and GHF. This place was originally used as a crèche for children from the area. Other NGOs besides GHF rented offices in the building, which functioned to serve a diverse range of needs for the people of Rosemary Gardens.

As mentioned, CRAAG employed three DVS members, providing them with an office, a material place that the entire group utilised. The history of NGOs having a physical presence in the neighbourhood of Rosemary Gardens aided people and groups who were oppressed by apartheid. NGOs continue to conduct community development work in this and other neighbourhoods, in the democratic period, impacting on the material space of these areas and providing services for residents. These physical places enabled young people like the Doodvenootskap to participate in specific kinds of educational practices and engage in a set of dialogues with NGOs and other groups that worked in the building and neighbourhood.

Imagined and Lived Space for the Doodvenootskap

The language and reference points used by CRAAG and other NGOs in the Global Hope Foundation building provided a rich set of ideas and concepts that DVS used in dialogues. This language and these concepts gave clues to the kind of imagined space inhabited by the crew. CRAAG staff regularly used children's rights discourses in their speech and in documents produced by the organisation, language that was related to the history of this NGO. A department of public health at a Cape Town university formed CRAAG in 1989, with the intention of using the NGO to conduct training and provide education on the prevention of child abuse. CRAAG was initially established as a research programme and later became part of a research unit at the university in question. Public health roots meant that a pervasive human rights discourse, couched in the language of 'empowerment', 'children's rights' and 'resilience', punctuated the speech of CRAAG employees. The Doodvenootskap was exposed to this discourse and a range of new concepts through their associations with CRAAG, shaping the imagined space in which the group worked.

Partnerships between civil society organisations, such as DVS and CRAAG, may combine liberal, rights-based discourses with forms of collective mobilization, generating rich dialogical learning places. These kinds of partnerships often lead to effective forms of political engagement in postcolonial contexts like South Africa (Robbins, 2008). While the existence of a relatively 'big' state has provided grants and constitutionalised social rights to citizens, access to these rights often requires pressure, advocacy and grassroots mobilisation, forcing the state to deliver on legislated promises. In post-apartheid South Africa some of the most effective forms of political mobilisation have been catalysed by partnerships between NGOs, other civil society organisations and social movements. These coalitions adopt pragmatic approaches to accessing state and donor funding, often through creating rich forms of dialogue in the public sector (Robbins, 2008). Examples of political alliances between civil society organisations and local people in post-apartheid South Africa include the Treatment Action Campaign forcing the state to provide anti-retrovirals for HIV-positive people. Abahlali baseMjondolo, the shack dwellers anti-eviction campaign for people in informal settlements, is another prominent case of this kind of partnership. For DVS, partnerships with NGOs meant potentially being exposed to new educational concepts and dialogues.

DVS' affiliation to global and local hip hop culture also provided it with rich imagined and lived spaces. Hip hop is a subculture and a set of practices that began in the Bronx in the early 1970s. It consists of rapping, breakdancing or b-boying, graffiti art and DJing (Chang, 2005, 2006). Young people, especially poor youth of colour, use hip hop to explore who they are and the world around them, engaging with rap songs and the life stories of famous rappers, like Tupac Shakur, to construct their identities, histories and a sense of community (Dimitriadis, 2009).

The Doodvenootskap identified with 'conscious' hip hop, a subgenre of hip hop started in the United States in the 1980s and 90s. Conscious hip hop is associated with American artists such as Afrika Bambaata, KRS-one and Chuck D. Conscious hip hop provides youth with the space to dialogue with mainstream popular culture and other aspects of society, prioritising the fifth element of hip hop, namely knowledge, particularly 'knowledge of self' (Haupt, 2008). 'Knowledge of self' is believed to be generated through intensive introspection, a necessary learning process according to emcees and one that needs to begin before meaningful hip hop art can be generated for political and social ends.

Part of this introspective knowledge of self is generated by hip hoppers outside of the United States translating meaningful hip hop practices, languages and values into their own local contexts, creating new imagined and lived spaces. The meaning of hip hop is reinterpreted in new contexts, as its practitioners try to stay true to the African-American version of the genre, not 'sell out' and, simultaneously, represent their own local contexts, languages and cultural practices. Hip hop is always used performatively, as youth give it meaning in their local times and spaces (Dimitriadis, 2009). Localization therefore involves a complex and often contradictory set of translations, as hip hop comes into contact with different class, race, ethnic and linguistic forces.

Research in Tanzania and Senegal showed how rappers initially mimicked American hip hop culture, before abandoning elements of US rap that were incongruent with the local context (Pennycook, 2007). In Tanzania rappers adopted aspects of American culture, including idioms, fashion and musical style. Soon thereafter Tanzanian hip hoppers began rejecting themes of violence and crude language because these were judged to be out of sync with local values (Perullo & Fenn, 2003). A similar trend occurred in Senegal, as rappers initially glorified popular American hip hop themes, like violence and chauvinism, before rechanneling their efforts to address local problems like poverty, racism and ethnic strife. Korean and Malaysian artists have expressed similar sentiments, saying that 'keeping it real' involves addressing issues of immediate concern and remaining true to values that exist in local contexts (Pennycook, 2007).

Conscious hip hop has likewise challenged Cape Town youth to explore aspects of their identities, engage with issues of common concern and to imagine new lived realities. It has provided them with a platform to enhance their critical and creative learning skills, which they have rarely acquired in the mainstream education system (Haupt, 2008). Towards the end of apartheid, Cape Town–based conscious hip hop groups like Prophets of da City and Black Noise used this cultural form to create a space for youth to express their resistance to the apartheid regime and question apartheid-era categories. Some of these groups utilised forms of Black Consciousness in their tracks, attempting to stimulate critical thinking. Consider the following lyrics from *Black thing* by the group Prophets Of da City:

> *The term 'coloured' is a desperate case*
> *Of how the devil divided us by calling us a separate race*

They called me 'coloured', said my blood isn't pure, but G
I'm not yakking my insecurity
So I respond to this and ventilate my mental state with black consciousness
...
And I believe in each one teach one reach one from the heart
Cause that's where beats are from
But racism's a trap and the nation seems to lack knowledge of self.
But it means what it seems
We're attracting anything but a black thing
(Quoted in Haupt, 2008: 146)

And from Black Noise:

Mandela can't set the 'coloured' man free, cause the 'coloured' man don't know who the hell he wanna be.
(Quoted in Battersby, 2003: 124)

Prophets of da City invoked forms of Black Consciousness through the creative medium of hip hop, generating powerful learning opportunities for Cape Town youth during apartheid. Apartheid functioned as an extreme form of restricting people classified as 'black', 'coloured' or 'Indian' from accessing public spaces and quality education. Conscious hip hop groups like Prophets of da City resisted this subjugation through forms of Black Consciousness (Haupt, 2008). The Black Noise lyric about Nelson Mandela indicates that other groups have used conscious hip hop to deconstruct the meaning of racial categories. Both groups demonstrate that this medium can be used to stimulate the interests and concerns of Cape Town youth, catalysing new imagined and lived spaces.

DVS form part of this rich tradition of learning through dialogue as it manifests in conscious Cape Town hip hop, although their politics was not aligned with Black Consciousness. In the post-apartheid era hip hop continues to provide the imagined space for South African youth to engage in forms of learning. Hip hop has therefore provided multiple generations of South African, and more specifically Cape Town youth, with a public space in which to resist oppressive political regimes, gain access to the public sphere and 'self-service' some of their developmental learning needs. NGOs and forms of popular culture enable alternative learning places for young Capetonians, both through developing forms of material space, like community centres and by imagining spaces in which youth may create and live alternative languages and ideas.

'Radio Material': Material Space and Youth Amplified

Unlike Rosemary Gardens High School and the Doodvenootskap, Youth Amplified's central activities took place outside of the local neighbourhood,

54 *Learning Places*

at the community radio station. The radio station, which was established shortly after the democratic political transition, broadcasted from a studio that was a big, unpretentious warehouse. It was born out of a project that the founder completed as part of an adult education course at a tertiary education institution in Cape Town in the early 1980s. The founder produced and distributed what he called a 'talking newspaper'—cassette tapes of the speeches of banned activists, politically charged music and revolutionary poetry. The station has subsequently established strong links to the University of the Western Cape's (UWC) journalism department. These founding influences that occurred during the apartheid struggle and current links to a university that contains a history of political activism are apparent in the practices that take place at the radio station. Such practices manifest in radio content and the kind of personnel who are employed by, and volunteer at, the station. This was the material space that shaped the birth and evolution of Youth Amplified.

Imagining a Form of Critical Pedagogy

My own role in organizing the radio show had an effect on the kind of imagined space that emerged. The practices that I introduced, such as insisting that the group engage with materials and that they generate questions prior to the show, had a substantial influence on the resulting place and associated forms of learning. My idea was that the radio show would be a form of critical pedagogy, an orientation to teaching and learning that follows Paolo Freire's (1970) philosophy that oppressed peoples gain liberation through recognizing the causes of their oppression. Critical pedagogy is not a method, rather it opens a space for students to act and assert themselves as agents, as they question their assumptions, develop an appreciation for history and critically interrogate the idea that education is value-neutral (Giroux, 2007). Underpinning the critical pedagogical approach is an assumption that schooling is a cultural and historical process that reproduces the structure of society, such that 'poor children go to poor schools and remain poor'.

I planned for the programme to revolve around young people engaging with materials, such as documentary films, newspaper articles, guests and music. These materials were intended to form the basis for critical discussions that explored the themes of 'education in South Africa' and other issues chosen by youth. During the 18 months of the programme we watched a number of documentaries, including *Testing Hope*, *Afrikaaps* and *Waiting for Superman*. *Testing Hope* is a story about township learners toiling in order to pass matric. *Afrikaaps* is a film that explores the possibilities of using a local, informal version of Afrikaans as a medium of instruction in Cape Town schools. *Waiting for Superman* explores inequality in the American educational context. The group read newspaper articles and an excerpt from *I write what I like* by Black Consciousness activist Steve Biko. We interviewed guests live on air, such as DVS and the junior mayor of Cape Town. Sometimes I made suggestions in terms of materials that I thought would stimulate vibrant discussion and on other occasions the young people suggested ideas for materials for the show. After watching, reading or listening to these different media, participants would write down 5–10 questions to be used in the discussion.

Other research has highlighted how the medium of radio production amongst youth and adults can generate democratic, participatory relationships between the different people that are involved and stimulate forms of learning. Chavez & Soep (2005) describe youth radio as a pedagogy of collegiality, characterised by joint framing, youth-led inquiry, mediated interventions and distributed accountability. The relationships between adults and young people were defined by collegiality, as each group relied on the other in order to produce a high-quality product for an audience (Chavez & Soep, 2005). These practices mean that a culture of cooperation may well underpin forms of learning linked to radio production, stimulating inclusive dialogue.

School Cultures and Imagined Space at Youth Amplified

Besides the physical location of the radio station and my own ideas about the value of critical pedagogy, Youth Amplified was also forged through the mixture of participating schools and their different institutional cultures. Participants were initially recruited from RGHS, where I was conducting youth leadership sessions at the time. Students from Lukhanyo High School were also invited. This school, a partner of my former employer, the Extra-Mural Education Project (EMEP), was reserved for black students during apartheid and consisted almost exclusively of isiXhosa-speaking learners. A group of students from the Cape Institute of Excellence (CIE) was also invited to attend. These students had attained good academic results, particularly in mathematics and science, and had been awarded scholarships in order to attend and reside at the CIE, outside of their township homes. The Western Cape Education Department established the CIE in 2004. It is an English medium school designed to enhance the academic development of gifted learners reared in the townships. A colleague of mine who was the director of an NGO called SAILI, an organisation that sponsored some students at the CIE, agreed to pay the transportation costs for these young people to attend the radio show.

A fourth school was invited into the emerging space, as the radio station did not want the show to become stigmatised as solely consisting of 'marginalised youth'. A former model C school that was the alma mater of the young woman who was providing me with technical support at the community radio station was decided upon. This school, Barry Hertzog High School (BHHS), agreed to select learners to participate in the show. Former model C schools in South Africa are generally associated with pedagogies and discourses of whiteness that originated in the colonial and apartheid eras. An example of these discourses of whiteness is the notion of 'standards' that are regularly described as needing to be upheld at former model C schools (Dolby, 2002; Soudien, 2012). This discourse is led by the old white middle class, which has morphed into a new multiracial middle class. Parents at former model C schools often disseminate notions of 'good schooling, quality and the maintenance of standards' (Soudien, 2012). This discourse of 'standards needing to be kept up' is used by middle-class parents to make exclusionary school fee policies.

Discourses of whiteness may be reproduced at former model C schools through practices such as sport and the enforcement of dress codes, creating imagined spaces with strong colonial associations. Dolby (2002) illustrated how playing rugby and wearing school uniform 'properly' functioned to maintain forms of whiteness, even though the school at which she conducted her study was comprised of a majority of black students. The 'image' of the school that Dolby (2002) researched—how it was perceived by others—was very important to teachers. Learning revolved around reinforcing a philosophy of control, based on appearance, forms of behaviour and discipline. Unlike former non-white schools, where school uniform policies are unevenly enforced, wearing school uniform 'properly' functioned in this context as a demonstration of respectability and 'standards being upheld'. This school's senior management attempted to use these discourses to maintain links to a network, an imagined space of Durban, South African and Commonwealth schools that perceived their heritage to be linked to the British Empire, distinct from Africa.

The BHHS learners who participated at Youth Amplified attended a former model C school similar to the one described by Dolby (2001, 2002), which impacted on their interactions with students from other, less well-resourced schools. The two elite schools that participated in Youth Amplified socialised their students with institutional practices and discourses that other research has shown may cause tension when these students interact with youth who attend township schools. Young people who, for example, speak English in public places, attend schools outside of the townships and incorporate academic identities through, for example, reading and carrying books, are teased for 'playing white' by their peers (Bray et al., 2010; Ramphele, 2002; Soudien, 2007). Jealousy and resentment may provoke youth who attend township schools to 'police' racial boundaries and shame individuals who go to elite schools.

As a learning place, Youth Amplified was therefore produced through the material spatial practices associated with the history of the community radio station and the fact that the show was broadcast live on air, meaning that it had consequences for the young people. Imagined space was partly produced by the critical pedagogy tradition, as well as the diverse mixture of elite and township schools which participating learners represented. Research has shown that the genre of 'youth radio' and media production more generally (see for example Chavez & Soep, 2005; Goodman, 2003; Mahiri, 2003), promotes lived space through notions of participation, child-centered discourses and adult-youth collaboration. However, the interaction of township-schooled youth with learners from well-resourced schools has created tension in other contexts.

Conclusion

Questioning how classrooms, rap groups and radio shows become 'places' helps to excavate the social relationships and historical conditions that make these sites what they are. Places are living, breathing constellations of social relationships that meet in time, enabling particular kinds of experiences and restricting others. Classrooms are often imagined to be sites where specialised knowledges are distributed in a self-contained, insulated setting. Examining the social relations that produce classrooms and schools shatters the classroom as container metaphor, allowing for a deeper understanding of the range of processes that shape school learning. Rather than viewing places as insulated, I have argued that places have porous boundaries that change with the people who enter them. These people bring with them fragments of other sites and relationships that shape their daily lives. The tumultuous neighbourhood of Rosemary Gardens, constructed during the apartheid era, affected learning at school, as students spent the vast majority of their time in this community. The different schools that participated in Youth Amplified shaped students' identities in significant ways and molded this new place, as these schools' values and practices 'travelled with' students to the radio station. The values underpinning global hip hop, a subculture that originated in The Bronx, New York City, had a profound influence on the Doodvenoodskap. Interrogating the concept of 'place' therefore allows for a radical analysis of learning, one that favours mobility over stasis and interaction over purity.

References

Battersby, J. 2003. 'Sometimes it feels like I'm not black enough': recast(e)ing coloured through South African hip hop as a postcolonial text. In S. Jacobs & H. Wasserman & S. Jacobs (Eds.), *Shifting selves: post-apartheid essays on mass media, culture and identity (pp. 109–129)*. Cape Town: Kwela Books.

Bray, R., Gooskins, I., Kahn, L., Moses, S. & Seekings, J. 2010. *Growing up in the new South Africa: childhood and adolescence in post-apartheid Cape Town*. Cape Town: HSRC Press.

Chang, J. 2005. *Can't stop won't stop: a history of the hip hop generation*. New York: St. Martin's.

Chang, J. 2006. *Total chaos: the art and aesthetics of hip hop*. New York: Basic Books.

Chavez, V. & Soep, E. 2005. Youth radio and the pedagogy of collegiality. *Harvard Educational Review*, 75(4), 409–434.

Dimitriadis, G. 2009. *Performing identity/performing culture: hip hop as text, pedagogy and lived practice.* New York: Peter Lang.
Dolby, N. 2001. *Constructing race: youth identity and popular culture in South Africa.* Albany: State University of New York Press.
Dolby, N. 2002. Making White: constructing race in a South African high school. *Curriculum Inquiry,* 32(1), 7–29.
Fataar, A. 2007. Educational renovation in a South African 'township on the move': a social–spatial analysis. *International Journal of Educational Development,* 27(6), 599–612.
Fine, M. 1991. *Framing dropouts: notes on the politics of an urban public high school.* Albany: SUNY Press.
Freire, P. 1970. *Pedagogy of the oppressed.* New York: Continuum International Publishing.
Giroux, H. 2007. Introduction: democracy, education and the politics of critical pedagogy. In P. McLaren & J. Kincheloe (Eds.), *Critical pedagogy: where are we now? (pp. 1–5).* New York: Peter Lang.
Goodman, S. 2003. *Teaching youth media: a critical guide to literacy, video production, and social change.* New York: Teachers College Press.
Haupt, A. 2008. *Stealing empire: P2P, intellectual property and hip hop subversion.* Cape Town: HSRC Press.
Lefebvre, H. 1991. *The production of space.* Oxford: Blackwell.
Mac An Ghaill, M. 1988. *Young, gifted, and Black: student-teacher relations in the schooling of Black youth.* Milton Keynes: Open University Press.
Mahiri, J. 2003. *What they don't learn in school: literacy in the lives of urban youth.* New York: Peter Lang.
Pennycook, A. 2007. Language, localization, and the real: hip hop and the global spread of authenticity. *Journal of Language, Identity, and Education,* 6(2), 101–115.
Perullo, A. & Fenn, J. 2003. Language ideologies, choices, and practices in Eastern African hip hop. In H. Berger & M. Carroll (Eds.), *Global pop, local language (pp. 19–51).* Mississippi: University Press of Mississippi.
Pinnock, D. 1984. *The brotherhoods: street gangs and state control in Cape Town.* Cape Town: David Phillip.
Ramphele, M. 2002. *Steering by the stars: being young in South Africa.* Cape Town: Tafelberg.
Robbins, S. 2008. *From revolution to rights in South Africa: social movements, NGOs & popular politics after apartheid.* Oxford: James Currey Publishers & Pietermaritzburg: University of KwaZulu Natal Press.
Samara, T. 2011. *Cape Town after apartheid: crime and governance in the divided city.* Minneapolis: University of Minnesota Press.
Sayed, Y. 1999. Discourses of the policy of educational decentralisation in South Africa since 1994: an examination of the South African Schools Act. *Compare: A Journal of Comparative and International Education,* 29(2), 141–152.
Scharf, W. 1986. *Street gangs, survival and political consciousness in the eighties.* Unpublished paper presented at the conference, Western Cape: Roots and Realities, Centre for African Studies, University of Cape Town, July 1986.
Sheehy, M. & Leander, K. M. 2004. Introduction. In K. Leander & M. Sheehy (Eds.), *Spatializing literacy research and practice (pp. 1–14).* New York: Peter Lang.
Soudien, C. 2007. *Schooling, culture and the making of youth identity in contemporary South Africa.* Cape Town: David Phillip.
Soudien. C. 2012. *Realising the dream: unlearning the logic of race in the South African school.* Cape Town: HSRC Press.
Willis, P. 1977. *Learning to labour: how working class kids get working class jobs.* Farnborough: Saxon House.

5 Dialogue and Learning at Rosemary Gardens High School

In those days we imagined ourselves being kept in some kind of holding pen, waiting to be released into our lives. And when that moment came our lives—and time itself—would speed up. How were we to know that our lives had in any case begun, that some advantage had already been gained, some damage already inflicted? Also that our release would only be into a larger holding pen, whose boundaries would at first be indiscernible.

Julian Barnes, 2011: 9

Teachers neither simply act within classrooms nor entirely act on the part of the school as an institution. Rather, teachers 'enact' classrooms in relation to other space-times and, hence, create social spaces in which one thing is more likely to be said than another or one position for participants is more available than another.

Leander, 2001: 642

'Guns, Words and Ordeal': Rosemary Gardens High School

The first stop on this journey across the lives of Rosemary Gardens youth is at the local high school. The disruptive effects of material space on the Rosemary Gardens community, and by extension the school, were extremely visible at this site. Overcrowding, systemic violence and families with low incomes, exhibited through learners coming to school irritable, hungry and without stationery or complete school uniforms, all impacted on learning, dialogue and language use in classrooms at Rosemary Gardens High School. Learning at RGHS was also hampered by representations of the school, produced through descriptions of the 'kinds' of learners who attended this institution and the 'quality' of the language that they had at their disposal. Students and educators alike described learners' languages as impoverished. Students said that the medium of instruction used in classrooms operated at a 'higher' level in comparison to the language that they spoke at home. The school was imagined to be a place where superior forms of language and culture legitimately existed.

Despite demonstrating a great deal of care for learners' physical well-being, educators reinforced depictions of deficient students. Teachers generally described learners as better suited to technical and vocational forms of education. Although the vast majority of both teachers and students would have been classified as 'coloured' under apartheid, differences in social class were apparent between middle-class educators and working-class students. A small number of students displayed interesting forms of lived space, either through enduring the school system and attaining academic success, or by continuing to attend school and being able to express extreme distrust with society at large, of which schooling was perceived as one component.

A Note on the Student Research Sample and School Discontinuation

In 2012, the year that I conducted the bulk of my research, there were 412 grade 9s and 60 grade 12s attending RGHS. The school principal stated that this trend of large numbers of youth discontinuing their schooling after grade nine had remained consistent over the many years that he had been an educator at the school. Reasons for the high numbers of young people discontinuing their schooling are explored in this chapter. However, it should be noted that most of the inputs from learners described here are taken from focus groups that engaged half of the grade 12 class (30 students). I decided to conduct dialogues with this group because of their set workbook for Afrikaans, *Map Jacobs' Christmas*, a script for a play that is written in Kaapse Afrikaans. Discussions on *Map Jacobs' Christmas* illuminated students' attitudes towards language. The students that predominantly feature in this chapter are therefore not representative of learners at RGHS, as grade 12 consists of the small group that perseveres through five years of high school. The grade 12 learners provided interesting insights into a group that endured the school system, its practices and ideologies, but they did not provide personal reflections on why students decided to stop attending school. I did interact with many students in the other grades during the four years that I visited the school to facilitate the youth leadership sessions and to participate in other activities. The group that attended Youth Amplified, who I got to know intimately, consisted of only one grade 12 student, enhancing my interactions with RGHS learners in a range of different grades.

"The Effects of That in the Learner": The Impact of Material Space on Learning at RGHS

Learning, dialogue and language use in RGHS classrooms could not be understood in isolation from the material spatial practices that played out on a daily basis in the community of Rosemary Gardens. This neighbourhood was plagued by poverty, high rates of unemployment, normalised violence and overcrowding. These distressing social challenges seeped into the school. The deputy principal who had been at the school for more than 30 years said:

Mr Konrad: What I don't like here is the effects of poverty. You see it everyday in your children. They come to school badly dressed, without having had breakfast, hungry, without the necessary stationery and books, without having slept last night because the neighbours had a party the entire night. I spoke about the width between the two doors (the front doors of apartments in the 'kortse'),[1] *if I step out of my flatlet I almost walk into your sitting room. The close proximity of one flat.* That has an influence on some of our learners. They come in noisy. You have to take a few minutes to tell them you are in a class now, I would like to do some work. This is not the street. So disciplinary problems would be another issue here that I don't like. Then the effect of gangsterism on our learners, the effects of drug abuse and alcohol abuse, that's the ugly side of my work.
Interviewer: By the learners?
Mr Konrad: The effects of that in the learners. It's sad to see a learner coming to school, single parent, mommy is a drug addict, alcoholic. That's the sad side of education. But I'm an optimist, I believe that out of the darkest corner, from the filth of the earth will come the whitest lily that you can imagine. I believe in every child, that they have the ability to become a lawyer, doctor, professor. I'm considered stern and very strict in my classes, but I would also like to think that I'm a very human person. I love to raise children, I love to lead them. And as a teacher we must remember that today's child is tomorrow's adult, today's learner is tomorrow your friend, that may even be tomorrow your husband or tomorrow your wife. That has happened.

This quotation provides a rich description of the ways that material and imagined space overlapped, impacting on interactions in RGHS classrooms and the wider community. Rosemary Gardens is a product of apartheid forced removals and is uncomfortably congested and overcrowded, making cohabitation frustrating for its residents. Material space in the neigbourhood of Rosemary Gardens influenced school learning, as overcrowded living conditions resulted in students becoming agitated and venting some of their domestic frustrations during the school day. For many learners the 'feeding scheme' school meal, which all students were entitled to receive, but many rejected due to the stigma attached to it, was their first meal of the day. Tired, unfed young people hampered attempts to conduct teaching and learning and impacted on the kinds of classroom dialogues that emerged.

Students' behaviour at school, which was often the result of overcrowding, noise and other forms of physical frustration that they experienced at home, provoked the deputy principal to impress on his learners that the school was not the "street". The "street" was a proxy for the homes and the community that learners inhabited, contexts that teachers implied were boundariless, unruly places of a questionable moral order. The conflation of learners' homes and community with the "street" is derogatory, as the "street" raises connotations that these students live like homeless people outside on the "street". It was therefore not surprising when one educator said that 'just about every single problem starts in the home'. Teachers at RGHS believed that part of their job was to insulate the school from the "street" and that doing so was a prerequisite in order to ensure that effective learning occurred. Teachers attempted to resocialise these young people with a different set of norms and values in the classroom, modifying the uninhibited behaviour that they believed was problematically learnt beyond the school walls.

Educators, like the deputy principal in the quotation above, regularly emphasised that 'discipline' was necessary in order to create conditions suitable for learning. Discipline was instilled through everyday spatial practices initiated by teachers. Students formed lines outside of classrooms before entering, their uniforms and grooming were inspected and teachers ensured that nobody was chewing gum or eating food. Once inside the classroom, teachers and learners greeted one another.

Corporal punishment, a form of discipline, melted into the normalised violence of daily life at RGHS. Corporal punishment was still used at RGHS, despite being outlawed as assault in the South African Schools Act (1996). I observed late learners getting a ruler on the hand or unruly students getting a little cane on the buttocks. The educator who matric learners unanimously named as the 'best teacher' admitted,

> "I still hit them, I give them a hiding because I love them. I hit them with that duster".

I do not believe that corporal punishment was used to inflict serious bodily injury on learners and I did not see any beating that looked particularly painful. It demonstrated an unquestionable hierarchy, maintaining discipline and order within a place that educators perceived as surrounded by chaos. This form of punishment may be counter-productive, as institutional support for resistance can be highly beneficial for marginalised youth (McFadden & Munns, 2002). Resistance is often a key component of identity formation in adolescence and a necessary outward expression of the cultural displacement working-class youth may feel at school (McFadden & Munns, 2002). Not only does corporal punishment suppress resistance and dialogue, it infantalises these young people who realise that 'we still get hidings at our school, you don't get that at the white schools', as one RGHS learner told the group at Youth Amplified. These observations were supported by the research report on school dropout written for the *School Is Power* project by the group of doctoral students from Vanderbilt University. The report stated that:

Several learners reported that one of the main aspects of school they did not like was being hit by teachers for coming in late or for having a wrong answer.

(Craven et al., 2012: 42)

Besides corporal punishment, students despised teachers regularly forcing them to leave classrooms. Learners said that their favourite teachers warned students prior to ejecting them from class, or allowed learners to sit at the front of the classroom, instead of removing them (Craven et al., 2012). Teachers perceived as students' least favourite educators removed learners without warning. The practice of requiring students to leave the classroom may lead to young people also leaving the school for the remainder of the day, seeking alternative forms of stimulation beyond the school walls. Banishment communicated that certain young people were unwanted in the classroom and silenced them from engaging in educational dialogues.

Educators wanted to maintain control and discipline in their classrooms, but they also desired to uplift these working-class coloured children from their current circumstances. The deputy principal's reference to the "darkest corner, the filth of the earth" and the possible emergence of the *'whitest lily'* was steeped in racial and evangelical connotations. This educator implied that the "filth", poverty and other social problems that existed within the boundaries of Rosemary Gardens, 'soiled' its inhabitants. Teachers understood a component of their role as educators to consist of uplifting and sanitising RGHS learners, eradicating the 'brownness' or "filth" from these working-class bodies and, in the best case scenario, producing "white lilies". Some educators therefore implied that these learners were in need of cultural uplift, including modification to their moral dispositions and, as will become clear in the next section, their use of language.

Doubts existed regarding whether it was possible to uplift these students. For example, in the quotation above Mr Konrad said that the effects of substance abuse were "in" the learner, meaning that, in response to the question, regardless of whether it was students or their parents abusing substances, the result was ultimately lodged 'inside' the students. These effects were insinuated to become a component of their DNA or biological makeup, meaning that efforts to modify associated behaviour and promote learning amongst students were somewhat in vain.

Mr Konrad did say that he believed in the ability of RGHS learners and that they held the potential to attain learned professions in law, medicine and academia. He expressed his passion towards aiding in the socialisation of these young people, using the word "love" twice. Rosemary

Gardens educators were generally thoroughly professional in their work and they appeared to be deeply emotionally invested in students, caring for their well-being. However, there was a patronising, hierarchical dimension to educator-learner relationships. Mr Konrad expressed his care for learners through concerns about their futures: through his "love" to lead/raise children, they may *become* doctors and lawyers and "today's learner is tomorrow your friend" or spouse. Future-oriented beliefs implied that educators did not validate or take an interest in learners' talents in the present. Dismissing learners' prevailing talents and resources, as the remainder of this chapter demonstrates, undermined students' aspirations for the future.

Returning to the material spatial relations between the school and community, attempts had been made to insulate the school from the violence and "filth" that existed beyond its borders, as one educator said:

> *15 years ago the school was burgled every night. Now we have panic buttons in the class and there are security guards. But there are still gang fights here on the school premises at night. The security guards locked themselves in a classroom. They grew up in the area so they can't apprehend the people.*

Erecting perimeter fencing and employing security guards were measures taken to protect the school and its resources from the threat posed by Rosemary Gardens residents. While physical divisions had been created between the Rosemary Gardens community and the school, these divisions remained permeable. The fluid boundaries between the school and community were demonstrated by the fact that the security guards were reared and lived in Rosemary Gardens, meaning that action taken against trespassers could lead to retributive consequences outside of the school. The violence that was widespread in the neighbourhood of Rosemary Gardens seeped into the school population and site, affecting its physical infrastructure and impacting upon learning at school.

Correlations between school and community violence have been confirmed by other research. A large South African survey (n=5939) conducted by Burton & Leoschut (2013) found that 60.5% of learners who claimed that crime was a problem in their neighbourhood had also experienced violence at school, whereas only 46.5% of those who were not victims of school violence said that crime was a problem in their neighbourhood. Young people who are victims of violent actions at school are therefore more likely to be reared in violent communities, meaning that the underlying social problems that lead to violence affect the same South African schools and neighbourhoods.

Violence affecting the school and community occurred regularly during my fieldwork in 2012. One grade nine learner was killed in gang crossfire

Dialogue and Learning at Rosemary Gardens High School 65

and a matric learner survived being shot in the face. A group of students was suspended for sodomising a boy on the school grounds and an educator was physically attacked by a group of learners. The principal named the worst school day of his career as the one in which he found a dead body of a six-year-old in room 72. I was asked to leave the school on one occasion and the school actually closed at noon on that day, due to potential violence, as it was known that the funeral of a former gang member was taking place during the afternoon.

Educators were regularly confronted with the realities of neighbourhood violence in Rosemary Gardens. Teachers often felt unsafe and, in addition to their core responsibility to deliver the curriculum, performed duties unimaginable to educators in middle-class contexts:

> *I was 22 years old when I began teaching at RGHS. There was no fence around the school at that time and the gangs would come and the back of the school was their battlefield. But I base everything I do on love, you can't achieve anything without it. I was brought up not to discriminate and judge people. One day a gang came to sort out one of the learners and they were armed. I went to face the leader. I taught that boy. I took him by the hand and felt up his arm . . . a machete and two guns . . . and I told him "Don't do this. Your mommy loves you and doesn't want to come and get your body here". I walked him away to the gate and the gang followed. When I taught him I didn't treat him differently to you or anyone else. But I don't do home visits anymore, it's too dangerous. A boy wanted to stab me once. He wrote ugly stuff on the board and I went to him and wanted to slap him and he took a scissors and wanted to stab me. And about a few weeks later they found that boy's body burnt in the bushes. I went to his parents' place . . . it was abject poverty. The mother pulled me in cause the bullets were just flying. And then I didn't visit homes anymore.*

RGHS teachers performed the roles of parent, social worker and psychologist, adding to their core work delivering the curriculum. These tasks often led to situations in which educators felt unsafe and threatened, both by learners and others who entered the school space. In the extract above the educator used the word love twice, as she tried to impress upon the young man that his mother valued him. bell hooks (2003), states that:

> *love in the classroom prepares teachers and learners to open our hearts and minds. It is the foundation on which every learning community can be created . . .*
>
> (hooks, 2003: 27)

At RGHS, teachers' 'love' for students was often wholly consumed by ensuring students' physical and emotional safety, meaning that pedagogical 'love' was of secondary importance. For these educators their love manifested through quelling threats to learners' material well-being, actions which often prevented them from 'going straight to the heart of the matter' of teaching. At times, pedagogical activities played a peripheral role, as educators were forced to deal with issues related to physical safety. Evidence exists that many educators at Cape Flats schools suffer from stressful working conditions. A recent piece of research that sampled 63 educators at four schools in this area found that in excess of 65% of the teachers studied were suffering from high levels of stress and burnout (Johnson, 2013). Some of the reasons cited for these worrying levels of anxiety and fatigue were role uncertainty, being overworked and the tedious bureaucratic processes to which officials subject educators (Johnson, 2013). The descriptions above of home visits in the midst of gunfire and the ashes of learners' bodies being found in the surrounds of this neighbourhood illuminate the kinds of issues that these teachers were forced to confront. Other RGHS educators reinforced this notion of not feeling safe at school:

Most of the time I don't feel safe at the school, physically and psychologically. Last week I was sitting in the computer lab alone. And a group of gangsters was sitting on the other side of the tarmac. They were smoking dagga (marijuana). A group of young men not from the school came onto the school during the DCAS (afterschool) programme. They were shouting remarks at me, some were ex-learners. I thought what if they come in and close the door. So I said something in the staff room the next day.

Dealing with gangsterism, school discontinuation, substance abuse and violence formed part of daily life for educators at RGHS, despite measures being taken to segregate the school from the community in which it was located. These social challenges shaped linguistic exchanges between students and teachers in classrooms.

Notwithstanding these contextual difficulties related to material space in Rosemary Gardens, in the past five years attempts have been made to upgrade the school infrastructure, with the support of the Rosemary Gardens Development Trust that was established by May Hughes. R750,000 was spent on building the school rugby/soccer field, a library was established with the support of the NGO Equal Education, a new computer laboratory was constructed, and Virgin Active sponsored the first South African school-community gym. Ten local young people were employed by the provincial Department of Cultural Affairs and Sports to facilitate sporting, music, dance and academic activities during the afternoons. These upgrades to school infrastructure have led to some positive attitudes towards the school:

> *Rosemary Gardens is one of the most awesome schools. They have a lot of activities for the youngsters to do.*
> Member of the Doodvenootskap (Translated from the Afrikaans)

And:

> *My principal Mr Williams . . . we're like the young Williams, he's making changes at the school . . . like in the toilets. I'm starting to feel proud of my school, I feel good in myself yooo I went to this school. That's why I say he's my role-model, he believes in me . . . like in the week they come and open up a gym in the week for the youth, supply us with gym equipment, so youth can exercise, play soccer. They got activities after school so they don't gotta worry about the guns and stuff . . . I don't think your principal is on the same point as mine. Mine is tough . . . Rosemary Gardens is a tough place to be a principal, you have to have a big brain. Gangs have ideas in their minds and he actually talks to them and changes them.*
> (Rosemary Gardens learner at Youth Amplified)

Students and others appreciated the activities and infrastructural developments at the school. Mr Williams, a man who was perceived as endowed with intelligence, courage and the ability to confront social problems that impacted on the school and neighbourhood, was respected as a role-model by many students. Some students' and community members' perceptions of the school were therefore becoming increasingly positive. Infrastructural developments at RGHS had not gone unnoticed by learners and others.

More time is required in order to assess the effect that these new activities and facilities have on students' overall schooling experience. However, it is likely that the deep-rooted social problems that exist in the wider Rosemary Gardens community, linked to the history of this area, will continue to impact on educators, students and learning at this school. Rosemary Gardens is a neighbourhood that was constructed during apartheid social engineering that physically segregated race groups in the early 1970s and placed people deemed to be inferior in overcrowded, undesirable areas, with few services. Forty years later, Cape Town is one of the most unequal cities in the world, with many of the neighbourhoods constructed during the apartheid era struggling to contain a range of social challenges. Rosemary Gardens' social problems, like violence, gangsterism, substance abuse and a lack of food and clothing, 'travelled' with students as they entered the school and attempted to engage in dialogues in RGHS classrooms.

'More Than Words': Imagined Space and Language Use at Rosemary Gardens High School

In addition to efforts to fortify the school from the effects of violence and poverty in the Rosemary Gardens neighbourhood, educators also attempted to insulate RGHS from some of the cultural practices associated with Rosemary Gardens' residents:

> *The biggest problem is that learners come with a cultural deficiency ... no books at home. The only proper English or Afrikaans they hear is from the teachers. Their oral tradition is good, but we need to get them studying and reading. It's the basis of the education. Once they have good command of the language, they can be fine.*

Educators believed that working-class students from Rosemary Gardens acquired inferior language skills in their homes and community. I agree with much of the sentiment expressed by the educator above, including that young people prosper from having access to books and that reading, studying and gaining a good command of language can be highly beneficial to their academic development. However, this does not mean that the language learners acquired at home was of a poor quality, or that it was useless for the purpose of school learning.

One form of language is not innately superior or inferior to another. Children arrive at school with a wide variety of linguistic experiences and resources that represent differences in cultural practices, not inherent deficiencies (Purcell-Gates, 2002). Vocabulary that is generally used at school is likely to be unfamiliar to them, as norms associated with language use at school more closely resemble language used in middle-class homes (Bernstein, 1964; Stubbs, 2002). Differences between linguistic practices at home and school do not necessarily imply deficiency, but at RGHS they were usually interpreted in this manner.

Culture-class differences between homes/communities and the school were sometimes expressed as differences in forms of morality. One educator said:

> *You can see by their accents that maybe my values and theirs doesn't merge because of their backgrounds.*

This teacher interpreted differences between her and students' accents to be related to differences in socialisation processes, values and moral codes. Differences in social class, language, ethics and assumed academic abilities had implications for the kind of education and learning that teachers felt was appropriate for students from Rosemary Gardens:

> *This school should have a curriculum where some learners are taught to be plumbers, electricians, carpenters. That is one reason for the*

dropout rate. What school presents is not what the learner requires. Those are all careers where learners make a living. Why must we flog a dead horse?

Some educators believed that the students that attended RGHS required an alternative, vocational form of education. The content of the curriculum was deemed to be inappropriate for 'these learners', and was pinpointed as one of the main causes of the school's poor academic results. The continued practice of corporal punishment was metaphorically referenced in "flogging a dead horse". The comparison between learners and an animal like a horse was derogatory to the intellectual potential of students.

Contrary to the educator quoted above proposing that the solution to learners' academic struggles is 'dumbing down' the curriculum, Ladson-Billings (2002) states that educators' genuine belief in their students' academic abilities is vital for student success. She names this as the first component of a three-pronged theory of a culturally relevant pedagogy. The other two components include educators supporting students' cultural competence vis-a-vis the school and promoting sociopolitical consciousness in learners, such that they become aware of the manner in which power operates in educational settings (Ladson-Billings, 2002). However, educators at RGHS believed that rather than demanding academic excellence, changing the content of the curriculum would be beneficial for learners. Some RGHS educators believed that regardless of their efforts in the classroom, the current curriculum would not enable these students to succeed academically. By contrast, Ladson-Billings (2002) argues that educators of working-class children and children of colour need to demand academic excellence and effort from their students, as holding students to these standards is key to their academic success.

Some educators did indeed acknowledge the academic abilities of students and understood links between the school and home/community spaces:

Interviewer: Why do learners leave school?
Mrs Ross: It's because of the family unit. It has nothing to do with the learner not being academically capable. Some of the brightest learners that get A's drop out. One of my brightest learners was sexually abused when she was 2 years old, by her stepfather. She went to drugs and tik (crystal methamphetamine) and couldn't deal with it. She planned to kill him. Her mom said she's talking nonsense. I'd say that 80–90% of dropouts are caused by a dysfunctional home.

While educators at RGHS often dismissed the linguistic capital of students, these sentiments were not displayed by all of the educators. Teachers' attitudes needed to be interpreted in the context of the dire social problems plaguing the Rosemary Gardens community. These overwhelming challenges limited what teachers believed was realistically possible for themselves in their role as educators and for these young people in terms of their academic careers.

Educators' opinions that learners brought substandard forms of language to school were mutually reinforced by grade 12 learners' sentiments regarding the medium of instruction used at RGHS. Learners imagined the school to be a place where 'higher' levels of language were used, in comparison to their mother tongue:

> *It's a high standard of words that they use and we've got to get the terms right. Usually the teacher says to us . . . they will give it just so to us, but then they will try to make it easier for us. They give it just so and then they explain.*
>
> (Translated from the Afrikaans)

and

> *The words are very high this year. We never hear those kinds of words. Everything we get is in Afrikaans but it's high Afrikaans. Not the Afrikaans that we speak. It's a higher level. And that's the Afrikaans that they train us in. It's the Afrikaans that we ought to speak but it's not the Afrikaans that we speak.*
>
> (Translated from the Afrikaans)

School was imagined to be a place where it was appropriate to speak and learn only in high, formal Afrikaans and it was interpreted as the fault of the learners if they were unable to converse in this version of the language. As one of the students said, "It's the Afrikaans that we ought to speak". The culture of the school was therefore conceived as 'high up' in comparison to learners, who were implied to be 'low down'. Students believed that if they wished to continue to 'play the school game', then it was necessary to 'raise' their linguistic standards. The language that young people spoke at home and in the Rosemary Gardens community was perceived as inappropriate for use in the school space. In this context educators were described as acting as intermediaries, people who made the terms and the curriculum easier for these youth, inculcating them with a different linguistic repertoire and 'dumbing down' difficult academic work.

Students understood the medium of instruction used at school to be a legitimate, elevated cultural product, describing an example of 'high' Afrikaans in the following manner:

Interviewer: Can you give me an example of 'high' Afrikaans?
Fiona: We are going to show Adam the high terms that they use in Afrikaans. . . . Go to those sicknesses in consumer studies (she is instructing her friend to look in the textbook).

Rasheeda: (Reading) Diabetes, what is diabetes? . . . (inaudible) . . . Insulin is a hormone produced in the pancreas and is essential to help the body to use digested food for growth and energy.
Fiona: Now that's the answer. Okay Adam, now comes the question, "what is diabetes?" Now why can't they ask it in an easier way?
Rasheeda: You can't (lots of laughter).

(Translated from the Afrikaans)

Students stated that it was impossible to explain the concept of 'diabetes' in a way that made sense in the language that they used outside of the school and, in turn, for them to 'double-voice' these terms in their own words. The definition of diabetes was said to be irreducible to simple language, providing an example of an authoritative discourse that needs to be 'wholly accepted or rejected' (Bakhtin, 1981). The students were resigned to the fact that learning at school meant memorising certain facts, in standardised Afrikaans, as they attempted to 'raise themselves up' to the level of the school.

All of the learners that I interviewed enjoyed the play *Krismis van Map Jacobs (Map Jacobs' Christmas)*, a Kaapse Afrikaans–dominated text that was a compulsory component of the grade 12 Afrikaans curriculum. When reflecting on the play, some interesting opinions emerged regarding the use of informal Afrikaans in the school place. A focus group led to the following exchange:

Pauline: In Christmas (with Map Jacobs' Christmas) they speak like us. I can relate to them.
Interviewer: Is it important to read books like that?
Pauline: Yes, yes. In a way yes and in a way no. That Afrikaans isn't right. It's not at the standard that it must be.
Interviewer: But isn't there a place for Kaapse Afrikaans?
Pauline: No.
Interviewer: Why not?
Pauline: Because you can't write in Kaapse Afrikaans in your (examination) question paper. The terms must be right.
Interviewer: Why? I know that's how it is, but why must it be that way?
Teresa: If it's about Map Jacobs I think it's all right because the book is written like that. But if we look at the other subjects. Like Vatmaar (the novel 'A place called Vatmaar') and so on. It's here and there maybe all right. Here and there is all right. But you can't mix your language. If somebody says to me . . . then I say "no it's cool I'm going to chill in the sun". We can't speak like that. Your marks go down immediately. They will penalise you [repeats in English], they will penalise you.

(Translated from the Afrikaans)

Young people at RGHS explained that it was a penalisable offence to answer school examination questions using the language that they spoke at home, stating that Kaapse Afrikaans is of a lower standard and it "isn't right". The statement that the "terms must be right" indicated that they believed that there was something wrong with speaking Kaapse Afrikaans in the school context. These students, who remained in the school system rather than 'dropping out', learnt how to maximise their points or 'score' through using context-specific linguistic codes. 'Playing the school game' meant accepting certain ideologies that were attached to the imagined school space, ideologies that prescribed how language should be used at school.

There were connotations of 'purity' associated with 'high Afrikaans', the 'appropriate' language of instruction, whilst it was insinuated that Kaapse Afrikaans comprised a 'bastardised' mixture of formal and informal Afrikaans and English. The learner above said that "you can't mix your language". The racial connotations of 'colouredness' as a 'mixing of races', associated with impure forms of language, comes to mind in reading this quotation. It is likely that these students, grade 12s who had persevered in the school system for five years, had to accept these societal and linguistic hierarchies in order to progress at school.

While many learners interpreted this hierarchy of language and culture as legitimate, some believed in a form of conspiracy, as the curriculum and its evaluation were interpreted as unfair attempts to expose RGHS students as ignorant:

Dane: *They use big words. Things that a person never heard before. We do an exercise in class. Furniture. We understand that language. But then the exams come and they ask the question in a different way man. You don't know. The word looks familiar, but you think "what are these people talking about?" You feel as if they are speaking in another language to you.*
Interviewer: *And why do they do that?*
Dane: *They want to catch you out man. They want to see if you're on that level man. How good is your Afrikaans, how good is your knowledge of consumers (consumer studies).*
(Translated from the Afrikaans)

Some students interpreted differences between language use at home and school as part of an oppressive system, which included forms of evaluation that attempted to undermine learners. Examination questions were supposedly intended to deceive these students and were not interpreted by some learners as testing whether concepts had been understood.

For some students, suspicion extended beyond the school itself, to the place of the school within a broader set of societal apparatuses. The following comment was made in response to the question, "Have things changed in the new South Africa?" The learner who answered felt that change has not occurred because:

They (social relations) have just turned around. We are still in the middle. The apartheid system is still there if a person looks. If you look at the cabinet. I don't want to be racist, but in the cabinet the high people are mostly black people. They motivate themselves, they want to go higher. People all have different views of each other. The apartheid system did that. . . . But white people are a little less mad now. They were mad in the first place to think that they were better than another person. "You can't sit next to me". That's a mad person. Now white people are a little less mad. In the back of their minds that's how they were programmed, that's how we were programmed. We are all products of society. They say which clothes to wear, what food to eat, they control you like a puppet. It's like religion, the same person that made religion is the person that set up the government, it's all the same people. Corrupt. They socialise you. Like here by us the gangsterism . . . but if you look out of the box there are other things that are going on. That's why they control our minds from grade R, they mould us to be workers for them. Like at the schools, the coloured schools, big windows on this side, the cold side, now we look, this is our lives. It's the way society is programmed.
(Translated from the Afrikaans)

For this student, school was understood to be one component of a social system that dictated young people's everyday practices, such as the clothes they wore and the food they ate. This 'system' was understood to mould young people's developing consciousness, determining the societal division of labour and reproducing wider power dynamics. It was clear, from these sentiments, that the school was not experienced as an empowering institution for these working-class youth.

This student clearly identified the apartheid system and the historical context as producing this state of affairs. His historical consciousness and understanding of social relations was well developed. This young man told me that *Map Jacobs' Christmas* had made a profound influence on this thinking and that he had proceeded to read Adam Small's other works. He had clearly developed a potent sociopolitical consciousness, which he used to make a sophisticated critique of the government and the history of race relations in South Africa.

I encountered a number of other students who complained about unjust social systems, but their explanations usually involved elaborate conspiracy theories, rather than historical and political analyses. On multiple occasions at Youth Amplified, RGHS learners made reference to the *Illuminati*, a nefarious power conglomerate apparently controlling the world through financial and political transactions and systems. Learners also mentioned the film *The Matrix* (as we will see later) as a meaningful text in their lives. The plot of this film revolves around a simulated reality in which people are unaware that their lives are being controlled by machines. The conspiracy theory of the *Illuminati* and learners' interest in *The Matrix* resonate with the sentiments portrayed in the excerpt above, illustrating the world views of many of these students. This world view was informed by high levels of suspicion, disempowerment and a sense that wider structures were systematically working against their success.

Students at RGHS therefore displayed three different responses to educators and the school denigrating their language. The first response entailed discontinuing their schooling, the second consisted of learners accepting language attitudes and ideologies as they appeared at RGHS and attempting to learn standard Afrikaans and the third response involved students remaining at school, but becoming vocally sceptical of 'the system'. To expand on these three responses, the first resulted in foreclosing the possibility of dialogue, as the vast majority of RGHS learners discontinued their schooling by grade 12, with the initial exodus starting in grade 10. School discontinuation is a form of suppressing dialogue, as youth who are likely to offer dissent and challenge school practices, policies and ideologies are ushered out of, or choose to abandon, the school system (Fine, 1991). There is little doubt that the messages that the school communicated to students regarding their use of language, one of the most intimate aspects of their identities, contributed to the high rates of discontinuation observed at this school.

A second, smaller group of RGHS learners accepted this linguistic, cultural and class-based hierarchy, committing themselves to working towards acquiring the language skills and knowledges that the school offered. These learners accepted the supposed inferiority of their language, as they chose to work towards obtaining a new language variety. This may have detrimental effects. Fine's (1991) research indicated that 'successful' low-income students who remained at school were more depressed, conformed to a greater extent and were less politically aware of poverty and racism than young people who discontinued their schooling.

A third set of learners remained at school, like the second group. However, instead of agreeing that their language was of a lower 'standard', these young people expressed extreme distrust in the system. The conspiracy theories developed by a small handful of learners who remained at school therefore demonstrated a form of resistance. Conspiracy theories indicated that Rosemary Gardens youth were aware of the ways in which society stacked the odds of success against them, the denigration of their use of language being only one example of this phenomenon. Although many of these young people were 'born frees', youth who were born in the democratic era, their lives continued to be dominated by inequalities related to South Africa's past. Some students were able to express these forms of social injustice verbally, producing forms of lived space.

"Jy Dink Jou Kak Stink Nie" (You Think Your Shit Doesn't Stink): Dialogue in the Classroom

Ubiquitous violence seeping into RGHS from the Rosemary Gardens neighbourhood, coupled with educators' beliefs that learners were more suited to vocational education and students' reticence that their language was inadequate, all led to restricted dialogue and learning in RGHS classrooms. Much dialogue never happened because the vast majority of learners discontinued their schooling prior to grade 12. The difficult neighbourhood conditions and learners' linguistic capital being dismissed as below-par by educators, amongst other reasons, resulted in an emphatic 'silence' as fewer and fewer learners returned to school in the higher grades.

I would like to emphasise that, although my findings have shown that educators were dismissive of learners' use of language and these young people's cultural practices, I did observe many instances of care for learners and attempts by educators to relate to the cultural worlds of students. I observed 16 educators teaching in their classrooms, 10 females and six males. Of the 10 female teachers whose classes I observed, five told their classes that they "love them". This demonstrated a remarkable level of open affection towards learners. On the other hand, this 'parental' or pastoral relationship did not necessarily promote high intellectual expectations and a belief in learners' ability to succeed academically. This culture of care contained a religious element, with prayer forming a regular part of classroom conduct. On one occasion I was sniffing in the classroom and the entire class was instructed to "pray for Adam to get well", demonstrating to the visitor that these young people were being socialised 'properly'.

Educators expressed their affinity for learners through the ways in which they pronounced words. I counted that seven out of the 10 female educators pronounced the word 'jy' (you) like the English letter 'j' or 'djy' and not in the more formal Afrikaans pronunciation, similar to an English exclamation of happiness: 'yay'. This is a typically Kaapse Afrikaans or working-class pronunciation of the word and I noticed some educators pronouncing 'jy' differently when talking to students in comparison to when they were conversing with one another.

Many educators tried to connect with learners through the use of humour and by making links between academic content and students' cultural contexts. For example, one life sciences teacher told her class that their mothers use calcium carbonate or bicarbonate of soda to make 'koeksisters', a popular sweet delicacy on the Cape Flats. The same teacher made a number of connections to learners' lives during the compulsory reading period that took place for half an hour at the start of each day. She had instructed students to borrow a book from the library, to be brought to class and read during the designated reading period. She complained about the fact that only a handful of students had actually complied with this instruction and then handed out a photocopied reading she had prepared. The reading was a piece from the magazine *Vrouekeur* entitled *Teesakkie se Moses* (roughly translated as 'Teabag go to hell') (see appendix A for the full article), a satirical piece about tea-party etiquette involving three people. In the article one guest at the tea party was trying to fit into high society, one was completely unconcerned with social norms and the final character was a member of the elite social strata. Ms Anderson read the article to the class and tried to make it relevant to the students, explaining the ironies and 'translating' statements such as 'jy dink jou sweet stink nie' (you think your sweat doesn't stink) to "jy dink jou kak stink nie" (you think your shit doesn't stink). She said this phrase meant that "jy hou jou kwaai" (you think you're cool). She explained an incident from the article regarding the host leaving the teabag inside of the cup, allowing a guest to remove it herself and said "we just chuck it out, throw it onto your mom's garden . . . it's good for compost".

Mrs Anderson's used a swear word ("kak" or "shit") and a slang term ("kwaai" or "cool"), attempting to break some of the usual school conventions and taboos in order to make schooling a comfortable, relevant experience for these young people. She said "we" would throw the teabag out, illustrating an attempt to decrease social divisions of class and education between herself and the learners. She made this interaction educational, transcending school subjects with her example of the teabag being used for compost: she was a life sciences teacher using this example during the reading period. Mrs Anderson demonstrated the lengths that some educators took to use their lessons both to connect with learners' worlds and to expose them to practices that would only occur outside of Rosemary Gardens, such as the etiquette of a middle-class tea party. These actions were carried out with love and care. However, throughout this reading period the educator did the vast majority of the talking; she directed the lesson, asked the questions and did all of the reading.

Similarly, during the teaching of the poem *Memento* by W. D. Snodgrass, Mr Williams, the principal, made a number of humorous remarks. For example, he linked the term "severed" hand to violence in the Rosemary Gardens community and explained the term "ambivalent" by encouraging learners to tell their mothers that "their feelings for her are ambivalent". He suggested that on a Monday night, when Spur restaurants offered a popular 'two hamburgers for the price of one' special deal, students should share that their feelings for their lovers are "ambivalent". He made fun of the poet's surname, making a mock telephone call and saying, "Hello, it's Mr Snodgrass here, I'd like two samosas and a pie".

These forms of humour were enjoyed by the students and relaxed the atmosphere in the classroom, something which learners said they desired in the school setting. However the lesson and the humour it contained were initiated and conducted almost exclusively by the educator himself. They did not provide the learners with opportunities to initiate interactions, ask questions or express their ideas.

These instances in which humour was used and efforts were made to relate to the life worlds of learners were not the dominant form of interaction, but they were certainly present and demonstrated the care that some educators at RGHS took to connect with the life worlds of students. However, these kinds of classroom interactions are still iterations of the initiation response feedback (IRF) type teaching style identified to comprise over two-thirds of classroom talk by international research (Flanders, 1970; Howe, 2010). Different degrees and forms of this IRF phenomenon were therefore observed in RGHS classrooms, ranging from the poem and reading period already described, to educators merely performing a prepared script and pausing from time to time for learners to insert a missing word. Pure dictation was also a common occurrence at RGHS, for example:

Change the following from direct to reported speech. Skip a line and make a bullet point. "Figurative language makes use of comparisons and suggestive ideas". Underline comparisons and suggestive ideas. Who still doesn't understand the difference between literal and figurative language? Put up your hand if you don't understand. Dis niks om nie te weet nie (It's nothing to not know). Please write down, "we use figures of speech to express ourselves, visually, imaginatively and powerfully".

and:

I will give you points and then you write them down. Write in your book: 'Grandpa Lewis' funeral. George Lewis received a Roman Catholic funeral. The entire Vatmaar community was there because he was one of the founders. Uncle Tjai prayed and sang the same prayers and songs that were recited every Sunday. Uncle Flip brought the coffin to the graveyard on his cart. He brought it on his horse 'Old Swaai'. A direct quotation indicates to the examiner that you know and your marks go up immediately. Open your quotation marks. "The coffin was good enough for King George. George Lewis was more black than white. He did more for the black people than for the whites". Use these as your key words. Turn forward to your characters. 'Pieter Bruin was a white man, married to Anna.'

(Translated from the Afrikaans)

These kinds of input from educators illustrated the opinion of one of the RGHS learners that attended Youth Amplified, who said that "the teachers tell us the answers, they tell us what we need to know to pass." Although the learner meant this as a positive contribution from teachers, dictation does not aid in students learning for themselves, as they merely regurgitate the words of educators. Dictation produces an authoritative discourse, a single answer that is neither reflected upon nor thought about and does not require that learners develop their own opinions. This pedagogical method ultimately ensured the repression of debate and discussion. However, these actions demonstrated to curriculum advisors, who visited the school in order to inspect learners' workbooks, that the curriculum had been delivered and that time had been dedicated towards completing required tasks. Ensuring that students received these dictated notes allowed educators to prove that if learners did not succeed in their examinations, it was not due to their being inadequately prepared by educators.

Learners did not enjoy classes in which they simply copied notes that teachers wrote on the board. They said that they desired to participate in discussions:

Interviewer: *What is a good teacher?*
Natasha: *She makes you want to do the subject. She makes actions, she moves. Not that they're not good, just not exciting.*
Interviewer: *And in what subjects would you say you really learn something?*
Natasha: *Tourism with Mrs Pearson. She doesn't write a lot of things on the board. She does verbal communication with us. She talks to us. She says communication is a better way to connect people in the world. If Adam goes to her class you won't see a lot of written work. We just write things down from the board in other classes.*

(Translated from the Afrikaans)

According to this student, a good teacher required that learners exercised their minds. There was also a significant amount of interaction and communication between students and the teacher in the classroom of the 'good' teacher and it was in these classrooms that learners felt that genuine learning took place. The student above stated that in other classes they merely reproduced information written on the chalkboard, which did not require learners to think or show initiative. There is clearly a need for students to be exposed to and absorb key ideas and base knowledge. However, this should be combined with interpersonal interactions in which that knowledge is used, explored and questioned by these young people. In order for learning to take place, it is vital that students actively engage in thinking and use their minds (Alexander, 2008; Mercer, 2002).

Contrary to what learners reported regarding educators' lack of willingness to engage in verbal communication, during my classroom observations I witnessed educators making limited attempts to create dialogue between themselves and the students. Almost all of the educators I observed encouraged learners to ask questions, with little success. When learners did respond to educators' questions, their responses were defended by educators, who often pleaded with the class to respect the inputs of peers and not to ostracise participating students. The reasons for student 'silencing' cannot, therefore, be solely reduced to the efforts and educational approaches of teachers.

Students' refusal or reticence to participate in academic activities may be partly due to fears of being exposed, as their academic progress, such as reading ability, may be lagging behind 'benchmarked standards' set by education department officials. There was ample evidence that students were sensitive to being exposed or shamed by teachers. Students said that 'good' teachers did not embarrass learners in front of their peers:

Interviewer: What makes a good teacher?
Melanie: The way they bring the work over. The way they make you understand. The relationship you have with the teacher. Maybe you don't understand the work na, now the way teachers are with you . . . maybe you scared to talk with that teacher cause you scared she'll give you an answer that won't be nice. And that happens when you don't even understand the work. Cause you scared that she'll embarrass you in front of the whole class. They like to make you feel bad jong,[2] in front of the whole class jong. You didn't do well in a subject and they throw it in your face, in front of everyone.

Situations in which students fear being exposed and embarrassed are not conducive to promoting forms of dialogue, as young people will be unwilling to speak freely, contribute opinions and ask questions if they fear humiliation.

Limited dialogue therefore took place in classrooms at RGHS. While some educators attempted to connect with the life worlds of learners using familiar cultural reference points and humour, the vast majority of classroom interactions consisted of dictation and educators performing predesigned scripts.

Conclusion

At RGHS dialogic learning was repressed due to the pressure on educators to deliver the curriculum. The master's thesis of the current Rosemary Gardens school principal, Mr Abdullah Williams, entitled *Towards participatory teaching and learning processes in the English language classroom*, demonstrated some of the difficulties contained in implementing alternative forms of pedagogy at schools, with their rigid curricula requirements. Mr Williams described two of his attempts to conduct action research projects that experimented with participatory, student-led forms of pedagogy. The first project utilised group work to foster cooperative learning amongst students in a second-language English classroom. The second project involved him teaching the novel *The Winslow Boy*. The plot of this text revolves around a naval college student who is expelled for supposedly stealing from a peer and the ensuing court case. Mr Williams led an outing to a magistrate's court and organised a film viewing of an adaptation of the text for the learners to observe. These projects demonstrated a deep commitment to his profession, as well as creativity and rigorous forms of analytical engagement with the subject that he taught. His project attempted to nurture students' political consciousness and critical thinking. However, neither of these projects tapped into the cultural or linguistic resources of the learners, as they failed to unearth students' everyday practices or capitals. Mr Williams ultimately required that the learners in his study conform to certain curricula requirements.

In addition to pressures created by the heavily structured curriculum, the material spatial forces operating in the neighbourhood of Rosemary Gardens, such as the effects of poverty and violence, combined with beliefs regarding the linguistic capital of learners, led to restricted dialogue and learning. At RGHS students learnt that the language they spoke outside of the school was inferior to the language that they were expected to use in classrooms. Educational settings provide many people with their first institutional encounters with language value judgements, as their words are evaluated and assumptions made about their intelligence, family background and future potential (Delpit, 2002). Denigrating the language learners speak at home implicitly insults students' families and other people close to them. Such value judgements lead to learners becoming highly suspicious of a system that belittles their most intimate identities and insinuates what their futures are likely to entail.

Many Rosemary Gardens learners rejected this state of affairs and discontinued their schooling. For those who remained, students needed to accept the status quo and adapt their practices in order to 'play the school game'. Some students that remained did so with extreme suspicion and expressed distrust towards the school and the world in which it operated, believing in a conspiracy that worked against their success. The appeal of these forms of conspiracy theory hinted that students desired a pedagogy that developed their political consciousness and directly engaged with issues related to social justice (Duncan Andrade & Morrell, 2008; Freire, 1970; Ladson-Billings, 1995). Rosemary Gardens youth did not need to be made aware of—or 'conscientised'—with regard to their oppression; they were already cognisant of the social hierarchy. They required new tools for interpreting the conditions in which they lived, concepts and language that could empower them to name these circumstances, to speak truth, as it were, to power. Neither the curriculum nor educators stimulated these learners' growing sociopolitical consciousness.

I would say that each of the three 'responses' to the conditions experienced at RGHS constituted a form of lived space. Youth negotiated the effects of material and imagined spatial forces that shaped their lives as they found ways of 'living' in the interstices of these structural conditions. However, some of these forms of lived space may not be empowering, such as school discontinuation, as these young people's future options are severely limited by not completing secondary school. Similarly, accepting that one's mother-tongue language is 'inferior', in the interests of acquiring linguistic capital to be used in future endeavours, is not an empowering process. While lived space may involve individuals exerting agency, actions such as leaving school or accepting inferiority do not necessarily empower young people.

Notes

1 Areas that were constructed by the apartheid state in the early 1970s, that were intended for habitation by people classified as 'coloured', are easily identifiable by the blocks of apartments that were built in these areas. These apartment blocks became known as the 'kortse' or 'courts'.
2 The term '*jong*' does not have an exact meaning, but is instead used for emphasis.

References

Alexander, R. 2008. *Towards dialogic teaching: rethinking classroom talk (4th ed.)*. York: Dialogos.
Bakhtin, M. 1981. *The dialogic imagination: four essays by M. M. Bakhtin*. Austin: University of Texas Press.
Barnes, J. 2011. *The sense of an ending*. London: Vintage Books.
Bernstein, B., 1964. Elaborated and restricted codes: Their social origins and some consequences. *American Anthropologist*, 66(6_PART2), 55–69.
Burton, P. & Leoschut, L. 2013. *School violence in South Africa: results of the 2012 National School Violence Study*. Cape Town: Centre for Justice and Crime Prevention, Monograph 12.
Craven, K., Doykos, B., Fisher, B., Geller, J., Maselli, A. & Wegman, H. 2012. *Rosemary Gardens High School: understanding and exploring reasons learners stop coming to school*. Unpublished report prepared for Youth Empowerment through School.
Delpit, L. 2002. No kinda sense. In L. Delpit & J. K. Dowdy (Eds.), *The skin that we speak: thoughts on language and culture in the classroom (pp. 31–48)*. New York: New Press.
Duncan-Andrade, J. & Morrell, E. 2008. *The art of critical pedagogy: possibilities for moving from theory to practice in urban schools*. New York: Peter Lang.
Fine, M. 1991. *Framing dropouts: notes on the politics of an urban public high school*. Albany: SUNY Press.
Flanders, N. 1970. *Analysing teacher behaviour*. Reading, MA: Addison-Wesley.
Freire, P. 1970. *Pedagogy of the oppressed*. New York: Continuum International Publishing.
hooks, b. 2003. *Teaching community: a pedagogy of hope*. New York: Routledge.
Howe, C. 2010. Peer dialogue and cognitive development: a two-way relationship? In K. Littleton & C. Howe (Eds.), *Peer groups and children's development (pp. 32–48)*. Oxford: Wiley-Blackwell.
Johnson, M. 2013. *Impact of stress and burnout interventions on educators in high-risk secondary schools*. Unpublished doctoral thesis. Stellenbosch University, Stellenbosch.
Ladson-Billings, G. 1995. Toward a theory of culturally relevant pedagogy. *American Educational Research Journal*, 32, 465–491.
Ladson-Billings, G. 2002. I ain't writin' nuttin': permission to fail and demands to succeed in urban classrooms. In L. Delpit & J. Dowdy (Eds.), *The skin that we*

speak: thoughts on language and culture in the classroom (pp. 107–120). New York: New Press.

Leander, K. 2001. 'This is our freedom bus going home right now': producing and hybridizing space-time contexts in pedagogical discourse. *Journal of Literacy Research, 33*(4), 637–679.

McFadden, M. & Munns, G. 2002. Student engagement and the social relations of pedagogy. *British Journal of Sociology of Education, 23*(3), 357–366.

Mercer, N. 2002. Developing dialogues. In G. Wells & G. Claxton (Eds.), *Learning for life in the 21st century (pp. 141–154)*. Oxford: Blackwell Publishers.

Purcell-Gates, V. 2002. "... As soon as she opened her mouth!": Issues of language, literacy, and power. In L. Delpit & J. K. Dowdy (Eds), *The skin that we speak: Thoughts on language and culture in the classroom (pp.121–141)*. New York: New Press.

Republic of South Africa. 1996. The South African Schools Act No. 84, 1996. Government Gazette, 15 November 1996. No. 17579.

6 Dialogue and Learning Amongst the Doodvenootskap

This is real,
*How can you a **nation** heal?*
*Everyone wants to be **Superman***
But no one wants to fight the battle
Babies lost their toys
Cause their mothers want to rattle,
Like chickens in a coop
Where everybody cackles
***Decisions** are made without us*
And now I must my bek hou (shut my animalistic mouth)
***Nowadays** everyone looks up to you*
*And you're an **infection**,*
You were born from a weak reaction
      (Translated from the Afrikaans. **English words that**
      were used in the original lyrics are in bold.)
From the album *Skollyhood Chapter One: reality's face*, by Ssslang, DVS member

... it (hip hop) also consists of graffiti and visual arts, dancing and different kinaesthetic movements, deejaying and being musicologically inclined. The fifth element of the culture of hip hop is knowledge ... the formulation and creation of knowledge ... all you have to do is look at what hip hop culture does in education systems ... we encourage young people to use and control language for their benefit, so it's empowering and liberating through the linguistic piece, but all these other elements are also a big part of this conversation. We're talking about a very full, robust culture here that has liberated young people and liberated their minds for almost four decades now.

                                Interview with Dr James Peterson
                        http://www.youtube.com/watch?v=TydqRM71eYo

> As is the case for cultural production generally, the politics of rap music involves the contestation over public space, expressive meaning, interpretation, and cultural capital. In short, it is not just what one says, it is where one can say it, how others react to what one says, and whether one has the means with which to command public space.
>
> Tricia Rose, 1991: 276

The Doodvenootskap: A Youth 'Movement' in Rosemary Gardens

The journey now moves away from the school to the next stop, where I introduce the Doodvenootskap. DVS is a crew of young hip hop artists from Rosemary Gardens who wrote their own lyrics, recorded tracks of music and attempted to highlight issues that they felt were social problems in their neighbourhood. Three members of DVS were employed by an NGO called the Children's Rights and Anti-Abuse Group (CRAAG). As CRAAG employees they helped conduct research with young people in Rosemary Gardens, advocated for the nonviolent treatment of children in this neighbourhood and promoted young people's participation in decision-making forums at school and in the wider community. The DVS crew consisted of approximately six to eight core individuals, however 20 people were regularly involved in DVS activities. One young person told me that up to 50 youth were loosely affiliated with the group. Of the core members of the crew that I interacted with, one was in his early thirties, one was 26 years old and the others were under 18 years of age.

Material, imagined and lived space shaped the emergence of DVS and influenced the ways that they used language in dialogues. DVS members described the crew as an intentional alternative to gang affiliation for young people. Apartheid laws disrupted material space, leading to the widespread emergence of youth gangs. Gangs formed in areas like Rosemary Gardens, as young men recreated social cohesion after the Group Areas Act (1950) dismantled many communities in the city. DVS members said that they hoped that Rosemary Gardens youth would rather participate in their activities than become involved in gangs. These material socio-spatial relations were intimately linked to how DVS was forged as an imagined space. The group conceived itself as a 'youth movement', providing an alternative education to what is learnt through gangsterism. This informal education consisted of young people leveraging and using new concepts through their involvement in and dialogues with NGOs and hip hop culture.

Acquiring concepts, ideas and language from global and local hip hop culture, as well as from NGOs, did not mean that dialogic learning took place. These youth needed to reflect on and interrogate these ideas, not merely use concepts without thinking. In the final section of the chapter I analysed the young people's use of concepts and language in discussions between DVS members and myself. I also looked at the meaning of the lyrics that they wrote. These spoken and written words illuminated how the group used language and engaged in dialogues across the multiple sets of social relations that they traversed.

Material Space and the Doodvenootskap

NGOs Help to Build the Community Centre

International and local NGOs' resistance to draconian apartheid policies led to a number of these organisations working in Rosemary Gardens, contributing valuable resources and helping to establish new educational places and practices. NGO involvement in Rosemary Gardens led to the erection of the community centre, a place where many educational activities took place and services were offered to the community. Specifically, a partnership between the United Reformed Church from Germany and the Global Hope Foundation (GHF), an American nonprofit organisation, led to the erection of the Global Hope Foundation building, the community centre as it was known, in the early 1980s.

DVS conducted most of its work in this building; a number of NGOs rented offices in this location, including CRAAG, who in turn provided DVS with a small office. The office and institutional base contributed to the group's overall professional identity and supplied DVS with a set of physical resources, such as a telephone, a computer and access to the Internet. The group held meetings in this office and observed and participated in interactions with interns, international donors and local government officials who moved through the physical space of the GHF building. This was the place in which I predominantly interacted with the group. The impact that NGOs have had on material space in Rosemary Garden therefore contributed to DVS emerging as a 'learning place'.

Apartheid Spatial Dislocation Leads to Gangs: DVS as Youth Imagining an Alternative Affiliation

The Doodvenootskap illustrated intersections and overlaps between material and imagined space. Material spatial forces in Cape Town led to youth gang proliferation, with DVS comprising an example of youth imagining an alternative to gang affiliation. In Cape Town the Group Areas Act (1950) dismantled local communities, which led to 150,000 people being relocated. This, in turn, led to some people who were relocated recreating new forms of social cohesion through establishing youth gangs or 'brotherhoods' (Pinnock, 1984). The emergence of DVS is related to turbulent material spatial conditions and young people's attempts to create alternatives to the effects of these oppressive structural forces. The life story of Hoppie, the founding member of DVS and role model for the younger DVS participants, illuminated how harsh material circumstances shaped his life trajectory:

Interviewer: How did it happen [that you got involved in gangsterism]?
Hoppie: *It was all my friends, family as well. They were the type of people that I looked up to. You speak about the exact same things.* **Gangsters** *have everything, clothes, cars. As I became*

older I realised that's not what makes a person. Before that realisation I moved in that energy. Stabbed people with a knife. Fought with people. I wasn't a gangster but I associated . . . it gave me street knowledge in terms of how **to communicate with youngsters**. And in the line of work that I'm involved in now, how to communicate with youngsters that are trapped in that same **energy**. I chose not to take a tattoo. For me it wasn't necessary because of my **religious beliefs**. But they said I know too many **secrets**. I was in wrong things. I went to jail also. The second time (I went to jail) I decided it **definitely** wasn't for me. I was at Pollsmoor. A **weekend was** like a month. I had (stabbed) somebody . . . with a knife. Attempted murder. I worked it all out, I found myself in **hip hop poetry**, **acting** and I lay there for a whole **weekend**. I thought I don't want to do that. I got my cards in a line. I booked myself into . . . not a rehab but with my people. With a **higher power**. I was **religiously involved** at the mosque. I was on my own for a whole month. I got **positive energy**. My **street knowledge** that I had, I put it all into my writing. My first song was about things that I often **imagined**. I was in America, courting Jennifer Lopez. The **song's** name was **imagination**. "You sit on the edge and it **corners** you, the kids sit in the park and play with yo yos.' I wrote that song and I was tripping. Tripping in the sense that I believed in myself. 'Collaborate with **J Lo, first class flight up to Chicago**. Now I have a CD and it hits on the radio." And so it began and the kids said this guy is awesome, he raps awesome. I wrote my second **song** and the second **song** was more **conscious**.

(Translated from the Afrikaans. **English words that were used by the speaker are in bold.**)

Hoppie's development as a musician and an artist was forged through constructing an alternative, imagined pathway—his first song was called *Imagination*—to the gang affiliation into which many young men on the Cape Flats are coerced. As a young man, Hoppie's influential relationships with family members and friends were plagued by social problems in Rosemary Gardens. Fortunately for Hoppie his religious background functioned as a support structure, aiding in his transformation from a lifestyle involving violence and narcotics to his pursuing a different set of activities, goals and dialogues.

Hoppie's resilience to the harsh material circumstances in which he was reared was further aided by his involvement in music and acting. His artistic career began when he was filmed as part of a documentary on recovery from crystal methamphetamine addiction. A prominent theatre director watched the film and approached Hoppie, asking him to help construct the script for an educational drama production that was taking place at the Baxter Theatre. After completing this project he proceeded to work on another play, collaborating with a different, established local playwright. Simultaneously, Hoppie wrote a number of songs that he uploaded onto YouTube. He is therefore a somewhat successful musician, music producer and playwright, a young man whose development has been influenced by interactions and communication with documentary filmmakers, playwrights and other artists. He served as a role model and educator for DVS youth, pioneering an alternative form of youth identity in Rosemary Gardens. All of the DVS members I interviewed described their initiation into the crew as revolving around an apprenticeship period in which Hoppie worked with them to improve their lyric writing skills.

The group's resistance to gang affiliation and their attempts to imagine an alternative place where young people acquire a different informal education were hinted at by the name *Doodvenootskap*. The name means 'funeral service', or quite literally, 'death partnership', implying that the group try to 'clean up' social problems related to gang involvement:

It's short for Doodvenootskap. That's the 'note' like the musical note and then the 'skap' for the brotherhood. In this rap game they (rappers) just wanna kill each other. Like I stand for something... I would rather collaborate than compete. **Because everybody in this game wants to compete. Funeral services we are here, we clean up.**

(Translated from the Afrikaans. **English words that were used by the speaker are in bold.**)

DVS differentiated itself from gangsterism, advocating for collaboration between different community organisations in order to help eradicate or "clean up" prevalent social problems in Rosemary Gardens. The group tried to achieve these ambitions through making music and performing in public, as well as by leading activities and research with young people. As a 'learning place', DVS was therefore produced as an imagined alternative to gangsterism, a phenomenon that resulted from the material spatial dislocation that occurred due to apartheid forced removals.

Imagined Space and the Doodvenootskap: A Youth Movement Shining "a Light Through the Darkness"

DVS was described by its members as a "youth movement", uniting young people in Rosemary Gardens through a 'positive' affiliation and, simultaneously, creating an alternative peer group identity and learning place:

DVS is a youth movement, we aim to empower youth with the knowledge to be future leaders instead of following. We believe in leading by example, so we taking the stand because there's a lot of poverty and

> gangsterism and negative stuff surrounding our community. We're making sure there's a light through all this darkness . . .

DVS encouraged young people to become involved in the activities that they facilitated, as they believed that associating with their group could help youth avoid social problems like gang affiliation, substance abuse and violence. By attracting a particular age-related cohort of young people rather to associate with DVS, the members of the group envisioned that they were constructing an alternative 'place' or youth movement. I was informed that the movement was aimed at youth in Rosemary Gardens and Riverside, areas that were designated for 'coloured' people under the Group Areas Act and which, more specifically, continue to consist almost exclusively of working-class coloured people. Geographically, for example, Pelican Park is positioned adjacent to Rosemary Gardens and was also restricted to 'coloured' residents during apartheid. However, in DVS members' descriptions Pelican Park was excluded from the vision for 'the movement', presumably due to its middle-class status. The 'movement' was therefore an imagined place where marginalised youth could create positive identities and engage in educational practices, like lyric writing, on their own terms.

Analysing the social relations between this hip hop crew and CRAAG further elucidated DVS as an imagined place. DVS members were exposed to new concepts through interactions with organisations like CRAAG, groups that worked in close proximity to them. The language, values and ideologies of NGOs that worked in the Global Hope Foundation building contributed to how DVS evolved as a 'learning place'. For example, CRAAG staff used a human rights discourse extensively, due to their founding links with a public health department at a tertiary education institution. Terms like 'empowerment' and 'freedom of speech' punctuated the talk of CRAAG staff and, in turn, DVS. Dylan Aprils, the young man who worked for CRAAG and was closely associated with DVS said:

> People or adults make decisions for children here. This isn't a child-centred community. If this were a child-centred community, bra, there would be parks, people in schools, camps over weekend, strong families. It's organised chaos here.

The material space of Rosemary Gardens was perceived as deficient in terms of facilities for young people and this attitude was tied to a set of discourses and practices that defined the neighbourhood as 'unchild-centred', a place where adults made decisions for children. Many DVS members also used this human rights discourse:

> CRAAG is an organisation aimed at children's rights. CRAAG stands for the children's rights and anti-abuse group. Like we . . . I work for them and we focus on empowering youth, the same as DVS. So it's a

combination of DVS and CRAAG. So we trying to fuse this whole thing to get youth off the street and we're trying to use the resources that CRAAG has, to uplift the youth. We trying to be what our ancestors wanted us to be. They wanted us to be this powerful nation in history. We believe in child participation that's our main focus, to see our community through the eyes of the children, the next generation, the next leaders.

The links between CRAAG and DVS are clearly stated in this quotation, with both groups working towards 'uplifting the youth', promoting 'child participation' and developing 'youth leadership'. DVS' work was therefore allied with the operations of CRAAG; the two groups' goals were aligned and they used similar concepts. Young people like Fabio (quoted above) utilised this rights-based discourse in their daily language, adopting concepts obtained from associations with CRAAG personnel. This discourse filtered down to the younger members of the group that were not employed by CRAAG, creating a form of imagined space within which DVS operated. Through this discourse the group attempted to alleviate some of Rosemary Gardens' social problems that were associated with "the street". Youth were therefore metaphorically taken "off the street" by DVS and CRAAG and led to a safe place, such as the Global Hope Foundation building. Through concepts linked to a human rights discourse DVS defined themselves in opposition to other peer groups, such as those that create their identities on "the street", groups like youth gangs that glorified criminal activities.

The human rights discourse propagated by CRAAG, and which is embedded in the South African constitution, introduced DVS to a new set of concepts, as illustrated by the following quotations:

I felt that was my responsibility as a elder brother to teach her her (his younger sister) rights, cause I was never taught that. I was always taught that whatever an adult say they right, you a child you wrong.

And:

I have a poet license, it's freedom of speech and I'm using mine now.

The young people involved in DVS perceived themselves as endowed with the responsibility to promote children's rights and guide other youth to militate against forms of injustice that they believed took place in Rosemary Gardens. The group used this rights-based discourse in their hip hop work as their "poetic licenses" and "freedom of speech" were expressed through lyric writing. These concepts were central to their advocacy endeavours for CRAAG, as they promoted the rights guaranteed to children by the South African constitution. DVS members utilised this discourse in their personal lives, in interactions with, for example, siblings, as one of the quotations above confirms. The work that DVS conducted with CRAAG therefore resulted in members of the group procuring a new set of concepts. Merely acquiring this discourse did not, however, necessarily mean that dialogic learning took place, as I will show in the next section. It was necessary for these youth to reflect on and question ideas related to a rights-based framework, in order for them to learn from these concepts.

The imagined space within which DVS members learnt was also produced by the concepts the group gleaned from global and local hip hop culture. For example, DVS members often described becoming 'more conscious' through hip hop, demonstrating their affiliations with international forms of conscious hip hop that originated in the United States:

Brad: *The best thing to do when you freestyle is rap a few things that you thought of before and when you run out of ideas, rap what is happening now or rap what you seeing. So if you sitting in this place you can rap over a chair and you can rap over your hair, cause you here and the chair's here. I'm not so good in freestyling, I'm getting better. I like to write lyrics. You have all the time to edit your lyrics and make sure they're more conscious lyrics.*

Interviewer: *What you mean more conscious?*

Brad: *When I'm freestyling and I'm running out of things you can say a lot of stupid things to just keep going with the freestyle. When you writing you have all that time to think and realise okay that doesn't sound right for a two-year-old. You understand?*

According to Brad, a conscious lyric is one that is reflected upon and thought about, not merely generated instinctively. He believed that "freestyling" was not conducive to rappers generating "conscious" lyrics, as it did not promote reflection and rigorous thinking. It was important to DVS members that lyrics made sense, were thought about and did not merely involve rhyming and using words gratuitously. These youth were therefore engaging with wider international discourses, practices and values that shape conscious hip hop, which they rearticulated in the local context and used to learn through the imagined space of DVS.

However, there was a strong affinity to local cultural forms in DVS' engagement with hip hop; through dialogic interactions with Hoppie, younger DVS members were able to obtain advice on how to write lyrics and rap, as they were encouraged to embrace forms of local culture and not the commercial American hip hop that they saw on television:

I said "look here Hoppie, how do you rap"? And he said I must write him a verse and so I wrote him a verse. I don't remember, I wish I had it right here right now to see how much I've changed. The verse was

> about "I wish I was a gangster, money, ladies, Tupac", and he told me "look here, man". He made me realise why do you have to go so far when everything is here at home. And I took it in and started writing and he started editing my verse, he showed me how much bars, how full the page must be. I practiced my verse everyday, I'm going over the song. He organised us a original beat. And we went to a studio in Hillview, Tyron's studio. And I was very excited I recorded my first song. My voice was very thin there.

And

> The first thing I wrote was "baby girl I like your style, I wish we could spend a little while. So I can press your numbers like I press a dial". All stuff like that. So Hoppie asked me "what's the message behind that"... so I was like... "I'm gonna knop this kind (have sex with this girl) and stuff" and he said "why do you wanna get that out there? Isn't 50 cent saying the same stuff? What makes you Fabio?" So I said I don't know and he said 'write a couple of things down'... and I owned that verse, that was my verse. And the message that came out was much bigger than talking about dating a girl and talking about a girl's private parts and I felt better writing a verse like that than writing about having sex with a girl. I don't want to be a pervert, especially now that I'm a dad. So ever since that day I've changed. There's a lot of other things I can talk about. Look at our government, corruption all the way. I have a poet license that allows me to say certain things.

Stories of initiation into DVS consisted of narratives of transformation; individuals grew from a naïve affinity towards American popular culture, materialism and misogynistic sentiments, to writing about their identities and the local context. In each of these stories the young people reflected on their values and their position in society and then expressed aspects of their identities through a public performance. This was achieved in relation to the challenges Hoppie set these individuals and the fraternal guidance that he provided. In Brad's case, the process culminated in his recording a track, a public event with a product of which he was proud. Fabio was able to use lyric writing to express a politically aware gendered identity that was congruent with the CRAAG work he was conducting and values that he had adopted. In both of these instances Hoppie challenged these young people to think about their values and cultural reference points, catalysing personal change in the process. Earlier Cape Town hip hop groups like Prophets of da City and Black Noise embraced local cultural forms in a similar manner, with DVS members aligning themselves with those practices and values. DVS' emphasis on local values illustrates similarities with how other hip hop crews outside of the United States have had to work to 'keep it real'. These groups have strived to express authentic identities that are congruent with local cultural contexts, as they avoid merely mimicking American words and values (Pennycook, 2007; Perullo & Fenn, 2003).

The imagined spaces of NGO discourse and hip hop exposed the DVS crew to many new ideas and concepts. DVS members used these terms in their daily life. Utilising these languages contributed to a form of informal pedagogy. However, as I have already emphasised, access to and the acquisition of these discourses and concepts did not mean that dialogic learning occurred. As the next section shows, DVS members needed to think about, question and reflect on concepts and ideas, in order to learn from them.

"My Porridge Bowl Is Now a Satellite Dish": Doodvenootskap, Dialogue and Other Dilemmas

So, what did members of the DVS crew learn through their interactions with NGOs and affiliations to hip hop culture? To answer this question I analysed examples of dialogues between the crew and myself from one-on-one interviews. I also examined the lyrics of an album produced by one of the crew, but to which the entire group contributed. The album, called *Skollyhood:*[1] chapter one, *reality's face*, illustrated how these young men used their written lyrics to reflect on dialogues in which they had engaged.

In interviews with myself, the DVS members often recited what they called 'punch lines' as examples of the sophistication of their lyrical abilities, without using these statements for the purpose of dialogue. On certain occasions DVS members used these punch lines, as well as concepts related to the human-rights discourse that they heard CRAAG recite, without thoroughly reflecting on the meaning of these terms:

Interviewer: ... *and what makes a good lyric?*
Raheem: **Freedom of speech.**
Interviewer: And what does it mean, **freedom of speech**?
Raheem: It means a lot for me, **especially** with the work that we're doing now. We're building resilience, now resilience for me is resistance. I am a resistance against gangsterism. The best lyrics instead of **accepting** it you rebel against it. The coolest lyrics in terms of **hardcore, commercial and underground** is to **manipulate** the mind . . . for example "without a gun I am a man, I will finish you reading a magazine".
Interviewer: But for example, **Nazi Germany had bad values and manipulated people in a bad way.** Is it good lyrics if it's used for bad purposes?
Raheem: That's because our people aren't **educated,** man. Now they misinterpret. Do you hear what I say "without a gun I am a man, I will finish you reading a **magazine.**" Hear that lyric. It's very **powerful.** He doesn't know if I am talking about a **magazine** like Huis Genoot[2] or a **magazine** that goes into a

Dialogue and Learning Amongst the Doodvenootskap 93

> gun. Now people can **misinterpret** that. And that's why we do **intros**. In most of our CDs we do **intros**. If you think I am a **gangster** I'm not. We make such things clear. But people misinterpret. Like I say "I will **chop off your arm then you can sue for armed robbery**." People interpret that **literally**, my bru. It isn't **literal** it's just a **pun**.
>
> (Translated from the Afrikaans. English words that were used by the speaker are in bold.)

In the passage above, Rico used the terms "freedom of speech", "resistance" and "resilience", which he had gleaned from his work with CRAAG, but he avoided engaging with me when I probed his understanding of the meaning of these concepts. He then produced two punch lines: "without a gun I am a man, I will finish you reading a **magazine**" (this punch line makes more sense in Afrikaans) and "I will chop off your arm then you can sue for **armed robbery**." The punch lines were intended to illustrate how local people misunderstand the nonviolent intentions of DVS' lyrics. They were pre-developed mantras, used as evidence of peaceful intentions. However, these punch lines did not stimulate debate in our interaction.

Rico began by saying that the value of a lyric is based on its potential to stimulate "freedom of speech", which can be used to "manipulate minds" and build 'resilience' in local communities by exposing youth to creative uses of language. When I asked him what "freedom of speech" meant, trying to stimulate discussion around this idea, he did not answer my question. Instead he said that the term was important to him and he linked it to other related human rights terms like "resilience" and "resistance". He did not expand on the meaning of those concepts either. Rico was able to use "freedom of speech", "resilience" and "manipulation" in his speech, but he did not attempt to analyse the complexities and context-specific implications of these terms. He had assimilated these ideas into his repertoire, but it was unclear whether he had fully interrogated their meanings.

Rico then recited his punch lines. Members of the group regularly used what they called 'punch lines' to illustrate their lyrical talents. A punch line is a lyric that is used in a rap battle, usually towards the climax, often to insult an opponent. While DVS' innovative punch lines were creative and intelligent, crew members normally uttered them in a predetermined manner, without debating the meaning of the terms or exploring the purposes of these statements. Rico used these phrases to demonstrate the power of DVS lyrics. It was a stand-alone statement, uttered without a context, and it did not invite a response that might have initiated dialogue.

Concepts like 'freedom of speech', 'resistance' and 'resilience' and various punch lines may therefore fail to stimulate forms of dialogic learning if they are not reflected upon and questioned in terms of their relevance to both local and wider contexts and used dialogically, in interactions with others. Dialogic learning occurs through questioning and debating issues, rather than reciting discourses and concepts that circulate amongst groups and networks like CRAAG and the global hip hop community.

Other members of the crew indicated that lyrics had value when they were used dialogically to assert creative language, raising questions and stimulating discussion. Brad described what it meant to defeat an opponent 'lyrically', in a hip hop battle, in the following manner:

Brad: *If I should battle a rapper, you should kill him lyrically, cause if you gonna push him down on facts that's not gonna mean anything to him, its just sounds he's hearing, he's not gonna hear any metaphors, puns, personifications, so he'll kill you easily if he must come back with all of that elements of hip hop.*

Interviewer: *Why does that make you win?*

Brad: *It's like the crowd knows about rapping. Either the crowd or him himself or the judges, but I was never yet at a battle, but I know if I should battle someone in the street, I'll spit something lyrical to show I know poems, I know what is a simile, what is a metaphor, I can make something dead alive and that's what people want to hear, they don't want to hear you reading a story or a article. That's the picture, but then you bring a bigger picture to the story . . . like I've got this line "I will break your arm off and then you can sue for armed robbery". Then the crowd won't laugh cause it's a shit joke.*

Interviewer: *So it's about beating the person by being creative with words not dissing them personally?*

Brad: *It's lyrical, lyrical . . . I get the opportunity to say what I want to say, freedom of speech, cause in most cases you won't get that opportunity.*

Brad explained that the value of rap lyrics was based on the figurative language one was able to use when 'spitting' one's lines; insulting somebody based on their appearance, life history or personality traits was not valued in this context. A "battle" therefore needed to be won "lyrically" and not by "putting somebody down on facts". Brad said that "facts" were merely sounds when used in a battle; they carried no weight as rappers needed rather to demonstrate linguistic creativity and innovation. This implied that good lyrics were actively created and used dialogically, responses to what other rappers "spat".

Lyrical sophistication was attained by 'making something dead alive', using innovative words and a message that extended beyond literal meanings. Brad added that rappers should be "bringing a bigger picture to the story": they were required to contextualise lyrics through analytical ability, creativity and linking particular lines to broader social contexts. Rapping necessarily entailed engaging with and building upon the existing story, 'dialoguing with the existing story'. Brad was therefore hinting at the links between the specific lyrics being created and a broader context, a bigger "story" that gave these lyrics meaning. He understood that words have meaning through the ways in which they are used, in context, and in answer to utterances that precede them—what I have described as the basic tenets of dialogue. As his reference to "consciousness" earlier in the chapter demonstrated, this process is enhanced by creating lyrics that can be thought about and reflected upon, not merely generated instinctively. Lyrics should not be predetermined and clichéd, like the joke about armed robbery; rather they need to be produced in response to what one's opponent is 'spitting'.

In this conversation myself and Brad participated in an exchange in which our utterances connected and created a joint product. Although Brad struggled to express the exact meaning of the concept of "lyrical" or to double-voice it into his own words, he was clearly grappling with the meaning of this concept, as he thought about the contexts surrounding the lyrics he was producing. He did not revert to his own internal thoughts and self-referential utterances, but engaged with me in a dialogue.

The lyrics of an album made in 2012 by one DVS member further illuminated how the group learnt through dialogue. The album was made by a young man known as Ssslang (Sssnake), but the entire group contributed to its production. A descriptive overview of the album's lyrics follows, before I conduct a more detailed analysis of one track, exploring some of the contradictions inherent in growing up in Rosemary Gardens.

The album's title, *Skollyhood: chapter one, reality's face*, is emblematic of many of the social relations that are referenced in the 13 tracks. The title is a tongue-in-cheek glamorisation of a potential Hollywood superstar, but also a self-mockery of Slang's 'lower-class' status ('lower class' is a self-referential term used in the lyrics of the album). This tension between 'glamour and nothingness', alluded to in the title, is reiterated at various points in the album, for example in the following lyrics:

> *In the evening I lie and I hear 500 thousand people scream my name*
> *Me, standing on a* **stage**, *because I'm* **complicated** *with a* **plan**
> *On a* **silver platter**, *sick of living up to other people's standards, why must I be compared to* **Brad Pitt** *if I've got my own life to live.*
> (Translated from the Afrikaans. **English words that were used in the original lyrics are in bold.**)

Ssslang engaged with the binary between fame and insignificance through philosophical musings about the meaning of life and mass media portrayals of success. These were interspersed with references to his social status, as he directly questioned the notion of "standards" and the processes and people that determine these social benchmarks. His social status inquisition was conducted dialogically and creatively. For example, at one point in track three a mock conversation plays out between Ssslang and a peer who calls him a "lower-class fuck". Although Ssslang stated at Youth Amplified, when DVS made a guest appearance, that many children in Rosemary Gardens idealise DVS, there was also an ever-lurking self-belief amongst these young people that they were simply 'common hooligans'. The album engaged dialogically with this tension between Ssslang's aspirations for self-definition through music and art and society's classification of Rosemary Gardens youth as lower class, badly behaved and uneducated. The title *Skollyhood* combines these two opposing identities or statuses, within the medium of rap, allowing Ssslang to explore and play with these contradictions.

The material context of Rosemary Gardens is described throughout the album. Everyday life in this neighbourhood and the violence that permeates it are vividly portrayed throughout the tracks. For example, the chorus of track nine reiterates: "Instant pudding, instant coffee, instant **death with** a once off guarantee", illustrating the fleeting and temporary value of life in Rosemary Gardens, which is compared to cheap consumable products.

The social effects of poverty and violence resulted in bodily references punctuating the lyrics, as living in Rosemary Gardens is an extremely corporeal experience. The violence that was commonly observed in the neighbourhood and which was lodged in the consciousness of youth from the area resulted in injuries to bodies, meaning that the body was a common reference point for this young writer. The subtitle of the album, *reality's face*, is an example of a reference to the most personally definitive of body parts, a face, as the album hinted that it would provide insight into life in Rosemary Gardens. The first line of track three, the song that is explored in more depth below, is: "my self-confidence se boosters het bruises" ("my self-confidence boosters have bruises"). The line is clearly a reference to narcotics, probably crystal methamphetamine (which he references at another point in the album), an addictive habit that marks the body, usually through visible weight loss. Ssslang was able to express, creatively, some of the pain associated with experimenting with recreational narcotics through the metaphorical use of the word "bruises", another reference to his body. The body is a marker of physical difference that has been used in South Africa to distinguish between groups of people in terms of their social status. Bodies define a person socially and personally, and youth from Rosemary Gardens were aware of this fact, as evidenced by the *Skollyhood* album.

As expected from a teenage boy, a number of the album's lyrics relate to romantic relationships. Some of these lyrics contained problematic misogynistic and homophobic attitudes. For example, track four consists of a fairy tale of a 'Cinderella' who he meets and has sexual intercourse with, despite her being part of a 'committed' relationship. In the chorus he tells her to "turn around touch the ground oooh la la". Even though Ssslang was an advocate for a children's rights and anti-abuse organisation, the glamorisation of a particular brand of masculine sexuality and women as objects of desire are unreflexively asserted in this track. There are also homophobic references to "faggots" and "bunnies" (slang for homosexual) at various points on the album.

Dialogue and Learning Amongst the Doodvenootskap 97

I would like to analyse the third track of *Skollyhood*, called *listen to your heart*, another bodily reference, in greater detail. I believe that it exemplifies some of the dialogic interactions that occurred between DVS, Hoppie, CRAAG and the Rosemary Gardens community and, more particularly, illuminates how these conversations impacted on this young man's expanding consciousness.

The track seamlessly amalgamates English and Afrikaans. This demonstrates the translingual practices used by these young men as they skilfully navigate the contexts through which they move. For example, the first line states that:

> *My **self-confidence boosters** have **bruises**, I am a **problem** if I want to be **unique***
>
> (Translated from the Afrikaans. **English words that were used in the original are in bold**.)

In this line Ssslang demonstrates his ability to alternate between English and Kaapse Afrikaans, almost on a 'word for word' basis, supporting Alim's (2009) statement that hip hop inverts Bernstein's (1964) codes, as youth actually expand a restricted, rule-based language. These youth produced an elaborate set of linguistic constructions. This implies that the rigidly prescribed codes of standard English are actually restricted in comparison to how they are used by youth.

Ssslang was aware of the paradoxes surrounding the NGO industry and the operations of organisations like CRAAG:

> *Organisations are competing, doing it for charity*

The irony of competing for charity is clear to this young man, as he questioned why groups would need to compete in conducting these activities, as charity is supposedly an altruistic act. The ironies of globalisation and the values it has disseminated also impacted on his consciousness. One sees rows of satellite dishes in Rosemary Gardens and yet hunger is supposedly widespread:

> *My porridge bowl is nou (now) a satellite dish*

Hoppie's critique of young people's idealisation of American consumer culture therefore stimulated these youth to think about and consider the contradictions that existed in their environments. This was underlined by another lyric:

> ***Babies lost their toys** because their **mothers** want to **rattle**.*
>
> (Translated from the Afrikaans. **English words that were used in the original lyrics are in bold**.)

In this line Ssslang comments on mothers' resources being utilised for personal entertainment, instead of contributing towards the developmental needs of their children. He used a creative and intelligent pun on the word "rattle", a baby's toy but also the mother's pleasure in 'rattling' or 'partying'. CRAAG's values and the dialogues he has shared with Dylan therefore stimulated Ssslang to think about parent-child interactions in Rosemary Gardens and some of the problematic elements of these relationships. He was then able to express these thoughts in his own language, demonstrating a form of double-voicedness and showing that he had thought about and understood these ideas, not simply accepted and reproduced the opinions of somebody else.

Ssslang illustrated how he had internalised the CRAAG human-rights discourse regarding children's decision-making, but that he had also thought about these ideas:

> *decisions* are made without us and now I must shut my bek *(mouth of an animal)*
>
> (Translated from the Afrikaans. **English words that were used in the original lyrics are in bold.**)

His understanding of young people's participation in decision-making processes was not reiterated in the clichéd children's rights discourse, but was translated and double-voiced in Ssslang's own language, as he denigrated himself ironically, saying that he is forced to shut his animalistic, 'lower-class' mouth. The ambivalence pertaining to whether his actions are truly path-breaking, or simply the pointless activities of a 'working-class coloured boy', is again observed towards the end of the track in:

*Jy's n (you are an) Infection, You Were
Born From a Weak Reaction*

The "weak reaction" has racial overtones, as racial mixing and being a 'coloured half-caste' is implied by the "weak" conception.

Ssslang's ideological consciousness developed through dialogues with Dylan and CRAAG, in relation to children's rights, and with Hoppie, who questioned how these young people engaged with forms of global consumer culture when their identities and most pressing concerns were located locally. These dialogues stimulated forms of questioning and thinking, as evidenced in the *Skollyhood* album. The value of these lyrics as cultural products and learning tools therefore lay in their potential to form part of ongoing dialogues and debates, interactions that occurred in the material and imagined spaces in which these young people lived. Through this album and its lyrics, Ssslang demonstrated elements of lived space and dialogic learning. He managed to avoid simply reiterating the words of others, without thinking, as he questioned and linked utterances to the contexts in which they were produced. The album therefore needs to be interpreted not only by decoding the meaning of the lyrics, but by exploring the social practices, the lived spaces and dialogues that preceded and resulted in its production (Hill, 2009; Hill & Petchauer, 2013). The processes through which young people translate concepts and ideas into their own forms of language are integral to dialogic lived learning. Ssslang's self-parody, observed in terms like "Skollyhood" and "weak reaction", illustrated his questioning of and engagement with the social contexts in which he lived. These lyrics were cultural products that emerged through ongoing conversations that had a formative effect on the members of DVS.

Conclusion

The Doodvenootskap's learning practices were buttressed by NGOs that erected sites for community development in Rosemary Gardens, organisations that resisted the oppressive apartheid regime and its policies of racial segregation. Supported by NGOs like CRAAG, DVS emerged in opposition to youth gangs, introducing an alternative education to what was learnt through gang affiliation. These activities endowed DVS members with positive self-esteem, building momentum for an 'imaginary' social movement that strived to improve living conditions for Rosemary Gardens residents. Doodvenootskap members learnt new concepts, such as those associated with the field of public health, through interactions with CRAAG. The language used in hip hop culture also introduced these young people to new ideas.

Simultaneously, members of the group often recited 'NGO speak' and hip hop punch lines, without interrogating the meaning of these concepts. Sometimes, DVS members wrote lyrics and made statements that were self-referential and closed, suppressing potential responses. In order for young people to learn dialogically, utterances need to be connected to broader contexts and used in conversation with other concepts, ideas and people. Otherwise they simply become authoritarian discourses that do not stimulate young people to think about the places through which they move. The *Skollyhood* album provided evidence that these young men were thinking deeply about and questioning the concepts and contexts which they traversed. The group confidently used forms of 'translanguaging', mixed linguistic resources, which they acquired through their heritage, to assert themselves as genuine actors.

Through their utterances and activities DVS comprised an example of a 'subaltern counterpublic' (Fraser, 1992; 1995; Haupt, 2008). 'Subaltern counterpublics' are arenas adjacent to but separate from the main public sphere, places where subordinate groups produce and introduce counter-discourses. The public sphere is the social space where citizens debate affairs of mutual interest and hold political conversations that affect the broader population. By first engaging within their own group, subordinate collectivities like DVS may agree on mutual interests, needs and standpoints, without the risk of these initially being co-opted and exploited by other, dominant groups, in the process creating forms of 'lived' space.

The concepts of a 'youth movement', 'dialogic lived learning' and 'subaltern counterpublic' make it possible to heed the call of some scholars who advocate for analyses of hip hop to move beyond the educational potential of rap lyrics. These researchers encourage linking hip hop to educational praxis, allowing hip hop to engage with issues of power, identity and policy. Hill & Petchauer (2013) urge for scholarly work on hip hop to broaden its range, extending to other aspects of hip hop cultural production, embracing places and communities where people actually create hip hop. In this chapter I have used a dialogic theory of learning and a spatial analysis, to analyse how the rap music of one group of young men is situated within a complex set of dialogues with relevant others. Decoding their lyrics and exploring the multiple contexts in which their words were produced generates a nuanced understanding of their social worlds. This type of analysis provides insights into the potential uses of these social practices in both formal and informal learning environments.

Note

1 A skollie is a Kaapse Afrikaans word that means 'hooligan' or a lower-class and badly mannered person.
2 *Huis Genoot* is a popular South African lifestyle magazine aimed predominantly at women.

References

Alim, H. 2009. Creating 'an empire within an empire': critical hip hop, language pedagogies and the role of sociolinguistics. In S. Alim, A. Ibrahim & A. Pennycook (Eds.), *Global linguistic flows: hip hop cultures, youth identities, and the politics of language (pp. 213–230)*. London: Routledge.

Bernstein, B., 1964. Elaborated and restricted codes: Their social origins and some consequences. *American Anthropologist*, 66(6_PART2), 55–69.

Fraser, N. 1992. Rethinking the public sphere: a contribution to the critique of actually existing democracy. In C. Calhoun (Ed.), *Habermas and the public sphere*, 109–142. Cambridge, MA: MIT Press.

Fraser, N. 1995. From redistribution to recognition? Dilemmas of justice in a 'Post-Socialist Age'. *New Left Review*, 212, 68–93.

Haupt, A. 2008. *Stealing empire: P2P, intellectual property and hip hop subversion*. Cape Town: HSRC Press.

Hill, M. 2009. *Beats, rhymes, and classroom life: hip hop pedagogy and the politics of identity*. New York: Teachers College Press.

Hill, M. & Petchauer, E. 2013. Introduction. In M. Hill & E. Petchauer (Eds.), *Schooling hip hop: expanding hip hop based education across the curriculum (pp. 1–9)*. New York: Teachers College, Columbia University.

Pennycook, A. 2007. Language, localization, and the real: hip hop and the global spread of authenticity. *Journal of Language, Identity, and Education*, 6(2), 101–115.

Perullo, A. & Fenn, J. 2003. Language ideologies, choices, and practices in Eastern African hip hop. In. H. Berger & M. Carroll (Eds), *Global pop, local language (pp. 19–51)*. Mississippi: University Press of Mississippi

Peterson, J. 2012. *Founder of hip hop scholars, versus debate.* Downloaded on 12 October 2013 from: http://www.youtube.com/watch?v=TydqRM71eYo.

Pinnock, D. 1984. *The brotherhoods: street gangs and state control in Cape Town.* Cape Town: David Phillip.

Rose, T. 1991. 'Fear of a Black planet': rap music and Black cultural politics in the 1990s. *Journal of Negro Education*, 60, 276–290.

7 Learning at Youth Amplified Radio Show

> *Radio's got this beautiful thing about it. You can hear your own voice on tape, it just gives you goose bumps, it does something to you. And so many people that never thought they'd ever be heard from the speakers of a ghetto blaster, heard themselves suddenly through the speakers of a ghetto blaster. And I recorded them, and I could look in their eyes and see this excitement in their eyes of recognizing their own voices on the air. And those small things were, for me, the most beautiful stuff.*
>
> Participant in Bosch, 2006: 256

Introduction

We now leave the Rosemary Gardens neighbourhood to follow a group of Rosemary Gardens High School students to a community radio station in the suburb of Salt River. I examine how these students used language and learnt through dialogues with peers from three other schools. I facilitated Youth Amplified for one and a half years, in which time 13 live shows took place. During this same period I conducted one-on-one interviews with all of the participants and made copious field notes based on my observations of interactions between students.

The live radio shows took place almost exclusively in English, although participants were encouraged to speak whatever language they felt comfortable using, with peers translating where necessary. Rosemary Gardens students predominantly spoke Kaapse Afrikaans at home, ID Mkhize learners spoke isiXhosa, Cape Institute students either used English, Afrikaans or isiXhosa at home and Barry Hertzog students mainly conversed in English. All of the students spoke some English, and this was the reason why this language was predominantly used for the show.

Language use and dialogue at Youth Amplified were bound up in broader social hierarchies related to race, space, schooling and the history of Cape Town. To illustrate this, the chapter is divided into four sections, beginning with a description of the RGHS learners involved in Youth Amplified. These biographical portraits illuminate the ways that race, language, schooling and relations with peers and adults intersected in their lives. I then unpack the two main themes that emerged from the radio shows, individual interviews with learners and participant observations. I have called these themes 'school institutional culture' and 'race talk'. Learners that attended the two elite schools transported their schools' institutional cultures with them to the radio show. These students spoke about the existence of 'standards', a concept that is regularly referred to at elite Cape Town schools (Dolby, 2001; Soudien, 2012). The discourse of 'standards' was linked to particular ways of speaking, as well as notions of race and class. Norms and values that operated at exclusive Cape Town schools entered Youth Amplified, catalysing particular kinds of interactions between students. Social hierarchies were also described in the form of 'race talk', a popular topic and reference point for participants at the radio show. In the final section of the chapter I analyse, in detail, one of the conflicts that took place during the programme, a heated discussion that explored the possibility of students using Kaapse Afrikaans as a medium of communication in classrooms. The idea that certain 'standards' related to language use, race and schooling exist was again central to this debate, affecting the production of dialogue and learning at Youth Amplified.

Rosemary Gardens High School Students at Youth Amplified

I recruited RGHS students for Youth Amplified through the school principal, Mr Williams, who instructed one of the teachers to select five learners to participate in the show. The teacher chose students that she was familiar with and to whom she offered a great deal of pastoral care, students who she regularly invited to eat meals at her house and transported to and from extra-mural activities. Although I would say that each of these five learners was highly intelligent, none were invited to the school prize giving in 2012, an occasion that honoured the 10 students from each grade who had achieved the best academic results. The students selected for Youth Amplified therefore represented the small proportion of young people that remained at RGHS for grades 10–12, but they were not exceptional students in terms of their academic results.

All five RGHS students attended the show regularly during 2011; however, only two of the five learners originally selected attended consistently during 2012. To expand on the three students whose attendance diminished, one young woman who was in grade 11 in 2011 stopped attending school and the radio show after she married a man from Pakistan. Mr Williams indicated that her decision was informed by family pressure and the bridegroom's need for a South African passport. Another young man attended regularly during 2011, however his school and radio show attendances decreased in 2012 after being badly beaten by a gang. A third young woman participated in many of the programmes that a few selected learners from the school were involved in, making it difficult for her also regularly to attend the radio show, as she was already over-committed. Whenever I saw her at school she spoke fondly of the programme and continued, verbally at least, to commit herself to participation. This meant that even though all of the RGHS learners regularly told me that they enjoyed their time at Youth Amplified, three out of the five students discontinued their participation in the programme or participated sporadically. Participation was limited due to the turbulent circumstances in the Rosemary Gardens community, restricting their learning at Youth Amplified.

I would like to describe the two Rosemary Gardens students that participated extensively in the programme in more detail. These young people's descriptions of their lives illuminated how they learnt in interactions with peers from other schools at Youth Amplified. Both students, Tracey and Mo, spoke excellent English. Tracey, an outspoken, quick-witted and articulate young woman, spoke English at home to her parents. When Youth Amplified began in 2011 she was a 16-year-old, grade nine student. In early 2012 she moved to live with her father in Mitchell's Plain, meaning that she endured an hour-long commute to RGHS each day. She insinuated that her mother consumed alcohol in abundance and was operating a small commercial sex enterprise from their home in Rosemary Gardens. Tracey's domestic situation was therefore volatile and this impacted on her emotional disposition.

One day I encountered Tracey at RGHS and she said that she needed R7 (approximately 50c US) for taxi fare to travel to the bus station. She said that she was unable to walk to the station because she feared being seen by her father's family. I did not understand why she was scared that her father's family would perhaps identify her en route to the station and I refused to give her the money. Tracey was very angry and she refused to attend Youth Amplified for a number of weeks thereafter. This example illustrates the tenuous and complex relationships that I shared with some of these students and the unequal power dynamic that existed between a white middle-class researcher and working-class youth from a low-income neighbourhood.

Power dynamics informed many of the relationships that Tracey described with older people and peers. In an individual interview she told me:

Tracey: I think it's the authority that makes children care. The older person will determine my action . . . If you gonna talk to me and tell me why I shouldn't do this and do that then I'm gonna respond better. I'm not racist or anything but I see it every day, a coloured mother is gonna tell her child, "moenie daai doen nie jy gaan seer kry" (don't do that, you will get hurt), but she's not gonna tell the child how the child is gonna get hurt, "ek gaan for jou bledy" (I'm going to bloody . . . you) then swear at the child. Then you get the white mother will say "don't play with the glass you gonna cut your fingers" and then the child's gonna listen cause the child knows my mommy said if I play with that then blood's gonna come out.

If you don't go the extra mile then the child won't listen. And at Prince Phillip they didn't have that . . . This school (RGHS) it's tough trying to survive. For me it's different, the other children they don't get discriminated because of the language they speak. We were the first English class after a few years and the Afrikaans children didn't like it cause English is so called 'sturvy'. And they look down on us cause we don't reach their level. And with the gangsterism on the school ground it's hard . . . there's corner boys and at Cresthill there's terror squads and so if I go there my life is in danger . . .

Interviewer: How did the decision get made for you to come here?

Tracey: *It's school fees, it's very cheap. It's R700 this year and R800 next year. It's R1200 or R1500 at other schools. The nearest most expensive school is Bothaville, that's 1500 a month and then 1000 for your books. At our school they say you must go on that trip. But if I get a affidavit to say I can't go then I stay at home. At Bothaville they just tell you this is the trip, this is the fees and you can't say no. . . . And my mom was late for applications at all the other schools.*

This extract provided some subtle insights into the home, school and community environments through which Tracey moved and the kinds of learning-related interactions that occurred in her daily life. Tracey's social world consisted of a set of complex hierarchies, related to race, class, gender and language. Her school and home spaces were characterised by adult-led, authoritative exchanges, resulting in intergenerational interactions that lacked joint decision-making and communication that generally involved adults talking and young people listening.

Tracey used a parent-child vignette to explain how relationships operated between students and educators at her primary school. One explanation for this comparison between educators and parents is that learner-educator relationships are based on pastoral care and not, primarily, on intellectual development at poor South African schools (Watson, 2011). For Tracey, communication with educators and parents, at home and at school, was often condescending in nature and rarely based on dialogue.

Tracey racialised this type of adult-child communication: she described differences in typical exchanges between adults and children in Rosemary Gardens by comparing these to similar interactions that she believed took place in white, middle-class schools and homes. As will become clear, students from all of the participating Youth Amplified schools constantly racialised objects and forms of behaviour. Although the description of the English-speaking, white mother's coaxing words did not constitute a dialogue, they were expressed kindly and without the threat of violence. It was unclear where Tracey had observed interactions between white mothers and their children. Perhaps it was in a public space or even on television. Whatever her opinions were based on, she certainly believed that teaching and parenting in Rosemary Gardens consisted of strict, hierarchical interactions and that white English-speaking children received teaching and parenting that contained higher levels of care. It is not my intention here to analyse the quality of teaching and parenting in different parts of Cape Town. Rather, I am trying to highlight that Tracey said that her interactions with adults, at school and at home, did not involve dialogue and that she was not given opportunities to contribute to discussions. Furthermore, she interpreted differences between adult-youth interactions in Rosemary Gardens and similar interactions amongst middle- and upper-class people, in racial and linguistic terms.

Her perceptions were interesting, not least of all because she actually spoke English at home to her mother, an invaluable form of linguistic capital that buttressed her participation at Youth Amplified, demonstrated by her outspoken contributions at the show. Census data shows that approximately 18% of Rosemary Gardens residents listed English as their mother-tongue language. However, at school Tracey felt persecuted for being placed in the English-speaking class, saying that peers labelled the English speakers as "sturvy", meaning 'exclusive', 'superior', or 'having aspirations for upward social mobility'. For township youth like Tracey, accusations of being "sturvy" were often related to educational aspirations and linguistic practices, especially speaking English. Peers ostracised young people like Tracy for not performing racialised identities in what was considered to be an 'authentic' manner.

Moving to Tracey's descriptions of the material space of RGHS, she said that the school was unsafe, as the area surrounding it was divided into a set of gang-controlled territories. Tracey clearly stated the reason why she attended RGHS and identified financial constraints as the primary mechanism of exclusion preventing her from attending a more affluent school. The humiliation of not being able to afford extra curricular activities, like outings, may also be a deterrent to some families, who choose not to send their children to what Tracey referred to as "the nearest most-expensive school" (Bray et al., 2010). Tracey had a clear picture of the local school-economy, with the different possibilities and options neatly demarcated.

For Tracey, home, school and community places were therefore characterised by hierarchical relationships and authoritative interactions, as race, class, language and intergenerational differences intersected. Learners from Rosemary Gardens, like Tracey, were constantly doing headwork (Soudien, 2007), assessing and positioning themselves in the social hierarchy. They held perceptions about legitimacy and inequality and sometimes resented the fact that they did not attend the "nearest most-expensive school", whilst other students attended these more affluent institutions.

The other learner with whom I became familiar, Mo, was 21 years old in 2012. He was slightly older than his classmates because he had discontinued his schooling for three years, flirting with gang involvement before returning to school after persuasion from a teacher. Mo was a warm, gentle person, with a subtle sense of humour. He wanted to become a certified carpenter (his father's profession) and study at a vocational college. He believed that 'papers', the word he used to describe certification, would help him to get a job. Mo said that:

> I'm excited to do matric (grade 12) next year. Matric is almost like a shovel. If you don't have a shovel you have to dig with your hands, but if you have shovel you can dig far.... At Chesterton high (his previous school) the teachers don't care, they say "I get my salary at the end of the month so what you do doesn't affect me". The teachers pushing you down, you got no self-esteem to do the work. They always telling you, you a nothing. You start to believe you a nothing. You got no motivation.

Mo valued formal educational qualifications, both matric and a carpentry apprenticeship at a Further Education and Training college and understood the value that these qualifications held in terms of aiding him to realise his aspirations. He used the metaphor of matric (grade 12) functioning like a "shovel", a tool that renders manual labour less arduous. His attraction to education was based on the utility that he perceived certification to hold, as he believed that qualifications could aid him in the labours of life. He did not speak about schooling or further education as exciting him or providing him with opportunities to stimulate his intellect. This lack of enthusiasm for schooling was partly due to his experiences with teachers at his previous school, who he described as regularly insulting students. Mo also described RGHS educators that did not grow up in Rosemary Gardens as lacking empathy towards students:

> The other teachers that come from other places, they don't really feel how we feel in this place, how it feel to stay here. It's messed up here. They (Rosemary Gardens residents) a group of crabs, crabs in a bowl, they grab and pull you down. They want you to be on their level. They ask me "why you go to school, you old?" I ask them "do you have money? Do you have work?" Then the other people that do have work they tell me "naai go to school". But problems at home make it hard to (do school) work. My mommy was in the operation room. Your daddy's a drunk, your brother's a tik kop (meth head). My brother's death was the worst family problem. My mommy still has wounds about that. The only reason the white children, the so called 'white' children have jobs is that they don't have problems. They can only focus on their books. Not worry about food, there's always food there. School fees is paid. You just have to do the work. Study, it's there. If everyone in South Africa have to pay the same money, from the doctor to the man in the street,

> everybody's life would have been nice and civilised. Most of the white people they not actually clever man I know more than they know about life. They just want to talk to me about stuff they learn out of a book. I say "don't talk to me about that, talk to me about life. What you see, what you experience". You can't talk about stuff you never experience. Anybody could have written a book, even me.

Mo described the material difficulties of life in Rosemary Gardens and the stressful experience of growing up in this area, including strains to physical health, drug addiction and financial constraints. These difficulties impacted on Mo's relationships, both with people from Rosemary Gardens and with outsiders, interactions that were dominated by antagonism. In terms of fellow residents, the social problems that plagued Rosemary Gardens' inhabitants resulted in jealousy towards the success of those who, for example, persevered with formal education, such as Mo. This form of resentment has been widely documented in other low-income Cape Town neighbourhoods (Bray et al., 2010; Ramphele, 2002). Mo countered this jealousy from others by referring to their lack of employment opportunities, expressing his belief that formal education and certification may offer him opportunities in the future.

The difficult circumstances in Rosemary Gardens resulted in Mo feeling resentful towards RGHS educators who were not able to empathise with learners' emotional and physical hardships, saying "they don't feel how we feel in this place". This emotional rift likely hampered teaching and learning, as students may have felt disinterested in learning from educators who they believed were unable to relate to their life circumstances. While educators were under immense pressure simply to deliver the curriculum and raise examination results, learners from Rosemary Gardens required a great deal of emotional support.

The harsh material space of Rosemary Gardens resulted in Mo resenting more affluent peers, rejecting the "book" knowledge that he believed white youth attain and which, in his opinion, did not enhance their intelligence. He believed that making sense of turbulent life conditions, like he had done from a young age, required a greater level of intelligence than simply reading somebody else's opinions in a book. Like Tracey, Mo made sense of social stratification in racial terms, although he also mentioned class-based divisions. Mo compared his circumstances to those of white children who he believed did not have to contend with the range of stressors that militated against his academic success. Mo's perception that educators and peers were unable to engage with what was meaningful to him and these people's lack of familiarity with the harsh realities of Rosemary Gardens, resulted in him dismissing the value of engaging in dialogue and learning with these people.

Race, class, language, schooling and neighbourhoods therefore combined to form part of a complex Cape Town social hierarchy. RGHS students constantly assessed these forms of stratification and their position within them, shaping their attitudes towards peers and their participation at Youth Amplified. The material spatial relations of Rosemary Gardens influenced learners' participation at the radio show, exemplified by the fact that only two students remained regularly involved in the show over the two-year period. Gang violence, volatile domestic relationships and families trying to ensure their own material survival were prominent factors in these young people's everyday lives. The attitudes and world views of these two students provided clues to the kinds of dialogic interactions that emerged at Youth Amplified, with peers who attended other schools.

"Like We're Taught at Our School, Your Success Depends on Your Own Hard Work and Effort": The Impact of School Institutional Culture on Learning at Youth Amplified

The Rosemary Gardens students were often annoyed and upset by learners from the former model C school and the Cape Institute of Education (CIE), especially in the initial stages of the programme. Students that attended these other institutions transported the norms, values, languages and discourses of their schools with them to Youth Amplified, shaping dialogue and learning amongst the group. All of the Youth Amplified participants were, to some degree, representing their schools at the show. They announced the schools that they attended at the start of each episode when they introduced themselves. These young people's opinions were therefore associated with the schools that they attended, as the show comprised a public forum. Other links with schools included the fact that participants were recruited through school staff, and I communicated with students through personnel at their schools. When the group met on Friday afternoons, many youth attended in their school uniforms. Because these young people were representing their schools, they were expected to behave in a manner that was congruent with their respective school's rules, its code of conduct and culture. Learning at the radio show was therefore shaped by the imagined space of the schools that learners attended elsewhere, transported into the new learning place of Youth Amplified.

As a means of further describing the institutional culture of the CIE, this predominantly residential school for talented township learners was portrayed by its students as an institution that promoted a culture of intense academic competition:

Greg: *Everyone wants to be in the top 10, so the competitive drive pushes you and it actually makes more clever people.*

Jake: *The typical example with me, the first time I met Greg I greeted him, but when I heard he wrote that essay and he achieved, I changed my view on him. And I respected him.*

Phumla: At school, I'm always in my own room studying. We all have to do hard work. To compete, that's part of my dream. At school there's a lot of competition, we eat competition, we need competition.

Greg: And that's what competition is, it's a great motivation, a great motivation.

(From a live Youth Amplified show)

At the Cape Institute of Education, students developed their identities and gained respect from peers through their academic achievements. This process occurred within a school culture of competitive intellectualism. Prestige and admiration from peers was publically acknowledged by regularly announcing the 'top 10' learners, those with the most excellent academic results in each grade. These young people, who attained academic 'excellence', were celebrated and respected by fellow students and staff. Respect was ritualised through integral components of the school's culture, such as announcing the 'top 10' students.

Phumla said that the learners "eat" and "need" competition. This comment hinted at the prevalence and all-encompassing nature of this culture, which functioned as an integral part of everyday school life, metaphorically 'nourishing' the students. It illustrated how these young people retained a strong sense of identity by demonstrating their academic superiority over their peers. The institutional culture of the CIE travelled with learners from this school to Youth Amplified, impacting on dialogues with students that were sensitive to appearing inferior, such as the RGHS students. Interactions between students from these different schools were therefore ripe for conflict, as illustrated in the final section of this chapter.

The CIE's institutional culture of competition and academic excellence instilled a sense of independence and self-sufficiency amongst students who were expected to demonstrate 'adult-like' behaviour. In an individual interview Themba, who attended the CIE, said the following:

The Cape Institute is not just a school, it's a sanctuary. In some of our communities there's violence and crime and problems at home.... This school doesn't have set rules, even with the code of conduct. We supposed to be responsible adults. Like our school doesn't have a bell. You have to check your own time at the end of the period. You are responsible for own learning and how you conduct yourself. If you don't study for a test you fail and then you out of Cape Institute and that's that.

There are distinct benefits to a school promoting a culture of independence and a sense of responsibility in its students. However, the CIE's code of conduct came with the threat that if students did not excel academically, not only would their independence be rescinded, but the underperforming learner would be excluded from the school. The CIE school culture was therefore based on competition, excellence, individualism and independence, with failure perceived as the result of individual inability.

The presence of the CIE institutional culture at Youth Amplified, particularly the notion that individual merit should be used to determine achievement, contributed to some of the conflict-ridden dialogues that emerged in this place. Tracey and Mo indicated that Rosemary Gardens youth believed that financial constraints and social problems, prevalent challenges for residents in their neighbourhood, prevented them from attending elite schools and accessing the opportunities that some of their peers received. Although there was certainly some truth to the belief amongst CIE learners that their success was based on hard work and individual talent, these were not the only factors that resulted in their attending this school, attaining good academic results and accessing valuable opportunities. Most of the CIE students came from working-class neighbourhoods; however, these areas generally had fewer social problems and more resources than Rosemary Gardens.

Moving on to the former model C school, BHHS, the attitudes of students that attended this school resonated with some aspects of the institutional culture of the CIE, although there were some subtle differences. BHHS learners also generally believed that success was due to individual choice, perseverance and hard work:

John (reading a Facebook message written by the educator in charge of leadership at BHHS during the show): *Mrs Small says "history shows excellent examples of youth from poor environments succeeding and achieving. Take a moment to find the motivation and develop whole happy youth. Baby steps create change!"*

And:

People they are blind-sighted. They miss the link between passing grade eight and nine and being successful in the future. You can't go and miss a whole lot of classes . . . and be successful. You have to put in the extra mile, like we are taught at our school, your success depends on your own work and effort and that's your responsibility.
(BHHS learner during a live show)

BHHS educators and students alike perceived success to be linked to the hard work ethic of individuals and their determination to overcome adversity. This attitude perpetuates the ideology of the school as a level playing field that is able to highlight individual talent (Bourdieu, 1977). It also reinforces Soudien's (2007) assertion that the 'official' discourse of the school, its values, practices and ideologies, are more prominent at formerly white schools. 'Official' school discourses were transported into the new place of Youth Amplified and presented by students as authoritative or uncontestable truths regarding success, justice and learning. These attitudes may have been insensitive to learners like Mo, who stated that more privileged learners did not understand the material, social and emotional struggles that RGHS students endured on a daily basis.

In terms of subtle differences between the CIE and BHHS, the attitudes of students indicated that the culture, values and norms of BHHS were more congruent with its former 'model C' heritage and the British colonial educational system:

John: . . . which is absurd to me coming from a school where uniform is of essence . . .
Bernadette: It's most important.
John: Even though it might be seen what has uniform got to do with you passing a test, it's about being part of a professional environment, and when you feel like you're part of a school then you are there to learn and there to educate, then obviously that's when education and knowledge flourishes.
(From a live Youth Amplified show)

At BHHS, education, knowledge acquisition, language use and personal appearance were linked to a form of conducting and presenting oneself that was based on colonial notions of respectability and conformity. The ways in which BHHS learners made links between their appearance at school, 'standards' and attitudes towards education more generally, resonated with Dolby's (2002) work at a Kwazulu Natal school. Dolby (2002) illustrated how playing rugby and compulsory adherence to dress standards functioned to reproduce pedagogies and discourses of whiteness: ways of teaching, speaking and behaving that are presented as 'better' than other ways of speaking and behaving. Pedagogies and discourses of whiteness represent the practices of a particular cultural tradition, which are not necessarily better than other school cultures. Dolby (2002) showed how the school that she studied created a form of imagined respectability through prescribed behaviours and traditions, utilising these discourses and practices to preserve the school's colonial heritage. Learning was therefore enmeshed with an imagined school institutional culture that was a product of colonialism. Similarly, BHHS students believed that particular colonial ways of dressing, behaving and speaking allowed 'education and knowledge to flourish'.

Learners who attended relatively more affluent schools therefore reproduced these institutions' values and norms, such as ideas about individual merit, reward and, as will become clear, appropriate language use, in the new emerging place of Youth Amplified. These attitudes differed from the perspectives of some Rosemary Gardens students, like Tracey, who realised that financial constraints, and not individual talent, prevented them from attending better-resourced schools. Schools that perpetuate discourses of hard work, individual achievement and competition may easily incense marginalised learners, such as those who attended RGHS. The ways that these schools embrace particular cultural practices and discourses, linked to colonialism, apartheid and the new state—and indirectly to privilege and aspirations for upward social mobility—may also enrage marginalised students in dialogic exchanges.

The Youth Amplified place therefore comprised an unusual junction or meeting point for students from different schools, institutions that have radically different histories, values, student demographics and languages. Urban Cape Town, with its history of forced segregation and continued inequality, results in these different groups of young people rarely encountering one another. When meetings do occur, the places that constitute these interactions can be rich sites for learning and transformation, but they also hold the potential for combustible conflict.

'There's Actually Different Standards of "Coloureds"': Race Talk at Youth Amplified

Schools were markers of social status, however the young people at Youth Amplified also used other powerful symbols to reproduce or challenge social hierarchies. All of the participants repeatedly used 'race' in descriptions of differences between South African people, institutions and other aspects of social life. As a simple example, one learner remarked after watching the documentary *Testing Hope*, a film which explored inequalities in the South African education system:

> We got to see how different the schools from different races are, black and white and all that.

The phrase "schools from different races" is somewhat confusing, but is in itself an interesting description. It is evident from this expression that places like schools are emphatically racialised in the language of post-apartheid youth, such that it almost seems natural that a school would 'have a race'. Apartheid-era segregation therefore continued to impact on perceptions of places that were important to post-apartheid youth. Neighbourhoods and shopping malls are other places that youth racialise, according to qualitative research (Bray et al., 2010).

Young people from Rosemary Gardens tended to assume that the schools which they classified as 'white' schools were inhabited by 'white' students. When the BHHS learners joined the group, after only approximately an hour of interactions, Mo proclaimed that he was going to sit with the 'white' children, despite only one of the five BHHS learners later classifying herself as 'white'. As Bray et al. (2010) state, 'colour' may not be referring to the hue of a person's skin, but may be used to symbolise style and aspects of youth culture, phenomena that in the post-apartheid South African context have become pertinently racialised. Similarly, Dolby's (2001) research illustrated that race, understood by the apartheid state as a set of biological, cultural and historical factors, has been redefined by globalised, post-apartheid youth, who speak about race in relation to choices, styles and tastes.

Post-apartheid youth actively reform meanings attached to race. Mo was aware of certain powerful symbols, such as the school that BHHS learners attended, the language that they used, their accents and their 'style', in the form of clothing and sense of humour, indicators that he used to classify students from BHHS in racial terms.

Youth Amplified therefore confirmed some of the findings that researchers have highlighted on youth and race in post-apartheid South Africa, in terms of race's prominence as a social category and the fact that young people reformulate apartheid-era meanings that were attached to this concept. However, the interactions between young people in this place also demonstrated how the students used 'race talk' in order to assign value to particular groups of people, as well as to include and exclude individuals. The following exchange is taken from a live Youth Amplified broadcast:

Ariel: *Ja because there is this thing between coloureds when you can be light of complexion and people say "no she's not actually 'coloured' cause look how she looks", so there's actually different standards of 'coloureds' for me cause I come from Strandfontein and if I step into Hanover park people will say "no she's not 'coloured'" but I actually am because of my background and heritage and things . . . it's just the way you look after yourself.*

Kelly (hostess): *You used the word 'sturvy' and Mo your eyes went so big in your head, so Mo what makes a person a 'coloured', cause Ariel's saying you sturvy. . . . You saying if you come from Rosemary Gardens you know how to steal and Karen saying that her mommy . . . economically she's been raised differently because there's more finance . . . What makes you 'coloured' in your definition cause clearly you're not sturvy?*

Mo: *'Coloured', it's funful people.*

Kelly: *Fun-filled how?*

Mo: *Like to make jokes, have fun, make a smile, even if there's no food in the house, there's a smile on your face cause we colourful people.*

(approximately one minute later)

Themba: *I spoke about apartheid and it's 17 years after that. Why are we still looking at people in terms of colour, why aren't we all human?*

Group: *Mmmmmmm . . .*

Tracey: *I think apartheid had a big role in this cause they made coloureds, so called 'coloureds' and so called 'blacks' feel inferior. They made us feel small as Letho said, they treated us that way, inferior, ja apartheid is gone, we have democracy and everything and still you walking in the street, the* so called 'white' people, the so-called more richer, more advanced people look down on us cause we were classed as 'coloureds' and 'blacks', which I think is wrong, Why say it's a free country, why say it's a 'coloured' nation, free world, when we still get treated the way apartheid used to treat us?

Kelly: So we gonna bring it back to the reason we all here, how does this apply to education? Is this a democracy and how does that affect us as the youth?

Themba: Seventeen years out of apartheid, but as Tracey says the majority of black people are still underprivileged and don't have access to education as white people do. We have to classify each other so we give equal opportunities, perhaps give more funding to the black people than we do to the white. However, should you say I am coloured because that person called me coloured, should you act underprivileged because that person called you under-privileged, are you inferior always or just economically inferior? Are you inferior because you have no money?

Kelly: I hear a word, the word of truth seems to be 'classification' out of your mouth.

Tracey: Coming back to what Themba and Ariel said, ja, people feel inferior and that's why I said so-called 'whites' and so-called 'blacks' and so-called 'coloureds': we didn't class ourselves as 'whites' and 'blacks' and 'coloureds'. We were called those by other people who were probably passed already. I wasn't even alive when apartheid was there but still I'm suffering. We as the new generation, as tomorrow, we should find a way of changing it even though we didn't start it.

(approximately one minute later)

Themba: I don't let the colour of my skin define me. It plays a role in opportunities. At CIE the coloureds and blacks click together and we're all children of the CIE. We write the same papers, same teachers, marking criteria the same, nothing different. But that's just to a certain individual. I think we should keep the racial classification thing for a government or a university to channel money to people previously disadvantaged. Cause look at the reality, people in Nyanga are suffering, coloured people are suffering. They're not getting the same opportunities as the white people. So it's right to classify, but in terms of you yourself it doesn't make it right to classify. Am I making any sense?

(From a live Youth Amplified show)

Three very different notions of coloured identity appear in the passage above. To summarise these three perspectives, Ariel's position originates from the aspirations of some Cape coloured people who aimed to assimilate with whites during the mid-19th century (Adhikari, 2005). By contrast, Mo produced a stereotypical account of 'colouredness' as 'fun and humourous despite living in poverty'. Finally, Tracey showed how 'colouredness' needs to be understood in historical context. The young people utilised these constructions of race for different purposes, none of which involved 'style, choice or taste'. The different perspectives showed that 'race talk' at Youth Amplified contained a definite political character, but that this topic held potential for rich dialogic learning.

To expand on these three perspectives, in the first part of the interaction Ariel grappled with her coloured identity and Mo's utterances, as she analysed the intersection of race and class. She contradictorily dismissed claims that she considered herself superior to families in working-class Hanover Park, while stating that "different standards of 'coloureds' exist", one criteria being that some, like herself, "take care of themselves". Her stance was somewhat defensive and was partly a response to Mo's statement that people judged him due to where he lived. Ariel described interactions with people from Hanover Park, a working-class neighbourhood similar to Rosemary Gardens, exchanges in which she felt judged for apparently attempting to attain an illegitimate, elevated status.

This notion of "standards of coloureds" demonstrated Adhikari's (2005) assertion that one strand of 'colouredness' has been forged through aspirations to assimilate with 'whiteness' and create distance from the African majority. This was pursued through liberal or colonial values of 'self-improvement, civilization and standards', including the desire to speak standardised forms of language. A discourse of 'standards' continues to create and maintain divisions between groups in contemporary South Africa. An informal, multiracial coalition of upper- and middle-class parents and teachers at former model C schools disseminate the notion of 'standards needing to be kept up' in the democratic period, using this discourse to set school fee policies and exclude poor students. It is likely that this discourse of standards is common at schools such as the one that Ariel attended, leading to her transporting it into the Youth Amplified space and fuelling potentially conflict-ridden interactions with peers from RGHS.

In response to Ariel's statement that coloured people may be differentiated through social class–based 'standards', the RGHS students offered vastly different contributions to the debate on the topic of coloured identity. Mo reverted to the caricatured stereotype of the coloured person as the laughing, carefree, happy-go-lucky joker. He described coloured people as "funful" and "colorful". This strategy was a form of conflict aversion; he used it because he did not want to become embroiled in an argument or be exposed as inferior in class-based or linguistic terms, especially live on air, in English. His response was partly due to Ariel referring to Hanover Park, an area not demographically dissimilar to Rosemary Gardens and her description of the ways in which working-class coloured people in that neighbourhood did not "take care of themselves". Such comments were likely to have offended and intimidated RGHS students like Mo. There were a number of occasions at Youth Amplified when learners attending high-status schools made insensitive and derogatory comments, leading to a 'backlash' from RGHS students, who complained that these learners were 'snobs', 'fake coloureds' and other pejorative terms. However, on this occasion Mo was simply unwilling to engage with this perspective.

Some learners from RGHS were able to reply to offensive comments from other learners without becoming defensive or silenced. In the discussion above Tracey explained how categories such as 'coloured' were imposed on some people through a historical process, in the form of apartheid. Through her repetitive use of the term "so-called" she showed how race was used as a way of categorising different groups of people for political purposes. Elements of Bakhtin's (1986) concept of double-voicedness were apparent in her endeavours: "so-called" indicated that others have categorised people in this manner, but that she had thought about this form of labelling and incorporated it into the formulation of her own perspective. The use of the term "so-called" consciously demonstrated different voices informing Tracey's thinking and illuminated how she had internalised an understanding of race as historically contingent.

Although at times she struggled to articulate her thoughts, by engaging with various abstract concepts and through personal reflection, Tracey was able to place herself in historical perspective, deconstruct the process of racial classification and be critical of the society in which she lived. There were other examples of double-voicedness in her response, as she played and experimented with concepts like "democracy", "coloured" nation (alluding to a "rainbow" nation), "free world", with words that were partly hers, partly garnered elsewhere. The internal dialogue that was operating in her consciousness was apparent in the range of terms she used and with which she struggled to make sense of her thoughts. The dialogic learning process was therefore observed in elements of double-voicedness, as Tracy attempted to assimilate concepts, ideas and words from relevant others, incorporating them into her repertoire.

Another indication that dialogic learning occurred was the three occasions when learners referred to the contributions of their peers or fellow participants by name. Naming other people's perspectives in the dialogue indicated that they had listened to these other positions, pondered their relevance and considered integrating them with their own opinions.

However, there was an even more unambiguous indicator that dialogic learning had taken place in the extract above, linked to the interaction between Themba and Tracey. Dialogic learning is demonstrated through a change of position, based on a person considering and thinking about other perspectives and then amending their original position. In order for learning to occur it is vital that students actively think for themselves and do not merely report the thoughts of other people (Nystrand, 1997). In the passage

Themba, a CIE student, originally stated that it had been 17 years since the demise of apartheid and that people continue to think in racial terms, when they should perceive each other simply as "human". Tracey's position on the historical process of racial construction then catalysed him to modify his argument. This culminated in a far more nuanced stance on the difference between using historical categories for redress in policy decisions, versus individual racial classification in the school context. It was apparent that Themba had considered his position in the light of other perspectives and developed it to form a more complex, context-specific set of opinions. Through their interchange Tracey and Themba were able to exchange ideas, build upon each other's perspectives, find a common language and co-construct knowledge. In the earlier, defensive interaction between Ariel and Mo, neither young person engaged with the perspective of the other, as they simply proceeded with their own line of thought.

Double-voicedness, referencing one's peers and changes of opinion therefore provided clues that on certain occasions dialogic learning occurred at Youth Amplified. This form of learning involved cooperation, not competition, and young people engaging with the perspectives of one another, co-constructing knowledge in the process. I would call this dialogic lived learning, as it is dialogical in nature and constructed out of combinations of material and imagined socio-spatial forces that manifested at Youth Amplified. These young people overcame material space by finding ways to continue attending the radio show, across vast distances, as they negotiated the social challenges that hampered their participation. Imagined space was dealt with by making sense of school institutional cultures, the different linguistic forms presented at the radio show and the racialised nature of interactions with peers. Through combinations of these material and imagined forms of space, some of the young people managed to produce utterances, as well as learn from one another, demonstrating instances of dialogic lived learning.

Youth Amplified therefore demonstrated how young people may use historical and contemporary notions of race in order to learn. However, 'race talk' amongst youth may have other, less positive effects. Race may be used to demarcate social hierarchies through stating that "standards" exist and that some people "look after themselves better than others". These authoritative, colonial and apartheid-era discourses often continue to be utilised at elite schools. Forms of dialogic learning are made possible when young people challenge the historicisation of these categories, as they find ways of creating open, persuasive voices, asking questions and catalysing dialogue. These forms of learning can be as beneficial for students from former model C and other elite schools, as they are for students from township schools. For some Rosemary Gardens youth, this kind of dialogue was too intimidating at Youth Amplified, live on air, in the presence of peers from more affluent schools who possessed powerful forms of linguistic capital.

This example of dialogic learning challenges Soudien's (2007) claim that spatial isolation results in township youth being able to understand their immediate environments, but that they struggle to make meaning beyond these spaces or to develop identities that usefully service them outside of these under-resourced areas. He states that township youths' lives are invariably dominated by everyday survival and meeting their own immediate needs, that for most of these young people "dependence is their key reproductive agency" and their contribution to society is often limited to their survival within it (Soudien, 2007: 103). An alternative explanation may be that safe and/or critically oriented places do not exist in which youth can engage with and challenge discourses that transcend their everyday 'survival'. Forms of critical pedagogy, such as Youth Amplified, may provide fertile ground for poor youth to engage with the society in which they live, question assumptions and buttress their conceptual development. It may also be that these young people do understand and make meaning beyond the immediate space of the township, but that they are often unable to communicate this understanding to others, as they do not have access to forms of linguistic capital that are valued in places of learning.

"No, It's Not Supposed to Be Like That": Conflict and Dialogue at Youth Amplified

The themes described in the previous two sections were both integral to conflicts that took place at Youth Amplified during the 18 months that I facilitated the radio show. Conflict can function positively, challenging young people to reassess their opinions through introspection and, in turn, stimulate learning. However, it can also lead to individuals being personally attacked through emotional confrontations.

I would like to describe, in some detail, a conflict that occurred after watching the documentary *Afrikaaps*, a film that explored the possibility of introducing informal Kaapse Afrikaans as a medium of instruction at Cape Town schools. Most of the RGHS learners primarily used 'Afrikaaps' outside of their schools, unlike the BHHS learners and the CIE students, although learners at these schools certainly used this vernacular sporadically. Lukhanyo High School students spoke isiXhosa at home and in their community.

The clash predominantly involved a CIE learner, Greg, and the two RGHS students described earlier in this chapter, Mo and Tracey:

Greg: *So look here, here's my standpoint right, so you, you people in support of Afrikaaps right, take you, you do Afrikaans at school right, that's your medium of ... so you say that you understand Afrikaaps and that at school you do Afrikaans and so that's a problem for you cause you have to come and do your subjects in that language. So you sitting with a problem. So here's the solution then, eradicate Afrikaaps, do the formal Afrikaans as it should be, then you won't have a problem at school.*
ALL TALK AT ONCE

Tracey: Why don't the teachers come down to my level?
Greg: No, it's not supposed to be like that.
Tracey: Why don't teachers come, okay they don't even have to come to my level. Why don't they just find a slight way of changing how they explain things?
Greg: That's the problem, you want to lower the standards. The standard has been set and now we want to lower it; it's wrong.
Tracey: Slow and steady wins the race.
Greg: Slow and steady might win the race but with this education system we're in now, is it time to be slow and steady?
Tracey: The thing is (ALL SHOUT AT ONCE). The thing is we are being taught, we have to learn to get to those standards. So they have to come to our standards to bring us up.
Greg: According to them Afrikaans is a very difficult medium of instruction and then we wanna come and simplify it in the most wrongest way by bringing this slang about . . . Afrikaans is the formal language. It's the legal language; it has its own set of grammar and everything of how it should be spoken. Now suddenly you want to come and say "no, it's a bit too difficult, I understand it better, let's make it that way".
Tracey: It's not that we want the language itself to change, but if the teacher finds a easier way of explaining, then we might learn the language better, don't you think? Take maths for instance. Your maths teacher always finds some way for the slower child to catch up. So why can't your language teacher do that? What's so wrong with that? How can we get to that level if we don't really understand?
Greg: So you saying the teacher should use some of your language in between?
Tracey: . . . and then give us the real meaning afterwards. Don't you think?
Greg: But then that's just gonna, that's just gonna . . . prolong things. You can, you just need to start reading baby Afrikaans.
(approximately one minute later)
Mo: My history teacher says you "coloureds" are nothing. I ask him, "Now what are you? You also a coloured". Then he say "ja, I'm just standing up for my rights". He think he something better. You a coloured, you running away . . . in your heart you're actually a coloured. A 'coloured's' a funful person, likes to make jokes.
Greg: Well if I'm not a . . . then am I not a coloured? I'm a very, very serious person.
Mo: Coloureds can act, that's why we actors.
Greg: No wonder I don't like acting.
Mo: People say coloureds steal. Coloureds don't steal, they fool you. My friend, he's a actor, you will believe him. That's why they say coloured people steal. They don't steal, man.

Themba: I think Greg has spent far too much time at school that has forced him to abandon his colouredness.

(From a live Youth Amplified show)

In the conversation above, Greg described how 'standards' relate to language, learning, education and implicitly to notions of race and class. He used the concept of 'standards' to argue that students who usually converse in Afrikaaps needed to elevate their linguistic abilities and become fluent in formal Afrikaans. In his opinion, standard Afrikaans was the appropriate medium of classroom instruction for learners who spoke local dialects of Afrikaans outside of the school. Greg argued that it was students' responsibility to attain "those standards" and learn formal Afrikaans, implying that hard work, perseverance and confidence were the only barriers to success. These sentiments demonstrated the culture and values of individualism and competition, which Greg was exposed to at the Cape Institute of Education.

The discourse of standards is authoritative, in Bakhtinian terms, meaning that it occluded alternative lines of inquiry that might have probed why specific varieties of Afrikaans have attained different statuses. This authoritarian discourse discouraged dialogue, as the "standard has been set" and "it's not supposed to be like that that". An authoritative voice is one that we must accept or reject, whereas a persuasive voice is one to which we must answer (Bakhtin, 1981). It was therefore difficult for the other learners to challenge what exactly these standards consisted of, as they were presented as predetermined and unchanging.

According to Greg, such standards exist due to Afrikaans' formal nature and the fact that it is a "legal language with a grammar". The legality of formal Afrikaans was therefore perceived as evidence of this version of the language being innately more sophisticated; the legal status of this variety of Afrikaans was not interpreted as part of a historical process, one that resulted in white Afrikaners ensuring that their version of the language became underpinned by the support of the state and the South African constitution. Yet, the argument that Afrikaans is superior to Afrikaaps because of its legal and constitutional status contains a weak logic: one cannot conclude that a language is inherently superior because it has obtained a superior status. The notion that Afrikaans has a grammar, unlike Afrikaaps, is inaccurate because all languages 'have a grammar' (Gee, 1990).

However, once Greg introduced the authoritative discourse of 'standards', the participants complied with the normative dimension of these standards and only contested how their own standards could be raised. In other words, the students did not interrogate the concept of standards; the criteria for 'high standards' were not explored. Instead, the learners debated whether the school system and educators should accommodate these students and their apparently 'substandard' language. Tracey argued that the most effective way for learners to raise their standards and social status is through the support of educators, who were encouraged, by her, to 'descend' to students' level. This implied that teachers should uplift these young people intellectually and linguistically. The language that RGHS learners brought to the classroom was assumed to be of an inferior quality in comparison to the language that middle-class learners displayed at school. Educators were not expected to use Rosemary Gardens students' rich reservoir of local knowledge in the classroom context. When Tracey referred to the "real meaning", she implied that the language which she used was not real, it was insinuated to be inauthentic and invalid. A large body of research in the United States has refuted this notion of marginalised students' supposedly inadequate resources. This research has demonstrated how skilled teachers can use the resources students bring to the classroom, linking these to discipline-specific forms of school learning, enhancing the education of marginalised and minority youth (Lee, 2007; Moll et al., 1992).

Greg's authoritarian discourse ultimately produced a backlash, as the RGHS students led the rest of the group to retaliate towards Greg. Greg was told that he had abandoned his 'race', as 'colouredness' was essentialised as something "in your heart", associated with a set of finite criteria, including the kind of Afrikaans spoken, acting and being humorous. Mo's reference to his history teacher was allegorically directed at Greg, who was proclaimed to be behaving in an illegitimate manner, based on his perspective with regards to Afrikaaps and his educational aspirations. Instead of responding to the authoritative discourse of standards by attempting to engage in dialogue and deconstruct the composition of these supposed standards, RGHS learners and others personally attacked Greg.

After the Afrikaaps discussion Greg sheepishly approached me, saying that he 'was not trying to be something which he is not'. His apology confirmed other research that has illustrated how township youth who attend schools elsewhere have to negotiate their identities, as they are constantly branded as 'coconuts' or black people accused of pretending to be white (Ramphele, 2002). Greg had originally emailed me to say that he was going to be absent during the first two sessions, but that he was very interested in the show. He attended one more show after the Afrikaaps conflict and then did not return, even though I telephoned him to say that I valued his presence. When I tried to conduct an individual interview with him at the CIE, he resisted participating in a one-on-one session and I did not persist in trying to interview him. The Afrikaaps dialogue therefore led to Greg feeling illegitimate and unwelcome at Youth Amplified and he withdrew from further participation. Dialogic exchanges in which participants carry out personal attacks on individuals may therefore prevent learning from taking place.

Some time after the Afrikaaps debate Mo said the following in an individual interview, in reference to the CIE learners:

> *Themba he's cool. I like his style. He's down to earth. The others they're coloureds but they're trying to keep them, like "I don't go to one of this*

local coloured schools", we get the same papers but now he wanna be like that guy. That wasn't cool. Why he like that? Cause he think he go to that school his stance more upper than us. I don't worry about him, I know a lot of people like that. They actually nothing. They think they're cleverer than you, they speak more English than you. He don't actually know the half of it. He just think he must stick with white people. White, black we all the same, we human being. Same blood, you bleed same as me . . .

RGHS students were therefore extremely sensitive to remarks that they felt implied that they were inferior to the CIE students and, at a later stage, the BHHS learners. Differences between themselves and other students were often observed through the use of language and the particular schools which students attended. These differences were consistently expressed in racial terms, for example: "he must stick with white people . . .". These statements illustrated how speaking in a particular manner, employing a discourse of 'standards' and denigrating 'Afrikaaps' were associated with aspirations to assimilate with 'whiteness', to not attend 'local coloured schools' and to embrace forms of 'book learning'.

The 'Afrikaaps' dialogue ultimately led to a number of the learners attacking and dismissing Greg, as he was perceived to be illegitimately seeking upward mobility. The young participants used constructions of race to discipline and exclude one student. This situation was partially caused by the authoritative, colonial-era discourses that continue to operate within the current South African education system and its elite schools, ideas that Greg attempted to introduce at Youth Amplified.

As a final example of how conflict functioned to limit learning in the Youth Amplified context, Appendix B contains a confrontation between a telephone caller and a number of participants in a live show. The caller had been listening to the young people interview the junior mayor of Cape Town. The fact that a member of the public took an interest in the show, telephoned the studio and stimulated discussion and debate was not interpreted as something positive by these youth. Instead of acknowledging the caller's perspective and analysing the dangers of corruption and party politics in South Africa, the interaction devolved into a confrontation in which the young people and the caller accused one another of failing to contribute to South Africa's development and transformation. In this context, evaluating the perspectives and arguments being asserted, not the individuals involved, would have been beneficial to the resultant dialogue. However, at school and at home, young South Africans are inculcated with values and practices that valorise competition, individualism, excellence and success, meaning that discussions such as this one can easily become a competition to demonstrate 'who is contributing more to South African society'.

Conclusion

Learning at Youth Amplified was influenced by the norms, values and discourses of participating schools, which traversed with learners into this new place. Particularly prominent in this regard were the powerful school institutional cultures of a former model C school and another new Cape Town school for 'gifted' township students. Students from these schools reiterated authoritative colonial and apartheid-era discourses and perpetuated values of competition and individualism at Youth Amplified.

Linked to, but separate from these school cultures, the construct of 'race' was a prominent tool that Youth Amplified participants used to differentiate between groups and to attribute social status to individuals. Race held much potential as a concept of interest to these young people, one that could be used to question social categories and understand historical contexts. However, race was also used in descriptions that reinforced taken-for-granted categories. It was clear that racial identifications did not only function to designate different styles and tastes, as other research with youth has found, but they were potent political practices that could serve to exclude or denigrate groups of people. Alternatively, 'race talk' may also be used for emancipatory purposes, for example, through historicising racial categories.

Rosemary Gardens' learners were particularly sensitive to comments that they interpreted as implying that they were inferior. They observed differences between themselves and other youth in the form of spoken language and the particular schools that students attended, and these differences were often expressed in racial terms. One of the challenges at Youth Amplified was to work with the young people towards acknowledging that when others disagreed with their opinions, this should not necessarily be perceived as a personal attack and that it could be interpreted positively because it meant that discussion was being stimulated. Many of the dialogues that took place were of a highly personal and sensitive nature, involving topics like race, language and intergenerational conflict. This made it challenging for youth to engage with issues conceptually and to not simply attack a person who uttered a remark deemed to be offensive.

References

Adhikari, M. 2005. *Not white enough, not black enough: racial identity in the South African 'Coloured' community*. Cape Town: Double Storey Books.

Bakhtin, M. 1981. *The dialogic imagination: four essays by M. M. Bakhtin*. Austin: University of Texas Press.

Bakhtin, M. 1986. *Speech genres and other late essays*. Austin: University of Texas Press.

Bosch, T. 2006. Radio as an instrument of protest: the history of Bush Radio. *Journal of Radio Studies*, 13(2), 249–265.

Bourdieu, P. 1977. *Outline of a theory of practice*. Cambridge: Cambridge University Press.

Bray, R., Gooskins, I., Kahn, L., Moses, S. & Seekings, J. 2010. *Growing up in the new South Africa: childhood and adolescence in post-apartheid Cape Town.* Cape Town: HSRC Press.
Dolby, N. 2001. *Constructing race: youth identity and popular culture in South Africa.* Albany: State University of New York Press.
Dolby, N. 2002. Making white: constructing race in a South African high school. *Curriculum Inquiry,* 32(1), 7–29.
Gee, J. 1990. *Sociolinguistics and literacies: ideologies in discourse.* London: Falmer Press.
Lee, C. 2007. *Culture, literacy and learning: blooming in the midst of the whirlwind.* New York: Teacher's College Press.
Moll, L., Amanti, C., Neff, D. & Gonzalez, N. 1992. Funds of knowledge for teaching: using a qualitative approach to connect homes and classrooms. *Theory into Practice,* XXXI(2), 132–141.
Nystrand, M. 1997. *Opening dialogue: understanding the dynamics of language and learning in the English classroom.* New York: Teachers College Press.
Ramphele, M. 2002. *Steering by the stars: being young in South Africa.* Cape Town: Tafelberg.
Soudien, C. 2007. *Schooling, culture and the making of youth identity in contemporary South Africa.* Cape Town: David Phillip.
Soudien. C. 2012. *Realising the dream: unlearning the logic of race in the South African school.* Cape Town: HSRC Press.
Watson, R. 2011. *The role-identification of teachers at a working-class school.* Unpublished MEd thesis. Stellenbosch: Stellenbosch University.

8 The Centrality of Language in Places of Learning

If you believe that children's language can be 'deficient', then you might be tempted to try to improve their language in some way. If you believe on the contrary that the concept of language deficit does not make much sense and that nothing is wrong with the language of any normal child, then you will probably believe that schooling should not interfere with children's dialects. And if you believe that linguistic disadvantage arises largely from people's intolerance and prejudice towards language differences, then you will probably try to change people's attitudes to language.

Stubbs, 2002: 79

Introduction

The journey across the three educational sites helps to expose how similar learning processes play out in different settings. This research method, known as multi-site ethnography, showed how students' language was received at school, versus how young people's words were interpreted and used in other educational sites. Traversing the three places illuminated how the school partly functioned to communicate to low-income students that the language that they spoke was inadequate and substandard, inappropriate for use at school. Other, famous studies in the sociology of education show similar 'sorting' processes at work. Classics like *Reproduction in Education, Society and Culture* (Bourdieu & Passeron, 1977) and *Schooling in Capitalist America* (Bowles & Gintis, 1976) demonstrate, powerfully, that schooling does not only provide young people with opportunities, as well as highlight and reward individual talent. Schools are part of society, and like other societal institutions, schools generally function to reproduce the status quo, such that powerful groups remain powerful and marginalised groups continue to be excluded. Schools claim to be able to determine students' individual abilities, demonstrated by their grades. However, deeper probing shows that academic performance is actually systematically structured by societal divisions that operate through, for example, race, class, gender, language and residential area (Apple, 2001; Bourdieu & Passeron, 1977; Bowles & Gintis, 1976; Gamoran, 2001). Willis' famous ethnographic study, *Learning to labour: how working-class kids get working-class jobs* (Willis, 1977), demonstrated how some marginalised youngsters refuse to be co-opted by this educational 'sorting' process. The genius of Willis' study lay in his analysis of how many young people unintentionally reproduce the existing social order despite, or even due to, their forms of resistance. Willis' 'lads' rejection of the school for what they believed to be authentic, masculine jobs on the shop floor ensured that they contributed to reproducing the class structure of that society. Research has found that South African schools reproduce inequalities more consistently than Morocco, Russia and the United States (Taylor & Yu, 2009). Studying learning amongst youth at RGHS, Youth Amplified and the Doodvenootskap demonstrated the central role that language ideologies played in the ranking of students' abilities. The use and evaluation of language was intimately linked to attitudes, values and prejudices that existed in the broader society.

Assessing the Value of Words

Educators and many of the students that remained at school for grades 10–12 concluded that the language that Rosemary Gardens youth learnt at home was inferior to standard Afrikaans and was 'inappropriate' for use at school. I have linked these attitudes and linguistic ideologies to the fact that the middle-class, historically white version of Afrikaans is the variety that informs the South African school curriculum. This version of the language is very different to the Kaapse Afrikaans that most Rosemary Gardens children and youth speak at home and in their community. 'Standard' Afrikaans is not more sophisticated than other varieties of this language; rather, it gained its superior status through political events of the 20th century.

Most schools are state-sponsored and administered institutions that resist local varieties that differ from standardised languages. School curricula repress deviations to what governments and international institutions recognise as legitimate uses of language. Teachers are mandated by the state to deliver a specific curriculum and to aid students in answering examination questions that test whether they have 'internalised' this curriculum. Students' supposedly 'inferior' language was therefore perceived as an impediment to curriculum delivery, a distraction in what was experienced as an already congested system. Teachers' affiliations and predefined roles contributed to their negative assessments of students' abilities, catalysing learner silence at Rosemary Gardens High School.

The young hip hop crew called the Doodvenootskap positioned themselves within an alternative international and local linguistic economy. In the late 1980s and 1990s Cape Town based groups like Prophets of da City and Black Noise used conscious hip hop to create Black Nationalist narratives on their own terms. These crews used linguistic codes that connected with the daily experiences of young South Africans classified as 'coloured' and 'black' by the apartheid state (Haupt, 2001). Since the 1980s Cape

Town hip hop groups have used subcultural practices, like lyric writing, to reclaim and reinvent local language. Some of these groups speak and write in what Brasse Vannie Kaap self-denigratingly call 'gamtaal', as well as nonstandard varieties of English, Xhosa and Zulu (Haupt, 2001: 173). Shaheen, a member of Prophets of da City, remarked:

> *When we do interviews and shit like that and we speak gamtaal or whatever, that shit's on purpose so the kid at home can say, 'Fuck they're speaking my language,' you know? They're representing, you know, what comes out of the township and shit. So if some middle-class motherfucker comes 'Oe god, skollietaal' ('Oh god hooligan language'), the shit's not for them, you know what I mean? I don't care if some white-ass dude at home thinks, 'Oh shit look at this . . . uncultured', you know? I want some kid from the ghetto to think, 'Naa, we can relate to that'.*
>
> (Quoted in Haupt, 2001: 178)

Cape Town hip hop crews like Prophets of da City used their language and music to create alternative values and standards of excellence in relation to language, rejecting the norms of middle-class, often white, youth and former model C schools. DVS did not write lyrics that directly confronted the issue of language status, as groups like Prophets of da City and Brasse vannie Kaap (BVK) did in the past. DVS simply wrote in the same language that they used for verbal communication, switching between English and Afrikaans as they used forms of translanguaging and asserted their own versions of language. However, their practices demonstrated parallels to the work of Prophets of da City and Brasse vannie Kaap. All of these Cape Town crews have used hip hop to validate their linguistic resources, encouraging pride in a marginalised identity, catalysing creativity and group solidarity:

> *They always show ugly pictures of our people*
> *Why must I always be a gangster or a coon?*
> *Like all that we see in the newspaper or TVs*
> *They hold their noses say "Sis you're a lower-class coloured"*
> *Your forefathers were whites and slaves. So it must be a bastard.*
> ***But, wait a minute, if you trust my story and not his story** you will see*
> *My forefathers were **a king and a queen and never knew drugs, guns** or a canteen*
> *They were always there to serve god*
> (Translated from the Afrikaans. **English words that were used by the speaker are in bold.**) (Brasse Vannie Kaap in Haupt, 2001: 181)

Like Prophets of da City and Brasse vannie Kaap, DVS created positive identities for themselves, subverting popular stereotypes and negative depictions of young people from the Cape Flats. These hip hop collectives have forged an alternative public space where they debate issues of relevance on their own terms, working within an ideological framework that promotes pride in their language. DVS was supported by the fact that the crew is 'descendants' of this line of Cape Town–based hip hop artists. The Doodvenoodskap created new forms and mixtures of language, whilst working with a sense of social justice. The group stimulated forms of solidarity by demonstrating strong allegiances to the community in which they were reared. Their use of language was catalysed by their local and global hip hop associations, which differed from the ways that language was used and endorsed by educators at the school.

The institutional culture that underpins many South African NGOs, like CRAAG, complemented the hip hop norms and values to which DVS was exposed. CRAAG supported DVS by providing them with a space to work, have their voices heard and participate in discussions that took place at the Global Hope Foundation building. Hoppie told me that:

These people (CRAAG) *have a cool way of doing it. Everyone **votes** collectively. It's **political**. This is my **opinion**, this is yours, I think it must be like this, you think it must be like that, come let's **vote**. Big people **decide** it.*

(Translated from the Afrikaans. **Words used in English by the interviewee are in bold.**)

Some South African NGOs practice forms of local democracy, militating against the silencing of youth. By working in collaboration with a democratic institution, namely CRAAG, the grassroots social movement of DVS developed into a caring educational place where young people were encouraged to speak freely. I observed DVS' confidence to contribute to discussions at the meeting at May Hughes' house, where members of the group spoke at length about their school experiences, in the presence of the school principal and seven doctoral students. Parent members of the School Governing Body did not speak on this occasion, as they were overwhelmed by the education and linguistic capital of others in the room of this white woman's house.

Through interactions with CRAAG, the group learnt a range of new concepts, discourses and practices, in the presence of more experienced and institutionally connected mentors. South African civil society organisations like CRAAG were born out of a mixture of Freirean popular education, faith-based institutions and large amounts of European donor funding, all of which aided in overthrowing apartheid and establishing the democratic state (Hendrickse, 2008). The value of civil society organisations asserting liberal, rights-based discourses, combined with forms of collective mobilisation, such as DVS, has led to liberatory forms of citizenship and inclusion in post-colonial contexts like South Africa.

The language that young people from Rosemary Gardens used at Youth Amplified was generally undermined by their peers. The mixture of schools that attended the show shaped how the group assessed language in that place. Particularly, the institutional cultures of the elite schools like the Cape Institute of Education and Barry Hertzog High School (BHHS), had a profound influence on the group. Students from these schools often asserted linguistic ideologies, stating that 'standards exist' and that it was the responsibility of RGHS learners to 'raise themselves up' and acquire these 'standards'. This discourse of standards circulates amongst educators and learners at former 'whites only' schools and other elite institutions, denigrating the language and culture of marginalised Capetonian youth. Learners who attended these schools transported this discourse into the Youth Amplified place. This led to students contesting the process of how 'standards' may be acquired, following their viewing of the *Afrikaaps* documentary and not debating whether or not 'standards' actually exist. The authoritative discourse of 'standards' was inherited from the colonial and apartheid eras and was used to denigrate groups of people and cultural forms, including language.

In contravention to this notion of 'standards', socio-linguists argue that the idea that some languages are more sophisticated or superior to others is a myth, as languages become standardised due to political and not linguistic factors. What is actually meant when people say that language is 'incorrect' or of a low standard, is usually that the language has been used inappropriately relative to the social context (Stubbs, 2002). Language develops norms and values at schools, in job interviews or in pubs and it may be used in ways that are considered to be inappropriate in specific places. At RGHS young people, who have inherited the complex tapestry of languages that overlaps with the history of the Cape, learnt that the language that they speak is 'lower', 'not proper', 'a mixture' and that they ought to speak a different version of the Afrikaans language at school. This contributed to mass school discontinuation, as these marginalised young people reciprocally dismissed the legitimacy of educators and the school. School discontinuation represents a mutual distrust, disrespect and abandonment between young people and the South African state. Young men and women from Rosemary Gardens symbolically told the school to 'go to hell', as this institution was unable meaningfully to engage with the social challenges they faced or the language they used.

In response to young people from elite schools demarcating acceptable and unacceptable forms of language at Youth Amplified, youth from RGHS attacked students who attended the CIE and BHHS, calling them "fake coloureds" and "snobs". In an individual interview with Tracey she repeatedly called Greg a "girl". Township youth attacking peers with greater opportunities and resources has been widely documented in South Africa. As the Youth Amplified facilitator I had my work cut out to create a context where the young people could cooperate and not compete and ultimately produce a show of which they could all be proud. This was further complicated by the culture of competition that existed at the elite participating schools. The dual tasks of promoting a sensibility for the ways in which history has

The Centrality of Language in Places of Learning 131

resulted in certain inequalities, as well as encouraging youth to reflect on themselves and the conceptual issues at hand, rather than personally attacking peers deemed to be offensive, made working with the Youth Amplified group a huge challenge.

Language and Social Hierarchies

The value attributed to different words was related to the social hierarchies that existed in each place. Relationships amongst DVS members were non-hierarchical, whereas tiered relationships between powerful educators and silenced learners, were most common at school:

> *Learning is different at school. The way the teacher explain something its proper, like the way you get it written in the textbook. Like at school it's straight learning, it's serious from the start of the period till the end . . . Hoppie will talk about a lightbulb. A teacher will explain it. Hoppie will come and say, jy weet mos na, gaan slap, sit die lug af (you know, you go to sleep, turn the light off). That's when you take the lightbulb out. A teacher will tell you "switch off the light when you take the bulb out". But then Hoppie comes and this is what we like hearing man, we like hearing at home, understand? Like Hoppie will do or the guys at home will do, when we want to learn something like they will always bring the way we do things at home in. Now at school it's not always that way. So at school pure English, not pure English but English all the way man . . . Hoppie he'll crack a joke about it and learning must be fun man. At school they will explain it to you they will show you a picture, how a pavement look. At home Hoppie will point to a pavement, say that's what I'm talking about.*

Hierarchical school relations were created through educators exercising their authority and validating language forces from above. School learning was described as "proper, like the way you get it written in a textbook", demonstrating how pedagogical interactions were set in stone, as students struggled to interact with school knowledge or develop their own opinions and ideas in this place. Aaron was the only DVS member of school-going age who did not attend RGHS. Learning at his school was associated with the high-status English language, a serious atmosphere and the use of textbooks. English has colonial connotations and is regularly regarded as 'the language of the oppressor', a language that often made learners feel uncomfortable, unfamiliar and inadequate.

Verbal interactions at school were portrayed as different to exchanges at DVS. Whereas the teacher **explains to** the learners, according to Aaron, Hoppie **talks with** the students, illustrating the difference between the authoritative discourse of the school and the internally persuasive discourse of Hoppie and DVS (Bakhtin, 1981). 'Explaining to' a person implies that a hierarchy exists between the knowledgeable person and one who is uninformed. By contrast, 'talks with', insinuates that learning amongst DVS was a collective exercise based on forms of equality, where knowledge was shared, reciprocally.

The equality experienced amongst DVS members catalysed relaxed interactions, allowing for a range of different opinions to emerge. Aaron said that "at home Hoppie will point to a pavement", creating an imagined affinity between DVS as a place and 'home'. DVS was described as a comfortable, unintimidating, homelike place that often contained forms of humour. On the other hand, the school was not associated with "cracking jokes", but with being "serious", rigid and formal. School-based dialogues between dominant educators and marginalised learners were hierarchical, whereas interactions between members of the DVS crew were portrayed as egalitarian. The social hierarchies and linguistic economies that existed in these places influenced the production of knowledge in the different sites:

> *A big thing at the school is that the misters/sirs don't kick off on the youngsters level. There's always that "I am the **adult** you are the **learner.**" I am right you are wrong. If you say "does sir know that Jan van Riebeek isn't the man in the portrait?", then the sir is going to fight with him. In the sir's book it isn't so. His **research** and his **intelligence** which he learns in other places is on a different **level**. "I am the sir, **studied** for 30 years to be the sir. Everything that you say doesn't matter." So he can **challenge** the sir on certain aspects but the sir isn't going to give him **credit** for that. Because there's only one way in the sir or madam's **mind.** I am the **adult.** You the **child.** And that ties into my work. We don't want to **permanently** make decisions for the youth. We teach the youth that their voices have weight. Their opinions count. They can be part of the **decision-making.***
>
> (Translated from the Afrikaans. **English words that were used by the speaker are in bold.** Hoppie originally used the word 'meneer', which I have translated as 'sir', but could also be understood as 'mister'.)

According to DVS members, a 'knowledge hierarchy' existed at school, as educators' knowledge and opinions were assumed to be superior to those of students. Hoppie's comment regarding educators acquiring their knowledge in a different place demonstrated the suspicion that young people in neighbourhoods like Rosemary Gardens felt towards institutions of higher education and the resentment they harboured towards knowledge gleaned in those places. The school was imagined to be a place that was linked to other elitist educational institutions, places that were unfamiliar to most Rosemary Gardens youth. Teachers' authoritative knowledge functioned as the ultimate source of power in the classroom. The knowledge hierarchy that existed at school reduced the potential for dialogue, as students felt that their contributions were not valued. By contrast, a range of opinions were valued and respected amongst the DVS crew.

Hoppie's reference to Jan van Riebeek, the Dutchman who led the colonisation project at the Cape, hinted at further resistance to, and suspicion of, the kinds of educational interactions that happened at school. I first heard DVS members mention Jan van Riebeek at a 'coffee bar' evening that the group organised for young people from Rosemary Gardens to meet and engage in discussions on the topic of 'identity'. A guest speaker called Bradlocks stated that no genuine portrait of van Riebeek existed; the two images commonly referred to—one on old South African bank notes and the other housed in the national gallery—were apparently images of an unknown person, according to Bradlocks.

It was interesting that Hoppie used this example as evidence that educators rejected students' knowledge. Jan van Riebeek is commonly referred to as the symbolic father of coloured people, having supposedly procreated with slaves to produce the 'coloured race' (Adhikari, 2005). By saying that nobody has actually seen van Riebeek's face and that educators would deny this fact, Hoppie was implying that educators and the education system collude with the colonial story and its main protagonist. School knowledge was associated, metaphorically, with defending the authenticity of the colonial project, as well as supporting the indoctrination and subjugation that accompanied it. Simultaneously, students' knowledge was apparently silenced at school, as teachers rejected their ideas, such as an alternative interpretation of their origins. Hoppie implied that the school system did not provide youth with opportunities to explore and develop their identities or take ownership of forms of knowledge linked to their heritage. School was therefore seen as a place that contained inequality in terms of opportunities to speak, the kind of language endorsed and the knowledge production processes that existed between educators and students.

The power relations and social hierarchies that existed at Youth Amplified were shaped by the participating schools which students attended. Learners from elite schools generally asserted broader linguistic ideologies, while RGHS learners opposed this state of affairs, often proclaiming that these young people were illegitimately seeking upward social mobility. The use of language and the social status of participants were continually contested by the young people.

This jostling for position in the social and linguistic hierarchy, amongst peers, could possibly be alleviated in informal learning contexts by encouraging forms of cooperation between diverse groups of young people, such that they, for example, translate each other's words. All of the participants could speak more than one language, providing a reservoir of available linguistic resources. A component of the critical pedagogical process at Youth Amplified therefore involved the students and myself learning to engage in forms of cooperation, instead of competing. This meant working with youth to reflect on instinctive reactions. Reflection led to a deeper exploration of the issues and perspectives being presented and generated new questions. Debates became democratic conceptual discussions, instead of 'circumstantial scuffles'. Debriefing and reflecting after the show were vital practices that helped the dialogic learning process.

The three places demonstrated that hierarchical, unequal relationships do not generally stimulate rich dialogue and often function to silence individuals or lead to conflict. Hierarchies were produced through the use of different varieties of language and the ways in which knowledge was validated in the three places. The nature of young people's interactions with one another, specifically, whether they competed or cooperated, also shaped whether or not such interactions were hierarchical. Linguistic ideologies and hierarchies influenced the kinds of speech genres that emerged in the three places.

Speech Genres

At Rosemary Gardens High School I saw first-hand the hierarchy between learners and educators that was described by DVS members. This hierarchy was maintained by a classroom speech genre known as Information Response and Feedback (IRF). Speech genres are the ways that utterances become arranged into fixed configurations that are repeated in particular contexts, becoming recognisable patterns of interaction. IRF-type classroom dialogues are partly caused by the practical difficulties encountered by the modern teacher. In contemporary society teachers are designated to disseminate cultural knowledge to large classes, armed with limited resources (Edwards & Furlong, 1978; Edwards & Mercer, 1987). Interactions characterised by IRF were also the result of social challenges in the Rosemary Gardens community, circumstances that led educators to believe that students were volatile. Predictable IRF-type interactions allowed teachers to maintain a thin veil of control in these challenging circumstances. Educators questioned Rosemary Gardens youth's values and moral conduct, using the rigid IRF format to prevent young people from hijacking discussions for their own ends. Finally, IRF-type interactions provided teachers with a framework to ensure that learners received forms of language that educators believed these young people needed to acquire. At this high school IRF was a particular classroom-based speech genre that allowed educators to shape the kinds of utterances, content, styles of speech and intentionality of both learners and educators.

A different speech genre emerged at Youth Amplified, one that was, at times, highly conducive to the production of dialogue and a talk radio show. Dialogic learning interventions at schools require thorough training programmes where educators and learners are introduced to sets of ground rules that explain how to take turns speaking, how to listen to others, ask questions and give reasons for opinions (see Dawes, Mercer & Wegerif, 2004; Mercer, 2002, 2005; Rojas-Drummond & Mercer, 2004). Talk radio shows are naturally oriented towards the facilitation of dialogue: a host or presenter controls the flow of talk, seeking out multiple perspectives. Participants learn to wait for their turn to contribute to discussions because interrupting one another prevents the audience from following the conversation. Students hosted the show themselves, enhancing this non-hierarchical, youth-led forum. Preparation for the show and the generation of questions beforehand improved the dialogues that emerged. The format and structure of a youth radio show can therefore be an ideal medium for the production and demonstration of forms of dialogue amongst youth.

Youth Amplified involved myself and the young people exploring a different set of 'rules of the game' and trying to stimulate dialogue through diverse opinions, critical thinking and asking pertinent questions. I learnt about different people's roles and responsibilities as the talk radio show unfolded. The particular roles that the young people were required to perform challenged them, as they needed to reflect on their instinctive responses and think about how to react, in order to make an effective contribution to the discussion. Students from all of the participating schools struggled to embrace this speech genre at Youth Amplified, as this kind of interaction is not commonly encountered or performed in other places through which South African youth move.

Youth Amplified demonstrated how speech genres that emerge in informal learning contexts and involve youth engaging with issues related to social justice, could differ from how these kinds of talk have been conceptualised as ideally existing in classrooms. Research has shown that dialogue can be most useful for classroom learning when young people are encouraged to conduct 'exploratory talk', a speech genre that is underpinned by the principles of the 'ideal speech situation' (Habermas, 1990). Exploratory talk promotes rational debate and multiple opinions. Researchers have constructed 'talk lessons' programmes to enhance classroom dialogue amongst educators and learners. These programmes develop fuller participation from students and encourage children and youth to give reasons for their views, as they critically but constructively engage with the opinions of others. Exploratory talk programmes repress personal identities and other factors that may hamper the operations of 'rationalism', encouraging participants to reach consensus, rationally, through the group agreeing on and pursuing the 'best ideas' (Wegerif & Mercer, 1997).

Youth Amplified highlighted how theories that advocate for the ideal speech situation and forms of classroom-based exploratory talk fail to acknowledge that language ideologies exist and that different people's words carry a range of values. The 'best ideas' being selected by groups for further inquiry cannot be separated from the ways in which these ideas are 'packaged' in language and the status that speakers carry, based on, for example, race, class and gender. The radio show also showed how the ideal speech situation is often neither possible nor desirable in informal educational contexts in which young people debate issues of intense personal and social relevance, where pertinent historical power relations are at play. When young people engage with social justice–related issues, the different perspectives presented are contingent on the identities of the speakers and the historical position of different groups. These identities and positions need to become conscious and integral components of the speech genres that are produced, otherwise a range of underlying issues, related to, for example, race, class and gender, will impact, unconsciously, on the ensuing dialogues, but these will not be acknowledged.

In informal learning contexts that use forms of critical pedagogy, young people need to be encouraged to reflect on the social positions from which they speak, something that will affect the speech genre that emerges. Reflection enhances dialogue as it increases people's awareness of their own perspectives and helps them to understand these in relation to their social position and the historical context. Dialogue in this situation does not simply involve the most rationally sound argument 'winning', but requires that people interpret different standpoints in relation to the social identities of the speakers. Whilst scholars that advocate for exploratory talk propose that rational debate and decision-making amongst equal parties benefits 'the common good', different groups of people have had different historical experiences and have not previously had equal access to 'the common good'. Dialogue that involves engaging with issues that are related to forms of social justice therefore requires that participants be aware of the historical context in which dialogue plays out and the ways in which different groups of people have been treated by each other in—and benefitted from—the past. Historical consciousness and social reflexivity may then produce a speech genre that is 'critical' in its orientation and not merely 'rational'.

DVS showed how speech genres produced by hip hop culture can both stimulate or hinder learning through dialogue. 'The cipha', which Alim (2009) describes as encapsulating the genetic make-up of hip hop, contains a unique speech genre. Ciphas are spaces where rap battles are fought, where opponents are felled through intelligent and creative uses of language. Although hip hoppers, including DVS, are quick to point out that pre-planned punch lines are not valued, some DVS members regularly used punch lines to demonstrate their creative talents. I have argued that hip hoppers 'spitting' pre-planned punch lines did not stimulate dialogic learning, as reiterating these plays on words did not involve actively questioning and engaging with the meaning of utterances. The values of the 'battle' may also result in participants using homophobic, sexist and other derogatory insults in order to fell opponents. Scholars state this is frowned upon in hip hop culture, however it appears to be a regular practice. On other occasions, DVS' interactions with NGOs and hip hop culture stimulated democratic dialogues in which all opinions were valued and space was created for each person to speak. This validated DVS' use of language and encouraged them to express their ideas.

To sum up, speech genres are patterns of utterances that structure dialogues. In RGHS classrooms dialogue was dominated by a speech genre known as Information Response and Feedback. IRF allowed educators to maintain control in the context of threatening external forces, large class sizes and pressure to conform to bureaucratic stipulations. While it may be important to disseminate important concepts and discourses to youth, this needs to be combined with allowing young people opportunities to explore forms of knowledge in ways that are empowering. The Doodvenootskap demonstrated verbal exchanges based on equality, allowing members to discuss issues on their own terms. On certain occasions DVS members used 'punch lines' from rap battles, a speech genre that did not invite responses or interactions between people. Youth Amplified showed that encouraging young people to reflect on their position within the society they inhabit, through introspection and personal positioning, enriches dialogues. Reflection catalyses young people to analyse their own perspectives in relation to other positions and the historical context, bolstering dialogic interactions and producing forms of 'critical' speech.

Conclusion

Language was central to dialogic learning at RGHS, Youth Amplified and amongst the Doodvenootskap, operating in distinct ways in the three places. Language is the medium through which knowledge, ideas and meaning are shared and communicated; it is a reservoir that is used for identity construction and development. However, language simultaneously distributes forms of power and status, both through the opportunities which people obtain to use it and in the form of linguistic practices: people's word choices and the ways in which they utter these words communicate their place in the social structure. Young people's use of language at school was entwined with the social hierarchies and linguistic ideologies that existed in the broader society and which are endorsed by the state. The cultural influences that produced DVS, with different associated histories, led to instances of the group reclaiming and reinventing varieties of language. Critical pedagogy at Youth Amplified laid the foundations for multiple contrasting perspectives to manifest. However, at times, school institutional culture and social stratification repressed dialogue. Both RGHS and Youth Amplified illustrated how schools reinforce broader societal hierarchies through validating specific varieties of language and colonial and apartheid era-discourses, in the post-apartheid period. The journey across the three places enabled a comparison of similar young people's use of language—and how their words were assessed—highlighting the ways that places inhibit or enable opportunities for young people to learn and how these sites show youth different futures.

References

Adhikari, M. 2005. *Not white enough, not black enough: racial identity in the South African 'Coloured' community*. Cape Town: Double Storey Books.
Alim, H. 2009. Creating 'an empire within an empire': critical hip hop, language pedagogies and the role of sociolinguistics. In S. Alim, A. Ibrahim & A. Pennycook

(Eds.), *Global linguistic flows: hip hop cultures, youth identities, and the politics of language (pp. 213–230)*. London: Routledge.
Apple, M. 2001. *Educating the 'right' way: markets, standards, god and inequality*. London: Routledge.
Bakhtin, M. 1981. *The dialogic imagination: four essays by M. M. Bakhtin*. Austin: University of Texas Press.
Bourdieu, P. & Passeron, J. 1977. *Reproduction in education, society and culture*. Beverly Hills: SAGE.
Bowles, S. & Gintis, H. 1976. *Schooling in capitalist America*. New York: Basic Books.
Dawes, L., Mercer, N. & Wegerif, R. 2004. *Thinking together: a programme of activities for developing speaking, listening and thinking skills*. Birmingham: Imaginative Minds Ltd.
Edwards, A. & Furlong, V. 1978. *The language of teaching: meaning in classroom interaction*. London: Heinemann.
Edwards, D. & Mercer, N. 1987. *Common knowledge: the development of joint understanding in the classroom*. London: Methuen.
Gamoran, A. 2001. American schooling and educational inequality: a forecast for the 21st century. *Sociology of Education, 74,* 135–153.
Habermas, J. 1990. *Discourse ethics: notes on a program of philosophical justification, moral consciousness and communicative action*. Cambridge: MIT Press.
Haupt, A. 2001. Black thing: hip hop nationalism, race and gender in Prophets of da City and Brasse vannie Kaap. In Z. Erasmus (Ed.), *Coloured by history, shaped by place: new perspectives on coloured identities in Cape Town (pp. 173–191)*. Cape Town: Kwela Books & South African History Online.
Hendrickse, R. 2008. *Governance and financial sustainability of NGOs in South Africa*. Unpublished doctoral thesis. University of the Western Cape, Cape Town.
Mercer, N. 2002. Developing dialogues. In G. Wells & G. Claxton (Eds.), *Learning for life in the 21st century (pp. 141–154)*. Oxford: Blackwell Publishers.
Mercer, N. 2005. Sociocultural discourse analysis: analysing classroom talk as a social mode of thinking. *Journal of Applied Linguistics, 1*(2), 137–168.
Rojas-Drummond, S. & Mercer, N. 2004. Scaffolding the development of effective collaboration and learning. *International Journal of Educational Research, 39,* 99–111.
Stubbs, M. 2002. Some basic sociolinguistic concepts. In L. Delpit & J. Dowdy (Eds.), *The skin that we speak: thoughts on language and culture in the classroom (pp. 63–87)*. New York: New Press.
Taylor, S. & Yu, D. 2009. *The importance of socio-economic status in determining educational achievement in South Africa*. Stellenbosch Economic Working Papers No. 01/09.
Wegerif, R. & Mercer, N. 1997. A dialogical framework for researching peer talk. In R. Wegerif & P. Scrimshaw (Eds.), *Computers and talk in the primary classroom (pp. 49–65)*. Clevedon: Multilingual Matters.
Willis, P. 1977. *Learning to labour: how working class kids get working class jobs*. Farnborough: Saxon House.

9 A New Educational Matrix

A bird doesn't sing because it has an answer, it sings because it has a song.

Anglund, 1967: 15

What kinds of educational and linguistic practice, what kinds of text and discourse, and what kinds of educated subjects can and should be constructed to forge new critical and contingent relationships with globalising economies and mass cultures—long after the departure of colonial masters . . . The issues of which languages, whose languages, which texts and discourses cannot be considered in isolation from these other questions about the amelioration and reconstruction of material conditions.

Luke, 2005: xviii

An alternative, democratic Afrikaans will be looked for in presentation, spirit and context. This democratising will lie in the introduction of an extended world in opposition to the narrow and demarcated world that school Afrikaans (and university Afrikaans) has so far presented. The departure point for this is that there is an Afrikaans world that is outside of the living world of apartheid.

Gerwel, 1988: 12

Learning Places as Intersecting Sets of Social Relations

When poor young people of colour enter educational places they are often suspicious—with good reason. White, middle-class youth are usually imagined to be the prototypical inhabitants of educational sites. In this study one young man at Rosemary Gardens High School said that:

They want to catch you out man. They want to see if you're on that level man. How good is your Afrikaans . . .

His words indicate that one of the most blatant indicators to youth that a place is likely to be humiliating, is the language that is used and valued in that setting. Lisa Delpit (2002) describes language as 'the skin that we speak', the medium we use to interpret our surroundings. It is the most intimate part of our identity that we hear while still in the womb when we listen to our mothers' voices. Her metaphor brilliantly captures that language use is a sensitive business. However, a skin belongs to an individual, whereas language is shared. Language is social. It is fluid, changing and linked to forms of power. It is a communal skin.

Past and present social relations structure how language is used in specific places, with consequences for how young people learn in these settings. In schools and classrooms language use is heavily influenced by the visions and aspirations that nation-states have for their citizens. Post-colonial nations have struggled to construct education and language policies that balance promoting national unity and respect for diversity, whilst ensuring that national economies are competitive in the global marketplace. Many post-colonial states were formed by social movements drenched in anti-colonial philosophies and politics that were pro-indigenisation. These states have been forced to reposition themselves in a rapidly globalizing world in which economic growth is believed to be stimulated by human capital that is 'globally competitive'.

Despite languages now increasingly being understood as mixtures of words from different sources, rather than discrete entities (Blommaert, 2010; Otsuji & Pennycook, 2010), national governments generally perceive language mixing to be a threat to producing citizens who will be able to command international respect and drive economic development. Examples include the Singaporean government resisting the mixing of Hokkien and English, Indonesian nationalists encouraging the use of a 'high' variety of Malay rather than creolised versions of this language and English and French being used in Cameroonian schools, rather than pidgin, Camfranglais or local dialects. A participant in the current study said that "your points go down if you mix your language". Whilst all languages naturally involve mixtures of words, state-supported language ideologies regularly endorse some forms of language as 'more pure' and of a 'higher quality' than others. Such ideologies are used by powerful groups to validate their own linguistic resources and denigrate people at the margins of society.

Valorising English and other language varieties that are elevated in status through, for example, associations with whiteness, like a specific version of Afrikaans, is not exclusively the prerogative of nation-states. Young people and their families aspire to attain the markers of success and attractive consumption lifestyles that dominate the global imagination. Students and parents acknowledge that financial prosperity is aided by English fluency. They have observed that the English-speaking middle classes are most empowered, a trend that exists in any post-colonial society (Lin & Martin, 2005). For many parents and students, school choice is swayed by language options such as English provision, as well as other enticing factors associated with upward mobility.

South Africa is not a typical post-colonial country, with large numbers of the descendants of colonisers and other white people who enjoyed colonial privileges remaining in the country through the apartheid regime and after the democratic transition. In order to avoid race-based conflict and appease and retain white skills and capital, the linguistic and cultural rights of minorities have been vehemently protected. The version of Afrikaans that remains enshrined in the South African constitution and taught at RGHS is the one spoken by white South Africans, a language tainted by privilege and dedicated to linguistic purity. Standard Afrikaans is not only foreign to Rosemary Gardens youth, but the endorsement of this version communicates to them that the language that they speak is worth less.

Caught in the crossfire between the state and its young citizens, teachers attempt to find temporary educational solutions, stitching together provisional strategies on a daily basis (Luke, 2005). Educators are pressured to deliver the curriculum in a predetermined manner and to 'teach to the test', as workbooks are regularly inspected and standardised tests and examinations are used to evaluate the quality of teaching and learning. Educators are tempted to dictate paragraphs of notes, as was evident in Chapter Five, as these practices demonstrate to officials that the curriculum has been delivered and that teachers have performed their duties adequately, creating an illusion that learning has occurred. At the same time, teachers at RGHS showed genuine care for young people's well-being, openly expressing love for students and comforting them in contexts of hardship. In 2011 the school achieved an 80% pass rate, even though approximately 75% of the students had discontinued their schooling by grade 12. These outcomes indicate the kind of temporary solution haphazardly constructed by Rosemary Gardens High School and its educators.

The social relations that shape schools and dialogic learning within them cannot be separated from the challenge of improving and redistributing material resources (Luke, 2005). Material and imagined space are always enmeshed. Material economic forces have resulted in Cape Town becoming a quintessential 'global city' and one of the most unequal societies in the world. The beaches and mansions of the Atlantic seaboard and the leafy suburbs and wine estates of Constantia coexist with the slums of Khayelitsha, Gugulethu and Nyanga. These divisions ensure that transnational capital and tourism are allowed to do business and pleasure as usual, buttressed by a cheap labour force that facilitates many of the needs of the wealthy. At the same time these inequalities lead to social problems that plague poor neighbourhoods. For example, the high levels of violence that exist in Rosemary Gardens traumatise young people and disrupt their schooling experiences. Almost all of the students I spoke to commented on the effects of violence. Both of the learners that featured in Chapter Five spoke about this issue. Mo said:

> *What happened to me this year, they called the police that come with these big black vans. If your place is too corrupt they send them out with guns. They start searching everyone. They put you on the ground, hands at the back of your head. They put a gun against your head and they search you. Everyday I got searched. That was the worst time in my life cause every day I got searched out. I went to the shop got searched out here. But it actually for a good cause cause the gangsters shooting everyone.*

And Tracey said that:

> *We don't know where and why the gangsters is gonna shoot against the other group. We just hear shooting and we have to run. We have to duck and dive for our lives day in and day out . . .*

In 2012, violence in Rosemary Gardens was so disruptive that Helen Zille, who was the premier of the Western Cape province at the time, asked president Jacob Zuma to deploy the military to the area. Zille claimed that 23 people, including seven children, had been murdered in a spike of gang violence. This violence seeped into the school. The silencing of young people in classrooms at Rosemary Gardens High School was partly the result of factors that originated *outside* of classrooms. Creating the conditions for learners to speak *in* classrooms requires dealing with the range of issues that perturb students, issues that originate in the wider society. Understanding learner silence and the lack of dialogue in Rosemary Gardens classrooms cannot be comprehended without perceiving these classrooms as linked to the web of places through which students move. These places were produced by apartheid, colonialism and global inequalities that play out in contemporary urban enclaves, such as parts of the Cape Town periphery. Low-income schools in other urban settings have also been described as inseparable from the social challenges that plague those areas. Giroux (2004) highlights the militarization of American public schools, places where drug raids and pointing guns at children are commonplace. In American schools children's rights are regularly negated and the criminal justice system merges with education to form the prison-industrial-educational complex (Giroux, 2004). In Canada poor urban youth labeled schools 'warehouses', sites where young people are 'stored' during the day with little concern for genuine learning (Dillabough & Kennelly, 2010). Learning that does or does not occur at schools cannot be analysed in isolation from the material and cultural factors that shape and produce these sites, both locally and globally. The dearth of dialogic learning at RGHS was related to the school 'game' that played out between the bureaucracy, educators and learners, in the context of a community constructed by and for apartheid South Africa, one that now forms part of a globalised world.

Dialogic learning amongst the Doodvenoodskap was related to another set of local and global social relations. Hip hop is underpinned by alternative norms and values, an alternative linguistic economy. Originating in The Bronx, New York City, but now a thoroughly global phenomenon, hip hop culture is an attempt by marginalised youth to reclaim public space through remixing and reinventing forms of language. This organically evolving, transnational youth movement that developed from the bottom up has germinated creative new mixtures of language, culture and forms of 'glocal', simultaneously global and local, citizenship. High-quality hip hop is defined as expressing global trends—definitive reference points from international hip hop culture—through local words, phrases and references. Hip hoppers are 'abo-digital', modern but in touch with their indigenous roots; they are intimately connected to both distant and immediate trends (Alim, 2007). Through this cultural bricolage hip hoppers demonstrate that they are aware of global trends, but are 'keeping it real', a quintessential hip hop phrase. 'Keeping it real' expresses that global forms of consumerism and imitation have not dictated a rapper's identity and that s/he is in touch with local cultural practices and objects. Outside of the United States 'keeping it real' often involves complex forms of translation, as rappers need to find congruent language, values and practices that maintain the original hip hop spirit, but do not clash with local linguistic and cultural forms (Forman, 2001; Pennycook, 2007). In these ways young people use hip hop to exert agency and play with language, as they navigate multi-directional cultural flows.

The Doodvenootskap used new ideas that they learnt from the NGO industry and glocal hip hop movements, within the medium of the language that they spoke at home, to produce lyrics that contested dominant linguistic ideologies.

This illustrates how, although hip hop culture has not created "an empire within an empire, a sub-space in which the laws of the dominant market are suspended" (Bourdieu, 1993: 63), it has, to some degree, interrogated and reversed how language is appraised (Alim, 2009). On a global scale, hip hop is now the largest youth subculture. Although all of its many varieties do not engage with politics and critical thinking, this subculture fundamentally involves youth experimenting with and asserting new forms of language. Hip hop ciphas, the human circles in which lyrics are 'spat' and 'battles fought', have become cross-national places where linguistic identities and ideologies are produced and contested, where language is altered and recreated, where space is lived.

But hip hop is not all liberation. As hip hop practices take root in new locations they become embroiled in local politics, identities, economics and prejudices. The Doodvenootskap are part of the Western Cape province, a region where people classified as non-white were pitted against one another under colonialism and apartheid and some clambered for relative privileges.

Some of the prejudiced attitudes and politics of DVS members can only be understood within this context. One DVS member told me that:

> I heard of a word, a supplanter, someone who studies someone else, to get into their position. Nelson Mandela was released in 1990. In 1994 he was the president for four years. He was de Klerk's supplanter. When he came out of jail he had this black suit on, he had this briefcase and his hair was combed, like he just came out of jail, he's got this degree in law. Who do they expect to believe that? I'm older than five, I know what goes on in jail. People don't have time to study cause they need to survive.

DVS' politics were rooted in a deep distrust of what they saw as the new black national government, which they associated with the same levels of corruption that were attributed to whites under apartheid. In addition to being highly suspicious of black South Africans, DVS strongly identified with the indigenous Khoi and San, the hunter-gatherer and herder groups that were all but obliterated by colonial forces. DVS members were learning Khoi language and had planned trips to the Namib dessert to interact with Khoi descendants. In the face of post-apartheid uncertainty, DVS retreated to identify with a group associated with a time before things 'got messy'. These local hip hoppers were therefore bound up in the local and global politics of the region, displaying attitudes of mistrust to black politicians and affinity with the Khoi.

Part of the reason why I raise this issue is to emphasise that I am not saying that school learning is uniformly 'bad', whereas popular educational places are simply 'good'. DVS could have benefitted from a rigorous history curriculum that explored how Nelson Mandela became a lawyer prior to his imprisonment. This hypothetical curriculum could unpack how the African National Congress has espoused non-racialism and analyse the ways that groups of people became entwined at the Cape, as well as the sad history and virtual extermination of the Khoi and San peoples. Hip hop is a form of "language ideological combat" (Alim, 2009: 11) that holds great potential for challenging oppressive language ideologies, but its practitioners form part of society, as well as its discontents and prejudices. While asserting local forms of language promotes confidence and a sense of pride, this could be supplemented, and its practitioners further empowered, by exposure to structured sets of knowledges from formal educational places.

Experienced practitioners working on critical pedagogy projects with youth have expressed similar sentiments, arguing that urban youth benefit from disciplined and structured educational sites (Duncan-Andrade & Morrell, 2008). This insight means that Paulo Freire's experiences and philosophies with adult education classes need to be carefully adapted to fit critical pedagogy interventions for urban youth. Freire (1970) was working with adults who chose to attend his classes and who were accustomed to dealing with marginalisation. By contrast—and depending on the age range in question—youth are still legally required to attend school, and many do not have a great deal of experience in long-term decision-making. Informal educational places need to work hard to make youth feel at home in these sites, affirming the language they use and acknowledging their experiences. This does not mean that these settings should have no rules, boundaries, or structured knowledge dissemination.

Aligning critical pedagogy projects, like Youth Amplified, with the material, cultural and linguistic needs of participants is extremely challenging in heterogeneous, post-colonial societies. Neat binaries between oppressed and oppressors are often blurred. In South Africa, some township youth are upwardly mobile, attending new and old elite schools, while other poor young people have acquired employment in organisations like CRAAG, without any formal qualifications. Some have found temporary wealth through forms of 'predatory capitalism' in the informal economy or forms of criminality (Standing, 2004). Many post-colonial contexts have experienced considerable 'internal colonisation' following independence, as specific groups within former colonies are differentially empowered. The deficit model of 'the oppressed' diminishes youth agency and is not able to describe the range of ways in which young people are, at times, simultaneously empowered and/or marginalised. Critical pedagogical interventions that involve diverse groups of young people therefore need to be careful not to alienate some participants or homogenise the groups with which they work. These kinds of programmes should also bear in mind that youth are affiliated to various institutions and group identities, like the schools that they attend. The three learning places therefore illustrated how educational sites are inextricably linked to the social relations that exist in the wider society. Understanding how and why learning does or does not occur requires careful analysis of how these social processes operate.

Changing Places

Using the concepts of 'place' and 'dialogue' as tools for conceptual exploration enables the classroom to be understood as one educational place amongst the range of sites of learning that exist within a poor community on the Cape Flats. The classroom is not envisioned as quarantined from society, an isolated place where educators perform unique pedagogical work. Learning places are constructed historically and they are shaped by relationships that exist inside and beyond their borders. This has implications for educational transformation, especially for youth on the periphery of society, a topic that is widely spoken about in many contexts globally. Educational transformation is usually associated with calls for increasing the efficiency and regularity of assessment practices and developing more sophisticated standardised tests. However, in addition to improving teachers' content knowledge and other traditional measures involved in school improvement, I believe that building links between educational places can empower low-income youth of colour and the communities in which they live, in a sustainable fashion.

Youth need the qualifications, exposure to high-status languages and knowledges that schools offer, if they want to become socially mobile. They need to master standardised languages that hold power in places like universities and employment settings. Local, peripheral forms of language may stimulate creativity, but they will often be regarded as inferior by powerful institutions and may ultimately function to reproduce social inequalities, unless they are developed in tandem with powerful languages and knowledges (Blommaert, Muyllaert, Huysmans & Dyers, 2005). To illustrate this point, 70% of South African youth with 13 years of schooling and over 85% with 14 years of education find employment, whereas, approximately 50% of people with 1–11 years of schooling find employment (Van der Berg et al., 2011). The certification, powerful languages and specialised knowledges that schools disseminate and their value to young people's future prospects cannot be ignored. If youth have ambitions to participate in universities and certain employment positions, it is important for them to learn about the codes, concepts and social evaluations that operate in those places.

In addition to the powerful and specialised knowledges, as well as the forms of certification that schools offer, marginalised youth also need places where they are affirmed and given opportunities to develop their sociopolitical consciousness, places that allow them to explore who they are and express their creativity. Most of these youth intuitively sense that society loads the odds against them; they need opportunities for those experiences to be validated and to be introduced to challenging concepts, ideas, books and films that help them to nurture and develop their already germinating critical faculties.

Informal educational places, like those related to hip hop and critical pedagogy, show how youth thrive in places that affirm whatever languages they use. Such places often provide them with non-threatening, creative opportunities to dialogue with the worlds they inhabit. These kinds of sites have been built on norms, values and institutional cultures that differ from, but are not necessarily incompatible with schools. They often emerge organically, as forms of resistance to oppressive structural forces, such as hip hop. They may be linked to organisations that have been established to support local communities, like NGOs. These educational places often contain invaluable local strategies, patchwork solutions that address social and political problems.

What might the educational project that I am proposing look like? If classrooms and other educational sites could be re-envisioned as junctions that facilitate a richer educational journey, the plethora of resources and people that are contingent to these places, and the overall expedition, could be utilised to enhance young people's education. This kind of educational project would require skilled and capacitated managers, and inter-sectoral collaboration. For example, in the Western Cape, this would need links between the Education department, the Department of Cultural Affairs and Sport, NGOs, community centres, clinics and the Health Department. American visitors were amazed by the fact that Rosemary Gardens High School had access to 10–15 young people, paid for by government, working at the school every afternoon facilitating sport, academic support, music and dance.

However, these young people were employed by the provincial Department of Cultural Affairs and Sport and they did not interact with the school or support its priorities, meaning that the Department of Education and Department of Cultural Affairs and Sport burrowed away in isolation, attempting to achieve their own sets of predefined outcomes. Many poor, urban South African schools and communities have access to a range of educational places that operate in their locales. In my work at EMEP it was common to find 20–30 NGOs working, uncoordinated, in one school. Schools are also almost always positioned in fairly close proximity to community centres, clinics and libraries. Unfortunately, each of these institutions has its own set of predefined outcomes to which it aspires, meaning that collaboration is often experienced as an impediment to achieving goals. Individually, these organisations and their associated government departments worked towards specified sets of 'deliverables', with minimal coordination or synchronicity and little planning in terms of what would be most beneficial to the young people and their educational journeys.

Lived, Dialogical Learning

Lived space opens up the conceptual room to explore how different sites offer youth opportunities to learn and express themselves and how these places may complement one another. Inserting oneself into conversations is the first step towards participation in dialogue and creating forms of what I have called 'lived space'. In educational places, lived space often involves who speaks, how they speak and why they speak. Young people like those from Rosemary Gardens need to speak and to be heard. The head boy, a leadership position designated by the school, described his favourite aspect of serving on the Cape Town junior city council in 2012 as follows:

Brett: *In the council chambers I am the junior speaker so I maintain the order and things like that.*
Interviewer: *Do you enjoy that kind of work?*
Brett: *I love it. I love it. The thing I love most is the mute button, Adam (both laugh). I love that mute button. What happens is, I need to make sure we keep to the rules and stick to agenda. When there's another topic on the agenda I read it out loud and then they debate about it. When the speaker makes a ruling that stays. So when I make a ruling that stays, which I love. When we in the chamber I'm in control. The*

> *reason why I love that mute button is when they talk too much or say something that's not on the agenda or they starting to argue then I press that mute button and it mutes all the mics in the audience and then only I can speak and say "okay, Adam you have the right to freedom of expression".*

Lived space is created by young people negotiating the *material* challenges of, for example, violence, overcrowding and unemployed parents, as well as the *imagined space* contained in language forces that shape identities. In between these forms of material and imagined space, young people may produce self-definitive utterances, in conversation with others. However, simply participating in dialogues does not produce lived space. Words may be used to oppress and exclude other people, to put them 'on mute', or to repeat an idea heard elsewhere. These words need to be used in the spirit of inquiry, knowledge co-construction and openness to changing one's opinion and not in order to assert a discourse without reflecting on its meaning. Dialogic, lived learning happens when a person actively engages with other perspectives.

Lived space was observed in each of the three places. At RGHS students adopted three responses to material and imagined space, either discontinuing their schooling, or stoically persevering with their formal education, whilst accepting the linguistic hierarchy as legitimate. A third group of students remained at school yet expressed extreme distrust in their society, identifying with a range of conspiracy theories and hinting at the ways that coloured youth are oppressed.

In Chapter Five I said that each of these strategies contained elements of lived space, as these young people negotiated material and imagined spatial forces and carved out a personal course of action. However, the first response, school discontinuation, is a form of lived space that forecloses a number of the options that could be available to young people. School discontinuation has dire consequences in the current economic context, in terms of potential employment and tertiary education opportunities.

Persevering with school, whilst accepting one's language as inferior, also displays aspects of lived space, but this option may well be damaging to young people's self-esteem. The third strategy of 'scepticism and perseverance' illuminates how young people yearned for engaging in dialogues that interrogated their historical circumstances and contemporary inequalities. Yet this form of critical, historical consciousness cannot be achieved by schools alone, as these institutions are too enwrapped in the tentacles of the state and its ambitions for national economic development. Collaboration between the school and other educational places is one way that sociopolitical consciousness may be developed amongst youth.

DVS wrote lyrics that directly engaged with their material and imagined circumstances, demonstrating elements of lived space. However, DVS' exposure to concepts related to NGO discourse and hip hop subculture often led to members of the group simply reiterating words that they had heard elsewhere, without these young men reflecting on their meaning. At times it felt as if the Doodvenootskap could have benefitted from being exposed to a different set of utterances and a more rigorous 'curriculum', one that would have challenged them to engage with some of the complexities of the concepts that they encountered.

At Youth Amplified young people from Rosemary Gardens displayed elements of lived space either through attacking their peers or by cooperating with diverse groups of youth to co-construct knowledge in a form of dialogic lived learning. The latter was a rare occurrence, one that needed to be built on through facilitated reflection and materials that connected with the life worlds of these young people. When it did occur, the experience was extremely rewarding for a number of young people, including myself.

Each of these educational places therefore held potential for lived space and dialogue. Building links and partnerships between educational sites would allow for cross-pollination of ideas and practices and show young people different kinds of futures. I am imagining a scenario where teachers would listen in to the debates at Youth Amplified and raise pertinent questions from the discussions during life orientation classes, history lessons and English periods. This would allow larger numbers of students to engage in vibrant dialogues. CRAAG could facilitate afterschool hip hop classes, in conjunction with the Doodvenootskap, leading sessions on lyric writing and discussions on identity. These sessions could be brought into similar classroom spaces like those mentioned in relation to Youth Amplified. School history teachers could lead community discussions on the Khoi, the history of Cape Town and on how communities like Rosemary Gardens were constructed. These interventions could help reimagine and reinvent educational places for the benefit of local communities, teachers and most importantly, young people themselves.

The proposed education project at the heart of this research extends beyond the walls of classrooms and takes power relations and history seriously. At the same time, it is uncompromising about the urgency for the acquisition of languages and knowledges that enable young people's success. It entails acknowledging that education is a truly social process that involves collective effort and reciprocal understanding. This approach demonstrates one example of how a piece of youth studies research in the Global South may simultaneously unpack the relationships between socio-historical contexts and young people's practices, whilst looking for solutions that mobilise the institutions and individuals that can potentially empower youth.

Beating the System

Like many of the people I encountered in Rosemary Gardens, Mo, the young man described in Chapter Five, was deeply sceptical towards broader societal powers that he believed oppress people in Cape Town neighbourhoods that were constructed through forced removals. On a number of occasions Mo's sentiments led me to conclude that he wanted to develop his sociopolitical consciousness, but he was not sure how to proceed with this desire. Mo's scepticism catalysed his interest in the film *The Matrix*, in which people were subdued and exploited through a simulated reality controlled by machines. Students like Mo understood that systemic, structural power relations functioned to reproduce the status quo, making it difficult for young people from his neighbourhood to realise their aspirations. However, Mo also insinuated that it is only by both interrogating this unjust system and utilising analytical skills and qualifications, such as those gained at school, that youth from Rosemary Gardens may overcome the structural conditions that militate against their success. To demonstrate these sentiments, Mo described what he valued, in terms of learning, in the following manner. It is appropriate that he, as one of the young people from Rosemary Gardens, has the final word:

Interviewer: *And what does learning mean to you?*
Mo: *In academics or life?*
Interviewer: *In anything, you choose . . .*
Mo: *It depends what way you take it. It's like people tell you stories and you must read between the lines, what's he actually trying to tell you. That's learning. I like to learn so. Like people telling me a story and I take that story and listen deeply and hear what they actually trying to say. I like that movie The Matrix. Like Morpheus with the blue and red pill. If you can see through the system you can actually beat the system.*

References

Alim, H. 2009. Creating 'an empire within an empire': critical hip hop, language pedagogies and the role of sociolinguistics. In S. Alim, A. Ibrahim & A. Pennycook (Eds.), *Global linguistic flows: hip hop cultures, youth identities, and the politics of language (pp. 213–230)*. London: Routledge.

Alim, H. & Pennycook, A. 2007. Glocal linguistic flows: hip hop culture(s), identities, and the politics of language education. *Journal of Language, Identity, and Education*, 6(2), 89–100.

Anglund, J. 1967. *A cup of sun*. New York: Harcourt.

Blommaert, J. 2010. *The sociolinguistics of globalization*. Cambridge University Press.

Blommaert, J., Muyllaert, N., Huysmans, M. & Dyers, C. 2005. Peripheral normativity: literacy and the production of locality in a South African township school. *Linguistics and Education: An International Research Journal*, 16(4), 378–403.

Bourdieu, P. 1993. *Sociology in question*. London: SAGE.

Delpit, L. 2002. No kinda sense. In L. Delpit & J. K. Dowdy (Eds.), *The skin that we speak: thoughts on language and culture in the classroom (pp. 31–48)*. New York: New Press.

Dillabough, J. & Kennelly, J. 2010. *Lost youth in the global city: class, culture and urban imaginary*. New York: Routledge.

Duncan-Andrade, J. & Morrell, E. 2008. *The art of critical pedagogy: possibilities for moving from theory to practice in urban schools.* New York: Peter Lang.

Forman, M. 2001. 'Straight Outta Mogadishu': prescribed identities and performative practices among Somali youth in North American high schools. *TOPIA: Canadian Journal of Cultural Studies*, 5(1), 33–60.

Freire, P. 1970. *Pedagogy of the oppressed.* New York: Continuum International Publishing.

Gerwel, J. 1988. 'n Besinning oor die vestiging van Alternatiewe Afrikaans op hoërskool. In R. Van den Heever (Ed.), *Afrikaans en bevryding.* Kasselsvlei: KPO.

Giroux, H. A. 2004. War on terror: the militarising of public space and culture in the United States. *Third Text*, 18(4), 211–221.

Lin, A. & Martin, P. 2005. From a critical deconstruction paradigm to a critical construction paradigm: an introduction to decolonisation, globalisation and language-in-education policy and practice. In A. Lin & P. Martin (Eds.), *Decolonisation, globalisation: language-in-education policy and practice (pp. 1–19).* Clevedon: Multilingual Matters.

Luke, A. 2005. Foreword: on the possibilities of a post-postcolonial language education. In A. Lin & P. Martin (Eds.), *Decolonisation, globalisation: language-in-education policy and practice.* Clevedon: Multilingual Matters.

Otsuji, E. & Pennycook, A. 2010. Metrolingualism: fixity, fluidity and language in flux. *International Journal of Multilingualism*, 7(3), 240–254.

Pennycook, A. 2007. Language, localization, and the real: hip-hop and the global spread of authenticity. *Journal of Language, Identity, and Education*, 6(2), 101–115.

Standing, A. 2004. Out of the mainstream: crime in the Western Cape. In E. van der Spuy & B. Dixon (Eds.), *Justice gained? Crime and crime control in South Africa's transition (pp. 29–57).* Cape Town: University of Cape Town Press.

Van der Berg, S., Burger, C., Burger, R. de Vos, M., Gustafsson, M., Moses, E., Shepherd, D., Spaull, N., Taylor, S., van Broekhuizen, H. & von Fintel, D. 2011. *Low quality education as a poverty trap: Unpublished report for the presidency.* Downloaded on 8 March 2014 from: https://www.andover.edu/GPGConference/Documents/Low-Quality-Education-Poverty-Trap.pdf.

Appendix A

sê amen

Teesakkie
se moses

Toeks kuier te lekker om haar aan high tea-etiket te steur en hoe meer ek haar waarsku dat mevrou Hoogenboezem in styl bedien wil word, hoe minder luister sy

Deur SOFIA SMIT

Die persoon wat uitvind hoe om van 'n pap teesakkie ontslae te raak, moet 'n Nobelprys vir vrede kry. Wees eerlik. Hoe dikwels was jy nie al in 'n situasie waar jy by mense tee drink en dan is die teesakkie nog in die koppie nie? Jy kan dit nie in die piering sit nie, want dan drup die teekoppie nes jy dit lig!

En dit lyk so onooglik – die ou pap sakkie wat soos 'n nat kladpapier in jou koppie dryf. Jy skep dit dapper uit, maar niemand weet ooit wat om daarmee te maak nie. Ek het al sulke fraai, piepklein bakkies gesien waarop daar "teesakkies" staan, maar hulle is so skaars soos tieners as die geute skoongemaak moet word. Met die gevolg dat die een wat ek het immer soek is.

So nooi Toeks vir mevrou Hoogenboezem vir tee. Toeks het altyd die hemel in haar hart, want, sê sy, mevrou Hoogenboezem het haar laas genooi en goeie boeremense nooi altyd die ander persoon terug.

Maar waar mevrou Hoogenboezem 'n mens uit haar fynste porseleinkoppies bedien ("Wat ek in Stratford-Upon-Avon gekoop het," Dan spreek sy nog die naam in Hoogingels uit), gebruik Toeks sommer gewone koppies. My vriendin kuier alte lekker om haar nog aan hoogdrawende high tea-etiket te steur en hoe meer ek haar waarsku dat mevrou Hoogenboezem, wat dink haar sweet stink nie, in styl bedien wil word, hoe minder luister sy.

Natuurlik word die uwe saamgenooi om die gesprek aan die gang te hou as Toeks nie by die verwaande dame se pretensieuse praatjies kan byhou nie.

"'n Mens het 'n graad in pretensie nodig as jy met mevrou H praat," het Mias, die dorp se mooi tandarts, nou die dag gesê.

So beland ek, Toeks en mevrou H om Toeks se eetkamertafel. Ek kon haar darem oortuig om die tee in die eetkamer te bedien en nie om die kombuistafel soos Toeks aanvanklik beplan het nie. Toe ons gaan sit, bekyk mevrou Hoogenboezem die teeservies krities.

"Nog van my oorle ouma geërf," sê Toeks en glimlag senuweeagtig, "maar 'n paar koppies het al uitgebreek."

Toe gebeur die onvergeeflike: Toeks los die teesakkies in die koppies! Gelukkig sien mevrou H dit aanvanklik nie raak nie omdat sy nie daaraan gewoond is nie. My teesakkie dryf sommer bo in die koppie rond, nes 'n opdrifsel. Ek skep dit vinnig uit en slaag net-net daarin om dit in my piering ágter my koppie te laat neerplons, terwyl die lywige dame haarself kort-kort moet regskuif om op die stoel te pas.

"Hulle maak nie meer eetkamerstoele soos in my dae nie!" kla mevrou H toe haar agterstewe oor die stoel se rande begin peul, nes die teesakkie oor my piering se rand.

"Ek sou ook werklik nie daardie soort kitsch kunswerk in my sitkamer toegelaat het nie," bedui mevrou H na 'n skildery teen die muur.

"Dis deur my oorlede moeder gedoen," kom dit floutjies van Toeks en ek sien sommer die trane in haar oë, maar die wrede mevrou H, wat net aan haarself dink, is onkeerbaar. Sy trek Toeks se huis uitmekaar.

En voor haar dryf die teesakkie in die tee. Ek mik-mik om dit uit te skep, maar mevrou H beduie so dat ek nie die koppie kan bykom nie. Ek besef desperate times calls for desperate measures en ek wys vervaard na die venster. "Spinnekop!" gil ek. "O, my alla, bring die Doom! Dat ek my in 'n huis begewe waar daar kruipende goggonoppers is!" snater mevrou H. Ek steek my hand uit om die teesakkie uit haar koppie te vis, maar die lywige dame draai presies op daardie oomblik weer terug om haarself met haar kantsakdoekie koel te waai. Daar keer die teekoppie op haar formidabele skoot om en die teesakkie trek uit my hand.

Nodeloos om te sê, het die dame verontreg opgevlieg (verbasend vinnig vir haar gewig) en geloop. "Ek het beter dinge om met my tyd te doen!" En net voor sy die deur dramaties toeklap, sien ek hoe die teesakkie in haar hare pryk met die toutjie met die etiket aan wat gesellig, nes 'n pendulum, oor haar voorkop heen en weer swaai. Vk

Illustrasie Dr Jack

Source: Teesakkie se moses, Sofia Smit, Vrouekeur, 3 February 2012.
Image: Dr Jack

Translation of Article "Teesakkie Se Moses": Teabags Can Go to Hell (Approximate Translation of the Title)

Toeks is too comfortable to try and impress high-tea etiquette upon her and the more I warn her that Mrs Hoogenboezen wants to be served in style, the less she listens.

By Sofia Smit

The person who discovers how to dispose of a used teabag must receive a Nobel Prize for freedom. Seriously. How often were you in the situation where you are drinking tea with people and the teabag is still in the cup? You can't put it on the saucer because then when you lift the teacup it drips! And it looks so bad, the old used teabag. You bravely get rid of it, but nobody knows what to do. I have seen those beautiful, tiny containers that say 'teabags', but they are as rare as teenagers when the gutters need to be cleaned. With the consequence that I am always searching for my one.

So Toeks invites Mrs Hoogenboezem for tea. Toeks has a golden heart because she says that Mrs Hoogenboezem invited her the last time and good Afrikaners always return the invitation. But whereas Mrs Hoogenboezen serves guests out of her finest porcelain cups ("that I bought in Stratford-upon-Avon", saying the name in high English), Toeks just uses ordinary cups. My friend is just too comfortable to try and impress pompous, high-tea etiquette to her and the more I warn her that Mrs Hoogenboezem, who thinks her sweat doesn't stink, wants to be served in style, the less she listens.

Naturally yours truly is also invited to try and keep the conversation flowing because Toeks cannot concentrate on the conceited woman's pretentious words. "A person needs a degree in pretentiousness to have a conversation with Mrs H," the town's nice dentist said the other day.

This is how myself, Toeks and Mrs H landed up around Toek's table. I convinced her to serve the tea in the dining room and not around the kitchen table, like Toeks originally planned. As we went to sit Mrs Hoogenboezem observed the tea service critically.

"On my dead grandmother's grave", said Toeks and smiled nervously, "but a few teacups have chipped".

And then the unimaginable happened: Toeks left the teabags in the cups! Luckily Mrs H didn't notice because she isn't used to such things. My teabag floated around on the surface like debris. I threw it out quickly, slotting it in just behind my cup, on my saucer, while the bulky woman rearranged herself on her stool.

"They don't make dining room chairs like they used to in my day", Mrs H moaned as her big bottom fell over the sides of the chair in much the same way a teabag falls over the edge of a tea cup saucer. "I also wouldn't have that kitsch artwork in my lounge", motioned Mrs H to a painting on the wall.

"It was made by my late mother", came the response from Toeks and I see the tears begin to well in her eyes, but the cruel Mrs H who just thinks about herself is unstoppable. She tears Toeks' house apart.

And in front of her floats the teabag. I plan to quickly nip it out the cup but Mrs H is positioned so that I can't get to the cup. I decide desperate times call for desperate measures and I point at the window yelling, "Look, spider!"

"Oh my alla bring the doom! That I landed in a house with creeping gog-gonoppers" announces Mrs H. I stick my hand out to fish the teabag out of her cup, but the woman turned around to fan herself down with her lace handkerchief at that exact moment. The teacup fell onto her big lap and the teabag fell out of my hand.

Needless to say the wounded woman stood up (surprisingly quickly for her weight) and walked off. " I have better things to do with my time!" and just before she dramatically slammed the door shut, I see the teabag adorned in her hair with the string and the label, like a pendulum, swinging back and forth over her forehead.

Appendix B

Youth Amplified hosted the junior mayor of Cape Town, who leads the Junior City Council (JCC). A caller telephoned the studio and questioned the integrity of the JCC in the following manner:

Kelly: . . . I have to jump in there, we have a caller online . . . Hello caller . . .
Caller: Hello.
Kelly: Who are we speaking to?
Caller: I'd rather remain anonymous.
Kelly: Okay . . .
Caller: The JCC has been labelled as an elite kind of organisation and DA (Democratic Alliance political party) based. What do you have to say about that?
Kelly: (To the other participants in the studio) The caller says it's been labelled elite and DA based.
Caller: Okay, I'll listen to the answer on the radio.
Mayoress: That is a very tough question and I understand why it would be labelled as a DA thing, seeing as though our municipal and provincial government provide assistance.
Kelly: Can I just jump in . . . to the anonymous caller, does it matter who is supporting it? Isn't the main aim to empower all youth?
Mayoress: Yes, I was just going to say.
Kelly: And that's what you just spoke about now . . . politicizing everything. Does it matter if it gets support from the ANC, DA, NP . . . what other political parties do you guys know? Does it matter? Its not the main aim to support different movements that we're trying to push.
Mayoress: And that ties in with that brain, that brain of our parents of 1976. That we are still living in the struggle. No, no, no! We are living in 2012 and . . . it doesn't matter whether we're getting assistance from the DA, ANC . . . and no caller, we are not an elite organization. Caller my name is Siphokazi Simunye,

I am from Khayelitsha, my school is Mondale High school in Mitchell's Plain. How elite can I be really when I live in the place that has the highest rates of HIV infection, highest rates of gangsterism and crime, how elite can I be? I'm going to explain to you the demographic in our . . .

(interrupted by Kelly the host)

Kelly: We have another caller . . . duh duh duh duh da da. Hello caller?

Caller: Hi its anonymous back again. I just want to clear things up right, if you are talking about a political party, because your guest said, before you interrupted her, that they have been helped by the DA government. Because the Western Cape is governed by the DA. But at the end of the day it does matter who funds or helps you because the DA makes sure that the JCC implements its policies. If I give you money, I want you to listen to me and to do what I say.

Kelly: Um caller . . .

Caller: The DA will make sure that the JCC implements its policies. Okay thank you.

Kelly: Caller I just want to ask you something. Is this based on fact or assumption? Saying that the DA would ask the JCC to carry out certain policies.

Caller: Why wouldn't they?

Kelly: Okay I'm going to quickly refer you to Themba (participant in the studio), because he is burning to ask you a question.

Themba: Hang on, I just want to answer your question with a particular question. What have you done to improve the situations that we face? Hmmm? This is a lady who is in school trying to deal with these problems. You're here criticizing, what have you done?

Caller: mmm mmm

Themba: What have you done?

Caller: That's great, but you're not answering my question.

Mayoress: Let me just answer you, we are apolitical, JCC. We are not mandated to be involved in any political issue. We are not answerable to any political matter in municipal government, in provincial government, national government. Now when it comes to receiving money and funds . . . no . . . yes . . . we do receive a particular assistance from the mayor because she is the one whose running our city. But she doesn't give us money to run . . . to carry out policies that we want to implement. The only reason that we're working with the mayor is that we're young people. We need assistance on running issues. (But) We are apolitical. We do not deal with political issues.

Caller:	Great now, in terms of the JCC, which schools do you choose from?
Mayoress:	I'm from Mondale High, which is in Mitchells Plain. We have . . . from . . . we have from Melkbostrand private high school, we have different schools in the Cape Metropole, all schools in the Cape Metropole. You probably asking cause you know someone in the JCC and (they) could not get picked. That is because the city council sends out nomination forms to the school and it is up to the school, if they want to carry out the duty to give the opportunity to the young person.
Caller:	And what I'm thinking, someone from Khayelitsha?
Mayoress:	I am from Khayelitsha mama.
Caller:	I think there are more disadvantaged schools and I think that students from schools like that would appreciate this platform.
Kelly:	I think we can answer your question in studio because the conversation is trailing but thank you so much for your question.
Themba:	Can I just finalise that quickly . . . you know . . . cause I appreciate people like the mayoress . . . because she is trying to change with the platform she's been given (in the background . . . "uuuuh what are you doing in your community"). They're given circumstances, they're given situations. You have never donated a single money, I presume, into the running of Cape Town and fixing this kind of stuff and you come and criticise, I think you should envy these people.
Kelly:	I think we should appreciate both the caller and Siphokazi today.
Caller:	I think that's very rude because, first of all, you don't know who I am and second of all you assume that I don't donate or play my part. I'm way older, I've done stuff. So what have you done, please tell me?
Kelly:	Caller I think we are going to have to end this conversation. Please do join our facebook group.
Caller:	No, the guy must answer. What has he done that is so amazing?
Kelly:	I think I'm gonna . . .
Caller:	Answer, please answer.
Kelly:	Themba, the caller is asking what have you done?
Themba:	Well the fact that I'm a part of Youth Amplified and the mere fact that I'm expressing myself and that I'm doing something for my community.
Caller:	(Laughing) . . . That's great, thank you (caller ends the call).
Kelly:	Woooo. Okay okay okay. I just need to clear something quickly. Firstly, this show is not here to criticise anybody. It is not the point of Youth Amplified. Please listen to our jingle

	and hear what is the point that Youth Amplified exists. It is here for upliftment and empowerment. Secondly, we appreciate all forms of comments and opinions and we respect them in every way and, thirdly, you can see that the youth in this studio is very passionate about the youth and upliftment. Fourthly we also respect adult opinions in every single way. Themba is going to give you a formal apology in a letter, if you want. Please post your address on our page and we'll see that it gets to you immediately, yes.
Mayoress:	And lastly JCC is non-political.
Kelly:	Okay, that is the thing we had to clear up, but I think you did. Respect to the caller that did phone in. Respect to Themba that almost lost us and I just want to say again that I just want to say that we can see again how passionate the youth is about this and we really trying, we really trying, guns blazing whatever we do. There's no encouragement . . . but here there is the breaking down thing and that's what saddens us as Youth Amplified. We not getting the maximum support, but we are getting the maximum criticism. If I may say so. And that is making us sad. So now we just gonna be sad . . . Done now. Mayor what have you done? Seeing as though we doing the whole "what I have done" thing. I have sat in this chair . . . Mayor what have you done or what has the JCC done?

Index

Adhikari, M. 27, 116
Afrika Bambaata 51
African National Congress 2, 144
Afrikaans 12, 21, 22–4, 25, 28, 30, 68, 93, 120, 122, 140; curriculum 71; formal 70, 75, 119, 121; informal 71; officially recognized 27, 29; 'pure' 31, 72; school version 130, 139; standardisation 35, 54, 71, 74; white version 127, 141; *see also* Kaapse Afrikaans; standard Afrikaans
Afrikaaps [documentary] 22, 54, 119, 130
Afrikaaps [language] 119, 121, 122, 123
Alim, H. 97, 136
alternative curriculum 8
Anglund, J. 139
apartheid legislation 9, 15, 28, 45, 46
Aprils, D. 88
authoritative and internally persuasive discourses 38–9, 71, 77, 105, 106, 118, 121, 122, 123, 124, 130, 131
Ayouch, Noureddine 31

Bakhtin, M. 38, 117, 121
Barnes, J. 59
Barry Hertzog High School 9, 55, 56, 102, 103, 111, 112, 113, 114, 119, 123, 130
Baxter Theatre 22, 87
Bernstein, B. 97
Biko, Steve: 'I write what I like' 54
Birmingham School 14–15
Black Consciousness 27, 52, 53, 54
Black Nationalist 127
Black Noise 52, 53, 911, 127
'born free' generation 3, 74

Bourdieu, P. 36; *Reproduction in Education, Society and Culture* 126
Bowles, S.: *Schooling in Capitalist America* 126
Bradlocks 133
Brasse vannie Kaap 128
Bray, R. 47, 113

Camfranglais 31, 140
Cape Dutch 25
Cape Institute of Education 8
Cape Institute of Excellence (CIE) 55, 102, 109, 110, 111, 112, 115, 118, 119, 121, 122, 123, 130
Cape Town, language, race and space in 21–33; Cape Colony case study connected to other contexts 31–2; differences between standard Afrikaans and Kaapse Afrikaans 30–1; emancipation of slaves 25–7; history of language 24–5; language and space after discovery of gold and diamonds 27–9; second-class citizens and language 29–30; South African languages 21–24
changing places 145–7
Chavez, V. 55
Child Justice Act 2
Children's Rights and Anti-Abuse Group (CRAAG) 7, 49–51, 84, 85, 88–91, 92, 93, 94, 97, 98, 99, 129, 145, 149
Christmas with Map Jacobs 60, 73
Chuck D. 51
ciphas 38, 136, 143; circular 38
City Improvement Districts 46
cognitivist learning theories 13–14

Index

coloured 2, 9, 26–7, 28, 60, 72, 98, 120–1, 122; areas during apartheid 17n3, 29, 30, 46, 47, 81n1, 88; demographics 10, 25; different standards 114–16; education 47; fake 117, 130; father of 133; language 29–31; rural 31; school dropouts 47, 48; violence 46; working-class 13, 46, 63, 117
corporal punishment 62, 63, 69
CRAAG *see* Children's Rights and Anti-Abuse Group
critical pedagogy 54–58, 54–5, 56, 136, 137, 144, 145, 146; *see also* Youth Amplified

DEIC *see* Dutch East India Company
Delpit, L. 1, 140
Democratic Alliance 27
demographics 10
dialogic learning 13–14, 17, 22, 35, 38, 39, 40, 41, 44, 45, 79, 84, 90, 92, 93–4, 98, 116, 117, 118, 134, 136, 137, 141, 142–3
diamonds 26
discontinuation 6, 7, 48, 60, 66, 74, 80, 130, 148
discourses of whiteness 56, 112
distrust 60, 74, 80, 130, 144, 148
Dolby, N. 56, 112, 113
Doodvenootskap (DVS) 4, 7, 8, 12, 14, 17, 34, 127, 143–4; alternative affiliation 85–7; apartheid spatial dislocation leads to gangs 85–7; authoritative and internally persuasive discourses 39; Children's Rights and Anti-Abuse Group (CRAAG) 49–53, 89–90, 99; competing for charity 97; 'conscious' hip hop 41; curriculum 149; dialogic learning 143; dialogue and other dilemmas 92–9; dialogue and learning 83–101; gangs 87; distrust 144; hip hop values 57; imagined and lived space 50–3, 87–92; language 37, 97, 127, 129, 137; learning practices enabled by material office space 50; learning space 49–50; learning through dialogue 40; material space 85–7; nongovernmental organisations 40, 49, 50, 85, 99, 143; persuasive discourse 39; places without borders 44–5; silencing 35; site of learning 49–50; *Skollyhood Chapter One* 83, 92, 95, 96, 97, 98, 99; speech genres 136; translingual practices 97, 128; verbal exchanges based on equality 137; 'weak reaction' 98–9
double-voicedness 39–41, 71, 95, 98, 98, 117, 118
Dutch East India Company (DEIC) 24, 25

educational places 1, 4, 8, 16, 85, 129, 139, 144, 145, 147, 148, 149; informal 146
electricity 2, 3
emancipation of slaves 25–7
EMEP *see* Extra-Mural Education Project
Erasmus, Z. 17n3
exploratory talk 36, 38, 135, 136
Extra-Mural Education Project (EMEP) 5, 22, 55, 147

Fine, M. 48, 74
Foucauldian discourse 41n2
formal dwellings 2
Four Weddings and a Funeral 49
Freire, P. 34, 54, 129, 144–5
fusing horizons 39, 41

Gadamer, H. 34
gamtaal 22, 30, 128
Gerwel, J. 139
Gintis, H.: *Schooling in Capitalist America* 126
Global Hope Foundation 50–1, 85, 88, 89, 129
graffiti 11–2, 51, 83
Group Areas Act 9, 28, 29, 46, 84, 85, 88

Habermas, J. 41n1
Hill, M. 100
Hinglish 31–2
hip hop 1, 17, 36; 'abo-digital' 143; alternative norms and values 143; American themes 52, 90; 38; 'battle' 94, 136; Bernstein's codes 97; Cape Town 53, 91, 128; ciphas 38, 136, 143; circular ciphas 38; 'conscious' 51–2, 53, 90; culture 40, 50, 51, 83, 84, 90, 99, 148; dialogic learning 93–4, 100; educational places 146; high-quality 143; high-quality 143;

Index

'keeping it real' 52, 143; 'knowledge of self' 52; language 4; 'language ideological combat' 144; language in places of learning 128; meaning 52; nonprofit organisations 130, 149; post-apartheid 53; punch lines 92, 93, 99, 136, 137; public space 128, 143; speech genre 136; 'spitting' 94, 95, 136; Tanzanian themes 52; values 57; *see also* Black Noise; Doodvenootskap; Prophets of da City
Hokkien 31, 140
Honwana, A. 15
hooks, b. 65
household income 2
Hughes, May 7, 34, 66, 129

ideal speech situation 41n1, 135
ID Mkhize 34, 102
Illeris, K.: *Contemporary Theories of Learning* 41
imagined space 11-2, 46, 48, 49, 51, 53, 54, 56, 61, 84, 85, 89, 90, 92, 98, 109, 118, 141, 148
income inequality 2
Industrial Revolution 26
Information Response and Feedback (IRF) 37, 77, 134, 136-7
IRF *see* Information Response and Feedback
isiXhosa 8, 22, 24, 55, 102, 119
isiZulu 22, 24

Jansen, E. 21

"Kaaps": as term 22
Kaapse (Cape) Afrikaans 12-13, 21, 22-3, 24, 25, 27, 29-30, 32, 60, 71, 72, 75, 97, 100n1, 102, 103, 119, 127; differences between standard Afrikaans 30-1
'keeping it real' 52, 143
Khoi 12, 17, 24, 25, 27, 144, 149
'knowledge of self' 52
KRS-one 51
KwaZulu Natal 24, 112

Ladson-Billings, Gloria 8, 69
language: centrality of in places of learning 126-38; history in Capetown 24-5; ideologies 14, 16, 35, 36, 44, 127, 135, 140, 144; social hierarchies 131-4; and space after discovery of gold and diamonds in Cape Town 27-9; South African languages 21-24; value of words 127-31; *see also* Doodvenootskap: language; hip hop: language; speech genres
Leander, K.M. 1, 59
learning, language and dialogue 34-43; authoritative and internally persuasive discourses 38-9, 71, 77, 105, 106, 118, 121, 122, 123, 124, 130, 131; building bridges and double-voicedness 39-41, 71, 95, 98, 98, 117, 118; speech genres 36-8; who spoke where 34-6
learning places 44-58; changing places 145-7; critical pedagogy 54-5; Doodvenootskap as site of learning 49-50; Doodvenootskap practices enabling material office space 50-3; imagined space 46-8; intersecting sets of social relations 139-45; lived space 48-9; material space, learning and Rosemary Gardens High School 45-6; places without borders 44-5; radio material 53-4; school cultures and imagined space at Youth Amplified 55-7
Lefebvre, Henri 11, 18n5, 44
Limpopo textbook crisis 5
linguistic capital 36, 37, 69, 75, 80, 81, 106, 118, 119, 129
lived space 11-2, 14, 15, 16, 18n5, 45, 48-9, 51, 52, 53, 57, 60, 74, 80-1, 84, 98-9, 100; dialogical learning 147-9
Luke, A. 139
Lukhanyo High School 8, 55, 119
lyric writing 87, 88, 89, 91, 128, 149

Mac an Ghaill, M. 49
Mandela, Nelson 53, 144
material space 11, 50, 53-4, 59, 61, 66, 88, 108, 118; disrupted 84; Doodvenootskap 85; RGHS 106
The Matrix 74, 150
Mcdonald, A. 3
mixed-race 26-7
Mountainview Primary 5

New National Party 27
NGOs *see* nongovernmental organisations

nongovernmental organisations (NGOs) 17, 40, 50, 51, 53, 85, 88, 92, 99, 129, 136, 146, 147; build community centre 85–7

'Old' National Party 27

Passeron, J.: *Reproduction in Education, Society and Culture* 126
Petchauer, E. 100
Peterson, J. 83
Phillips, N. 1
places, learning *see* learning places
Population Registration Act 28
precious minerals 26
Prophets of da City 52–3, 91, 127, 128
punch lines 92, 93, 99, 136, 137

radio material 53–4
Ready D 30
Rose, T. 83–4
Rosemary Gardens High School (RGHS) 5, 6, 7, 12; *Map Jacobs' Christmas* 60, 73; community violence 64–5; conspiracy theories 73–4, 80, 148; corporal punishment 62, 63, 69; Development Trust 6, 66; dialogue and learning 14, 39, 59–82, 142; dialogue in the classroom 75–9; ethnicity 30; graffiti 11–2; Illuminati 73, 74; imagined space and language 11, 68–74, 148; kinds of learners 59–60; language 37; language and imagined space 11, 68–74; lived place 11; material space and learning 45–6, 59, 60–7; physical space 50; place produced by history 11; place without borders 44, 45; school discontinuation 60; silencing 117, 127, 142; teachers 141; who spoke 34–5; *see also* Youth Amplified
Rushdie, S.: *Chutnifying English* 32

San 12, 17n3, 24, 27, 144
school discontinuation 6, 7, 48, 60, 66, 74, 80, 130, 148
School Is Power project, Vanderbilt University 63
School Improvement Programme (SIP) 6, 7
silencing 35, 39, 48, 63, 75, 78, 117, 127, 129, 131, 133, 134, 142

Singlish 31
SIP *see* School Improvement Programme
slavery 31; abolishment 25; history 32
Small, A. 22, 73
Snodgrass, W.D.: *Memento* 76
social grants 2, 3
social hierarchies 13, 80, 102, 103, 106, 108, 113, 118; language 131–4, 137
Soep, E. 55
Soja, E.W. 18n5
South African languages 21–24; history at Cape Town 24–5
South African Schools Act 2, 62
Spanglish 32
speech genres 14, 36–8, 39, 41, 44, 134–7; classroom-based 134; exploratory talk 36, 38, 135, 136; Information Response and Feedback (IRF) 37, 77, 134, 136–7; 'spitting' 94, 95, 136
Ssslang (Sssnake) 83, 95–6, 97, 98, 99
standard Afrikaans 21, 22, 29, 74, 127, 141; differences between Kaapse Afrikaans 30–1
symbolic domination 36

talk radio 38, 134, 135
Taylor, K. 1
Testing Hope 54, 113
translingual practice 12, 31, 32, 97
Treatment Action Campaign 51

unemployment 10, 15, 60
United Reformed Church 50, 85

van Riebeek, Jan 132, 133
Virgin Active 6, 66
Vrouekeur: 'Teesakkie se Moses' (Teabag go to hell) 76
Vygotsky, L. 14

waithood 15
Waiting for Superman 54
Webb, V. 21
Western Cape Education Department 6, 8–9, 55
Williams, A. 67, 76, 80, 103; 'Towards participatory teaching and learning processes in the English language classroom' 79
Willemse, H. 21

Willis, P.: *Learning to Labour* 48, 126–7
The Winslow Boy 79
words, value of 127–31
World Bank 15

Xhosa 24, 128

Youth Amplified 4, 7–9, 12, 17, 60, 102–25; authoritative and internally persuasive discourses 39; conflict and dialogue 119–23; critical pedagogy 133, 137, 145; dialogue 14; dialogue and conflict 119–23; imagined space 55–7; impact of school institutional culture on learning 109–13; language varieties 12; learning through dialogue 40, 62, 73, 95, 137; lived space 149; material space 53–4; physical space 50; language and dialogic learning 37, 39, 40, 130, 131, 135, 137; place without borders 44, 45; race talk 113–19; school cultures and imagined space 55–7; social hierarchies 133, 137; speech genres 38, 134; students from Rosemary Gardens High School 103–9; speech genre 134, 135; teachers 77; who spoke 34–5

Zille, H. 142
Zulu 24, 128